'A very interesting and informative dialogue amongst three expert theologians that covers a wide range of topics from the perspective of Abrahamic faiths. The dialogue is engaging, thought-provoking and eye-opening in relation to the sources of scripture, God and man's relationship with the divine, daily life, ethics, morality and eschatology. A frank conversation like this, conducted with mutual respect, is rare in our atmosphere of exclusivist discourse, and we need more of this. I very much hope that this worthy book will inspire and encourage further such encounters.'

— *Sheikh Dr Salah al-Ansari, Egypt and UK-based Imam for 20 years, including at the Regent's Park Mosque (London Central Mosque, UK)*

'Great stories, memorable jokes, profound theory – all are interwoven in this wonderful record of what happens when a Jew, a Christian and a Muslim talk together about their scriptures. You could call it Scriptural Reasoning; or you could call it a conversation among friends of God. Whatever you call it, this book will enlighten, enliven and engross your spirit.'

— *Rt Revd Dr Michael Ipgrave, Bishop of Lichfield, UK*

'Rich and fascinating, *People of the Book* will undoubtedly be used as a reference book by those who are involved in interfaith engagement. Members of each faith group will surely learn new things from this book, not just about the other religions but also about their own religious heritage. Just as surely, those outside of the interfaith arena who are seeking to understand diverse religious worldviews among their constituencies, or in the wider global environment, will benefit from this profoundly informative and thought-provoking work.'

— *Farhana Mayer, Former Lecturer at the School of Oriental and African Studies and the Institute of Ismaili Studies, London, and author and translator of classical Islamic texts on Qur'anic hermeneutics and Sufism*

D1546030

'In this most illuminating and engaging volume, three authors, from (their) committed standpoints as Jew, Christian and Muslim, present their informed positions on a wide range of topics, ranging from the interpretation of the Word of God to gender and ethnicity, aspects that vitally affect how we live, communicate with, and understand each other in today's world. Dispelling ignorance and misunderstanding, the volume will surprise the reader as to the extent of those values and beliefs we actually share in common rather than what keeps us apart. This is a most readable, and informative book, usefully divided into helpful sections so that it can act as a reference volume as well as a work to be read in one sitting. It is an ideal resource for those engaged in interfaith dialogue, at either an academic or pastoral level, and is a major contribution to promoting understanding and respect for others, whose beliefs we may not personally hold ourselves.'

– Martin O'Kane, Professor Emeritus,
University of Wales Trinity St David, UK

'The book offers a useful trialogue between the authors – as well as between the Hebrew Bible, the Christian Bible and the Quran – concerning the views of these three scriptures on a variety of topics, from creation to afterlife, and from land to God. As such, it not only offers the readers a glimpse into each scripture, but also a background for understanding the differences and similarities between the three scriptures, and the religions which they represent.'

– Dr Zohar Hadromi-Allouche, Lecturer in Islam at
The University and King's College of Aberdeen, UK

PEOPLE OF THE BOOK

of related interest

Exploring Moral Injury in Sacred Texts
Edited by Joseph McDonald
Foreword by Rita Nakashima Brock
ISBN 978 1 78592 756 0
eISBN 978 1 78450 591 2

Learning to Live Well Together
Case Studies in Interfaith Diversity
Tom Wilson and Riaz Ravat
ISBN 978 1 78592 194 0
eISBN 978 1 78450 467 0

Ageing and Spirituality across Faiths and Cultures
Edited by Elizabeth MacKinlay
ISBN 978 1 84905 006 7
eISBN 978 0 85700 374 4

Christian Ashrams, Hindu Caves and Sacred Rivers
Christian-Hindu Monastic Dialogue in India 1950–1993
Mario I. Aguilar
ISBN 978 1 78592 086 8
eISBN 978 1 78450 347 5

Re-enchanting the Activist
Spirituality and Social Change
Keith Hebden
ISBN 978 1 78592 041 7
eISBN 978 1 78450 295 9

Muslim Identity in a Turbulent Age
Islamic Extremism and Western Islamophobia
Edited by Mike Hardy, Fiyaz Mughal and Sarah Markiewicz
Foreword by H.E. Mr Nassir Abdulaziz Al-Nasser
ISBN 978 1 78592 152 0
eISBN 978 1 78450 419 9

The Role of Religion in Peacebuilding
Crossing the Boundaries of Prejudice and Distrust
Edited by Pauline Kollontai, Sue Yore and Sebastian Kim
ISBN 978 1 78592 336 4
eISBN 978 1 78450 657 5

PEOPLE
OF THE BOOK

An Interfaith Dialogue about How Jews, Christians
and Muslims Understand Their Sacred Scriptures

DAN COHN-SHERBOK,
GEORGE D. CHRYSSIDES
AND USAMA HASAN
FOREWORD BY MARCUS BRAYBROOKE

Jessica Kingsley *Publishers*
London and Philadelphia

First published in 2019
by Jessica Kingsley Publishers
73 Collier Street
London N1 9BE, UK
and
400 Market Street, Suite 400
Philadelphia, PA 19106, USA

www.jkp.com

Library of Congress Cataloging in Publication Data
A CIP catalog record for this book is available from the Library of Congress

British Library Cataloguing in Publication Data
A CIP catalogue record for this book is available from the British Library

ISBN 978 1 78592 104 9
eISBN 978 1 78450 366 6

Printed and bound in the United States

Contents

PART 4: SOCIAL AND POLITICAL ISSUES

PART 5: HOPE

Foreword

This book is particularly important at a time when isolated verses from holy books are used to justify violence or suppress human rights. I hope it encourages the faithful to read their scriptures for themselves rather than relying on what preachers say. It may even come as a surprise that the Word of God is transmitted to us through human beings and that the Creeds too did not drop down from heaven, but were composed by church leaders. An added bonus is that besides fresh insights into their own scriptures, the reader will learn something about the beliefs of other 'People of the Book' as the three authors – Dan Cohn-Sherbok (Jewish), George D. Chryssides (Christian) and Usama Hasan (Muslim) – share information and opinions. This they do, both concisely and honestly.

Besides explaining how we come to have Holy Books and the authority given to them, the authors explain what the scriptures say on key subjects such as the Creation of the World by God, Marriage and the Family, War and Peace, and Life after Death. They make clear the different interpretations within a faith community and, refreshingly, also tell us their personal interpretations and spiritual practices. They also speculate on the possible conflicts between future discoveries of space exploration and our old religious beliefs. Would extra-terrestrial beings, who obviously were not descended from Adam and Eve, be tainted with original sin? Maybe, as the poet Alice Meynell suggested, this would add a new dimension to interfaith dialogue as 'we compare together...a million alien Gospels'. As it is too few Jews, Christians and Muslims have read each other's scriptures let alone the Upanishads.

There is a traditional Muslim teaching (hadith) in which God says, 'When someone recites or reads the Qur'an, that person is, as it were, entering into conversation with me and I into conversation with him or her.' Scriptures have also been called 'love-letters from God'. May this book help us to listen more attentively and as we listen to recognise that the God who assures us of divine love has the same love for other people, even if it is expressed in different texts and languages.

Marcus Braybrooke

Revd Dr Marcus Braybrooke,
Joint-President of the World Congress of Faiths

About the Authors

DAN COHN-SHERBOK

My great-grandfathers were immigrants to the US from Hungary at the end of the nineteenth century. Initially the family lived on the East side of New York City. One of my grandfathers was a kosher butcher, and I have a photograph of him standing in front of his shop. After my maternal grandmother married my grandfather, who worked initially as a cigar-roller, they moved to Denver, Colorado. He worked there as a clothing salesman, and the family belonged to a modern Orthodox synagogue. My father, an orthopaedic surgeon, came to do medical research at the National Jewish Hospital in Denver, and met and married my mother. They joined a large Reform Jewish temple where I had a *bar mitzvah* and was confirmed. I went to a typical American high school, and then studied philosophy at a small, all-male, liberal arts college, Williams College, in Massachusetts.

From a young age I wanted to be a Reform rabbi, and subsequently I was a student at the Hebrew Union College-Jewish Institute of Religion, the largest Reform seminary in the world. During the five years I was there I studied biblical and rabbinic Hebrew, Aramaic, the Hebrew Bible, *midrash*, Mishnah, the Talmud as well as other related subjects. I also served small congregations as a student rabbi in Jasper, Alabama; Galesburg, Illinois; Harrisburg, Pennsylvania; Boulder, Colorado; and Denver, Colorado. After ordination I was a rabbi in Melbourne, Australia before embarking on a PhD at Cambridge University. During these years I also served as a rabbi at West London Synagogue, and in Johannesburg, South Africa.

These rabbinic experiences, however, convinced me that I am more suited to academic life, and in 1975 I became a lecturer in theology at the University of Kent; subsequently I became Professor of Judaism at the University of Wales, where I am now an Emeritus Professor. Over the years I became increasingly interested in interfaith encounter and dialogue, and I have written a number of books dealing with this subject, including *Judaism and Other Faiths*. I also edited several books concerned with world religions, including *Islam in a World of Diverse Faiths*, and *World Religions and Human Liberation*.

Judaism has always been central in my life. In this connection I should say something about the notion of Jewish identity. Unlike Christianity and Islam, Jewishness is determined not primarily by belief but by ethnic descent (although it is also possible to convert to the Jewish faith). According to tradition, a person is Jewish if that individual's mother is Jewish – in other words, Jewish identity is based on maternal descent. In modern times, various branches of non-Orthodox Judaism have redefined this criterion to include patrilineal descent as well. Yet, even with such flexibility, Jewishness is perceived as a form of inherited ethnic identification. Ever since I was a child, I have seen myself as Jewish in this sense. In addition, I am loyal to Reform Judaism. From its origins in the nineteenth century, this branch of the faith – which is the largest worldwide – has championed prophetic ideals as found in Scripture and is also open to change and development based on modern knowledge. It is, I believe, the most reasonable and sensible form of Judaism – ideally suited to the modern world. As far as Christianity and Islam are concerned, although I admire Jesus' and Muhammad's moral teachings, I disagree with the theology of both religions. I do not believe that Jesus is God incarnate, nor that the Qur'an is God's revelation to Muhammad.

GEORGE CHRYSSIDES

I can't remember ever not knowing the Bible's stories. When my brother and I were children, our mother always read a Bible passage to us at night, and we were expected to attend church and Sunday School regularly. Having been born in Glasgow, we belonged to the Church of Scotland.

In my early teens I remember a minister preaching a sermon about Ezekiel and the dry bones. I hadn't heard the story before – it was quite scary, but it made me realise that there was much more in the Bible than the stories of Jesus and the Old Testament tales of Abraham and Isaac, Joseph and his dreamcoat, and the Israelites' journey to the Promised Land.

In my later teens I went away on a church mission with some other young people in my congregation. One evening a local minister spoke to us about the Bible, and urged us to get to know it better by reading a chapter a day, until we had read it in full. I took up the challenge, and systematically read a chapter – sometimes more – daily, with the help of *The New Bible Commentary*. My home congregation was quite conservative theologically; the minister was a fundamentalist Christian, and this commentary was much favoured in such circles for its fundamentalist leanings.

I later came across a book in the Teach Yourself Series (now out of print) called *A Guidebook to the Bible* by Alice Parmelee.[1] This book opened my eyes to more liberal biblical scholarship, introducing me to theories of multiple authorship of the books attributed to Moses, the synoptic problem, biblical poetry, prophecy and biblical history, which put all my childhood stories into proper perspective.

My growing acquaintance with the Bible and the Church made me want to make this my life's work, so I decided to become a minister in the Church of Scotland. I studied philosophy at the University of Glasgow, and then went on to complete a Bachelor of Divinity degree at Trinity College, Glasgow. This involved studying the Old and New Testaments (including Hebrew and Greek), Church history, systematic theology and pastoral theology. The last of these involved practical training – constructing sermons, preaching, and some counselling.

As the course progressed, I began to have second thoughts about a career in the Church. My academic work was going well, and there was a prospect of substantial funding to study for a doctoral degree. I went to Oxford in 1970, where I resided in a Church of England theological college, and was introduced to the Anglican tradition. I was fortunate in gaining an academic post in 1972 in Plymouth Polytechnic (now the University of Plymouth), and later moved north to the University of Wolverhampton, where I eventually became head of a small group of Religious Studies staff. In 1978 the Open University introduced its new course entitled 'Man's Religious Quest' (later retitled 'The Religious Quest' in the interests of political correctness). I was taken on board as a tutor, which involved taking students on field visits, meeting members of other faiths rather than simply reading about them.

My move to England caused me to join the United Reformed Church, which is closest in ethos to the Church of Scotland. I served on its national Other Faiths Committee from 1981 to 1987, which brought me into further contact with faith communities, especially Buddhists and new religious movements, the latter becoming my specialist research interest. Having married an Anglican, I eventually decided to move across to the Church of England, and we attend Lichfield Cathedral regularly on a Sunday.

USAMA HASAN

I was born in Nairobi, Kenya, in 1971 to parents of Indian/Pakistani origin. Our original ancestors were Arabs who immigrated to India centuries ago. I was blessed to be born into a family of devout Islamic scholars: both my parents are scholars, teachers and preachers of the Qur'an and hadith according to the salafi or *Ahl-e-Hadith* interpretation, as were their parents, grandparents and many previous generations. My father and paternal grandfather are/were amongst the most senior Islamic scholars in India, Pakistan, Saudi Arabia and the UK.

My parents moved with their five children to London in 1976. Growing up in London, English became my first language, although I still speak to my parents in my mother tongue, Urdu. We had a devout Muslim upbringing at home, observing the five daily prayers and daily Qur'an study from a young age. We visited the extended family in Pakistan annually during the summer holidays, always travelling via Saudi Arabia and the holy cities of Mecca and Medina. Aged 11, I had completely memorised the entire Qur'an in Arabic under the supervision of my parents, mainly my mother. As a hafiz, I first led mosque prayers during Ramadan at the age of 11 or 12, thus becoming an imam. I have served as an imam ever since then, for about 35 years.

I continued my Islamic studies at home and mosque in the traditional way, learning from a number of teachers, of whom my father was my main one. These studies included Arabic, Qur'an-commentary, hadith and its analysis and commentary, and fiqh (jurisprudence). At school, my favourite subject was mathematics. I held the John Carpenter scholarship for sixth-form studies at the City of London School for Boys, where I scored 100 per cent in the internal mathematics exam and won the maths prize. I also played for the school First XI cricket team there, having played for my primary and preparatory school football teams.

Although I could have followed in my father's footsteps and studied at the Islamic University of Medina in Saudi Arabia, he was keen for me to earn a living independently of religion if possible, especially since I did well in all my academic subjects at school. Thus, I gained MA, MSc and PhD degrees in theoretical physics, mathematics, engineering and artificial intelligence from the universities of Cambridge and London between 1989 and 1998.

Throughout my university career, I continued leading mosque prayers and also began leading Friday prayers regularly. I was also elected President of the students' Islamic Society at all three of the higher education institutions that I attended. I had also been a leading member of the UK's largest salafi youth movement (JIMAS) since my teens, and, whilst an undergraduate at Cambridge, I even briefly took part in military jihad against communist forces in Afghanistan. Other friends of mine fought military jihad in Bosnia, Kashmir, Chechnya and Burma during the 1990s.

I got married towards the end of my PhD studies – our marriage was entirely arranged, and my wife and I only met on our wedding day. We have been blessed with three sons and a daughter.

After university, I worked in UK industry (artificial intelligence) from 1997 to 2003. I then taught artificial intelligence at university for a decade, 2003–2012: one year in Pakistan and nine years at Middlesex University in London. Since 2012, I have held a full-time role in Islamic studies at Quilliam International, a counter-extremism organisation. Throughout my adult life, I have been an imam, teacher, preacher and Muslim community activist with organisations including JIMAS, mosques in London and Cambridge, the Muslim Council of Britain, Islam Channel, City Circle, Cambridge Muslim College,

Muslims for Progressive Values, the Muslim Reform Movement and Quilliam. I have over two decades of interfaith experience, and have published translations of a number of Islamic texts from Arabic and Urdu into English. I am a regular contributor to national and international media.

Introduction

Jews, Christians and Muslims have each been called 'People of the Book'. The three 'Abrahamic' faiths, as they are frequently called, differ from those other religions that either have no defined scriptures, or who acknowledge sacred texts but do not have an agreed canon of scripture. Aboriginal religions would fall into the former category, while Hindus and Buddhists are examples of the latter.

The scriptures of the three Abrahamic faiths are connected. Christians are unusual – not quite unique – in appropriating the entire scriptures of their parent faith, Judaism, while Muslims hold that both the Jewish and Christian scriptures were corrupted, and that the Qur'an restores the authentic word of God. In what follows, three scholars who belong to each of these three faiths discuss points of difference and points in common between their respective traditions' sacred writings.

We have arranged the topics under five broad headings. First, there are questions *about* our scriptures: How did they come about? Are they divinely inspired, or are they the work of human hands? How have they been transmitted and interpreted? If they are not to be taken literally, in what sense do they have authority? The ensuing four parts discuss questions about what is *in* our scriptures: the nature of God; the guidance they offer for life; social and political issues; and what hope they offer for the future – life on earth, and possible life beyond.

The book is a kind of conversation, each chapter having six exchanges in all on its designated theme. It differs from an everyday conversation, however, in that we frequently refer to our respective scriptures and cite our sources; we would not be quite as proficient at this if we were simply chatting over lunch! However, we believe that anchoring our conversation down by giving precise references is more helpful to the reader, even if it is at the price of naturalness and spontaneity. As with most conversations, there may be places where we seem to have strayed slightly off topic, and places where the discussion could have been taken further. This is because we imposed on ourselves the discipline of confining each exchange to between 500 and 600 words – otherwise the book would simply have got out of control. Those who engage in interfaith dialogue themselves can, of course, continue the discussion where we have left off, and we very much hope this will happen.

The tone of the discussion is intended to be friendly, yet frank. In the early days of interfaith dialogue, participants tended to emphasise points of similarity rather than difference, probably because they wanted to demonstrate that they were not as different as they might initially have seemed. However, harmonious co-existence does not consist of finding similarities; on the contrary, it involves locating differences, but nonetheless discovering that our differences are not barriers to living and working together.

We decided that we should take it in turns to start off and end the various topics. We thought this was better than letting our faiths speak in chronological order, with the Jew going first, being the most ancient of the three religions, and Islam coming last, as the youngest. Having a more or less random, yet equitable, ordering ensures that the same discussant does not always set the agenda, and that the same person does not always have the last word.

We should make it clear that we are not official representatives of our various faiths. Although all three of us have undergone professional training in them, the ensuing discussion is not sponsored by any faith or interfaith community. We speak on our own behalf, and the opinions expressed are our own, although we have attempted to acknowledge the spectrum of opinion that exists within our three faiths. Our discussion aims to identify issues that are important in our traditions, to highlight our similarities and differences, and to help to remove prejudice and stereotyping that one so often finds in the media and from the general public.

One or two points of fine detail should be mentioned. Our different traditions created slightly different ways of referring to scriptures. Many Jews react unfavourably to the Christian term 'Old Testament', preferring the terms 'Hebrew Scriptures' or 'Tanakh'. Although a small number of Christians have begun to use the preferred Jewish terminology, George has retained the term 'Old Testament' because of its continued prevalence within Christianity. The term is not meant to imply that the Jewish scriptures are out of date, superseded, or inferior in any way, and the relationship between Hebrew Scriptures and the Christian New Testament will be explained as the discussion proceeds.

Another small point of diversion was the writing of pronouns referring to God. Both Dan and George are accustomed to using lower case where words like 'he', 'him', and 'his' refer to God, and this convention has typically been used in Jewish and Christian literature – even as far back as the 1611 King James Version of the Bible. By contrast, Usama believes this practice is irreverent for the Muslim. We have therefore decided that each faith should use its own conventions in this regard. A further issue related to referring to the *suras* of the Qur'an. Usama tells us that it is best practice to include the name of the *sura* when citing Scripture, rather than – as Jews and Christians have been accustomed – simply the chapter and verse numbers. We have been happy to adopt the convention that Usama has recommended: part of interfaith dialogue is about getting to know how one can best respect a different faith from one's own.

Questions of authorship have loomed large in Christian biblical scholarship, and – to a lesser degree – among Jewish scholars. In particular, most Christian scholars are confident that Paul did not write the Letter to the Hebrews and the so-called 'Pastoral Epistles' (to Timothy and Titus). The Letter to the Ephesians is also in some doubt. We wanted to avoid the discussion becoming over-technical, so George has avoided using expressions like 'Paul' or 'pseudo-Paul', simply attributing the pastoral epistles to the declared author. Readers who wish to explore questions of authorship further should consult a reputable scholarly biblical commentary, such as the *Oxford Bible Commentary*.[2]

Finally, when referring to individuals in the text, we have sometimes used pseudonyms to preserve name anonymity.

PART 1

QUESTIONS ABOUT SCRIPTURE

Chapter 1

TRANSMISSION

What do our three faiths believe about the origins of their scriptures and how they were transmitted? Orthodox Jews hold that Moses received the Torah directly from God on Mount Sinai, together with an Oral Torah, which was passed on to Joshua. The American evangelist Billy Graham said that the Bible was dictated by God to 30 secretaries. Muslims traditionally hold that Muhammad was instructed to 'recite' what the Angel Gabriel spoke to him. Other more liberal believers – certainly in Judaism and Christianity – are not so sure, regarding their scriptures as human works, but nonetheless 'inspired' by God.

DAN

For Jews, Scripture is of fundamental importance. Sections of the Torah (the Five Books of Moses) are read every Sabbath, and biblical characters play a critical role in the spiritual life of the Jewish nation. According to the Bible, Abraham was the father of the Jewish nation; Moses led God's chosen people out of bondage; the prophets called the people to the highest religious ideals.

According to the Jewish tradition, the Hebrew Bible is referred to as the *Tanakh*. This term is formed from the initials of the three divisions of Scripture: *Torah* (Law), *Neviim* (Prophets), *Ketuvim* (Writings). The Torah consists of Genesis, Exodus, Leviticus, Numbers and Deuteronomy. The *Neviim* are composed of the Former Prophets (Joshua, Judges, 1 and 2 Samuel, 1 and 2 Kings) and the Latter Prophets (Isaiah, Jeremiah, Ezekiel, Hosea, Joel, Amos, Obadiah, Jonah, Micah, Nahum, Habakkuk, Zephaniah, Haggai, Zechariah and Malachi). The *Ketuvim* consist of liturgical poetry (Psalms and Lamentations), love poetry (The Song of Songs), wisdom literature (Proverbs, Job and Ecclesiastes), historical books (Ruth, 1 and 2 Chronicles, Esther, Ezra and Nehemiah) and apocalypse (Daniel).

In traditional Judaism, all the books of the Bible are viewed as sacred and inspired, yet the Torah is of pre-eminent importance since it is viewed by the Orthodox as revealed directly by God to Moses on Mount Sinai. This means that all the words of the Five Books of Moses are regarded as true, even though their meaning is interpreted in a variety of ways. This fundamental belief was explained by the twelfth-century philosopher Maimonides in this way:

> I believe with perfect faith that the whole and complete Torah
> as we now have it, is one and the same as that given to Moses...
> I believe with perfect faith that the Torah will never be changed,
> nor that any other law will be given in its place by the creator.[3]

Because the Torah is of divine origin, its 613 laws are viewed as binding. This legal code is referred to as the 'Written Law'. Alongside this legal corpus, traditional Jews also believe that there is a God-given 'Oral Law'. These laws were not written down, but were said to have been passed down through Moses to the elders, from the elders to the prophets and from the prophets to the Men of the Great Assembly. Eventually this oral code was finally written down in the second century CE in an anthology of law called the Mishnah and supplemented by the Palestinian and Babylonian Talmuds.

It should be noted, however, that non-Orthodox Jews do not view either the Written or Oral Torah in the traditional way. Non-Orthodox movements (such as Conservative, Reconstructionist and Reform Judaism) regard the Torah as inspired by God but written by human beings. Hence, they view the Bible – not as the word of God – but as the inspired record of Jewish history. And they do not feel bound to accept the rabbinic interpretations of scriptural law as binding.

GEORGE

Christians are distinctive in appropriating the entire scriptures of another faith. We accept the entire Jewish Bible, but most Christians would not recognise the term *Tanakh*, traditionally preferring the expression

'Old Testament'. To this we add our own distinctive set of scriptures, the New Testament, which we believe the Old in some sense foreshadows.

Like the Jews, there are fundamentalist Christians who believe that the Bible is free from any error – historical, scientific, doctrinal or ethical. The majority of academic scholars, however, are not so sure, and suggest that the books attributed to Moses are really an edited collection of earlier writings by several authors, and they are divided on the question of how much we can rely on the Gospels and the Book of Acts as reliable history about Jesus and the early church.

How we come to have the Bible in its present form is less controversial. The earliest sets of scriptures had to be copied by hand, and when scribes painstakingly transcribed the text word by word, errors inevitably occurred. We do not possess the original manuscripts that came directly from their authors. Instead, we possess a variety of scrolls and codices (sheets of handwritten parchment sewn together in the style of a modern book), which are not totally identical with each other, and scholars have exerted much time and energy into attempting to reconstruct the original text. Most errors can be identified and corrected, and where alternative versions appear to have equally good pedigrees, they are usually about unimportant points. For example, some manuscripts record that Jesus healed two demon-possessed men in 'the region of the Gadarenes' (Matthew 8.28), while other versions read 'Gergesenes' or 'Gerasenes'. Discrepancies like these are relatively unimportant, and only in a very few instances are points of significant fact or doctrine at stake.

The Hebrew Bible was translated into Greek, and this version is known as the Septuagint – *Septuaginta* being the Latin for 'seventy', the number of legendary scribes who are credited with the translation work in the third century BCE. Some of the New Testament authors, especially Paul, quote from the Septuagint rather than the original Hebrew text. In the fourth century CE St Jerome (c.347–420 CE) translated both Testaments into Latin, and the Vulgate – as the translation is called – was used in the Roman Catholic Church from the sixteenth century until just after the Second Vatican Council (1962–1965). Until the 1960s, most English-speaking Protestant churches used the 1611 King James Version, but most churches now prefer modern translations.

The vast majority of present-day English versions are directly translated from the original languages of Hebrew and Greek, thus ensuring that the meaning of the most ancient texts is preserved. Some translations are fairly literal, for example the New Revised Standard Version, while others – such as the Good News Bible – aim for readability rather than precise rendering.

The care that has gone into Bible translation and biblical scholarship should inspire confidence that our scriptures are authentic and reliable, and it is difficult to see in what sense it might be suggested, as Muslims do, that Jewish and Christian scriptures became 'corrupted'.

USAMA

The traditional Muslim account of the origin of the Qur'an (meaning: 'recitation' or 'reading' – thus emphasising its oral aspect) is that it was revealed by God to the Prophet Muhammad, peace be upon him, over a period of 23 years: from the first revelation in Mecca, marking the beginning of Muhammad's prophethood, until shortly before his death in Medina. The Meccan and Medinan phases of this revelation lasted ten and 13 years respectively, totalling 23 years and mirroring the Prophet's monotheistic, social, political and social mission.

The revelation was sometimes direct, but usually via the Archangel Gabriel (Arabic: Jibril), who would come to the Prophet in angelic or human form, just as he had done so previously with Prophets Abraham, Moses, Mary and Jesus Christ, according to Islamic tradition.

The revelations came in varying lengths, from one verse (*ayah*) to dozens of verses (*ayat*),[4] at a time. Sometimes, a complete chapter (*surah*) was revealed in one go. The Prophet would recite these revelations to his disciples, known as his 'Companions', and in the strongly oral culture of seventh-century CE Arabia, these were immediately memorised and transmitted widely through word of mouth. He would also dictate the order of the revelations, with some groups of verses organised into chapters. The Qur'an has 114 such chapters, of varying length between the shortest and longest *surahs*, three and 286 verses respectively. The *surahs* are named after major themes within them, and some *surahs* have more than one name. For example, some *surahs* are named after:

- the 'Most Beautiful Names of God' (24 Light,[5] 40 Forgiver, 55 Most Merciful)

- prophets of God (10 Jonah, 11 Hud, 12 Joseph, 14 Abraham, 19 Mary, 47 Muhammad, 71 Noah)

- natural or created phenomena (13 Thunder, 76 'Human' or 'Extended Time', 85 Zodiacal Signs, 86 Bright Star, 89 Dawn, 91 Sun, 92 Night, 93 Forenoon, 95 Fig, 103 Time)

- animals that feature in various Qur'anic stories and parables (2 Heifer, 16 Honey-Bee, 27 Ant, 29 Spider, 105 Elephant).

The Qur'an was preserved during the Prophet's life in mainly oral form, although parts of it were also written down. Soon before or after the Prophet's death, the Qur'an was collected into one written text for the first time, with Sunni and Shia Muslims disputing the details and giving the credit to their respective leaders. Since that time, the Qur'an has been transmitted meticulously through memorisation and writing, as exemplified by my own personal and family tradition, described in my short autobiography for this book.

Whilst the Qur'an is regarded as the direct word of God, there are also the hadiths or traditions relating to the Prophet, that contain the second source of Islam after the Qur'an, that is, the *Sunnah* or 'Way' of the Prophet. The hadiths were also, like the Qur'an, preserved orally and in writing, and transmitted with chains of narrations for centuries afterwards. The massive, voluminous and major canonical collections of hadiths were compiled by various scholars between the first and third centuries of the Islamic calendar, or seventh to ninth centuries CE. The authenticity and interpretations of these hundreds of thousands of hadith traditions are hotly disputed amongst the various schools of Islamic theology and jurisprudence, in contrast to the almost unanimously agreed purity of the Qur'an. I say 'almost' because a handful, a tiny minority, of Shia theologians over the centuries have accused the early Sunnis of distorting the Qur'anic text to omit references to basic Shia beliefs.

DAN

For thousands of years Jews viewed the Torah (Five Books of Moses) as revealed by God to Moses on Mount Sinai. This doctrine is referred to as *Torah mi Sinai* (Torah from Sinai). Thus it is not simply the

Ten Commandments that were disclosed to Moses during his 40 days and 40 nights atop Mount Sinai. Rather, Orthodox Jews believe that God revealed to Moses every word in Genesis, Exodus, Leviticus, Numbers and Deuteronomy (including the account of Moses' own death). How God did this is a mystery, but it is a cardinal belief of traditional Judaism.

This means that every word in the Torah is of divine origin. Therefore, biblical narratives about creation, the flood, the Exodus, the sacrifice of Isaac, revelation, etc. are all true and sacrosanct.

Such a conviction parallels the Christian fundamentalist belief in the holiness of Scripture. Yet unlike Christian fundamentalists, rabbinic sages employed a range of hermeneutical principles to explain the meaning of the biblical text. Alongside the literal understanding of Scripture, rabbinic scholars believed that deeper meanings could be discovered through various exegetical methods.

Alongside the narrative sections of the Torah, the 613 laws contained in the Five Books of Moses are similarly viewed as of divine origin. These commandments – which are to be observed as part of God's covenant with Israel – are classified into two major categories: (1) laws concerned with ritual performances, characterised as obligations between human beings and God; and (2) laws that would have been adopted by society even if they had not been decreed by God (such as commandments regarding murder and theft). The 613 commandments consist of 365 negative (prohibited) laws, and 248 positive prescriptions (duties to be performed). According to tradition, all are binding on the Jewish community.

Through the centuries rabbinic sages discussed the interpretation of these biblical laws. Their deliberations are recorded in the Palestinian and Babylonian Talmuds, which were codified by the sixth century CE. Both Talmuds incorporate the Mishnah (a second-century compilation of rabbinic discussion) and later rabbinic discussions known as the Gemara. According to traditional Judaism, these rabbinic interpretations of the law should also be regarded as God-given. This is based on the belief that the Oral Law was first given to Moses, and then to the elders, from the elders to the prophets and from the prophets to the Men of the Great Assembly. Therefore, both the Written and Oral Torah should be viewed as divinely revealed either directly to Moses or indirectly through the teachings of generations of rabbinic scholars.

Through the centuries Jews universally viewed Scripture as sacred, and biblical and rabbinic law as binding. Yet, since the beginning of the nineteenth century, modernist Jews have adopted a more radical approach to the tradition. Non-Orthodox branches of the faith sought to liberate themselves from the religious restrictions of the past. In time a number of different movements emerged within the Jewish community (Reform Judaism, Conservative Judaism, Reconstructionist Judaism and Humanistic Judaism). In different ways they distanced themselves from the belief in *Torah mi Sinai*. Today it is no longer the case that the vast majority of Jews view the Torah as the divine word of God. Instead, the Five Books of Moses are understood as the inspired record of the history of the Jewish people. Both in Israel and the diaspora Jews accept only those elements of the tradition which they regard as personally spiritually significant.

GEORGE

There are two aspects to the transmission of Scripture – the human and the divine. Dan and Usama have discussed both, while so far I have focused on the former, and argued that the written texts of Jewish-Christian scripture have been faithfully copied, with only a small number of fairly insignificant inaccuracies.

Christians call their scriptures the word of God, and therefore in some sense they are the result of divine inspiration. The famous evangelist Billy Graham once said, 'The Bible is a book written by God through thirty secretaries.'[6] However, the picture of God standing over Matthew, Mark, Luke and John as they transcribed his words is not one that would be acceptable even to many fundamentalists.

Some of the biblical text has blemishes, which have largely been covered up in English translations. The Gospel of Mark and the Book of Revelation, for example, are stylistically infelicitous in Greek. As the German philosopher J.G. Hamann (1730–1788) wrote, 'God speaks bad grammar.'[7] Hamann's point, however, was not to disparage the Bible, but rather to contend that God could inspire those of lesser ability than the great literary writers of their time, to convey his truths.

This does not mean, however, as is popularly believed, that John, James and Peter, who are credited with various New Testament books, were unlettered Galilean fishermen, whom Jesus called away from their trade (Mark 1.16–20). The titles of the Gospels ('The Gospel according to Matthew', etc.) do not appear in the original manuscripts, but are editorial additions in some versions of the Bible. The tradition that Matthew, Mark, Luke and John wrote the four Gospels arose in the second century, and may well be guesswork by early Christian leaders. Most, although not all, scholars believe that Mark is the earliest Gospel, and that Matthew and Luke used a sizeable amount of his material, probably with another independent source, which scholars refer to as Q. The manuscript Q, if such exists, has never been discovered. John's Gospel is substantially different from the others, and he may not have known the synoptic writings.

Because we do not know the gospel writers' real identities, we cannot be sure how close they were to the events surrounding Jesus' life. However, the purpose was not to convey historical biographical information, as we would expect today, but rather to transmit Jesus Christ's teachings and – most importantly – the message of salvation that he offers.

The Bible states that all Scripture is inspired by God (2 Timothy 3.16). Christian fundamentalists take this to mean that the Bible is totally inerrant. Other more liberal Christians, such as myself, would wish to distinguish inspiration from infallibility. I cannot therefore accept Usama's Muslim notion of direct divine delivery and a prophet's subsequent recitation. I have more sympathy with Dan's Reform Jewish position, that we have an inspired record of the history of the Jewish people and – as a Christian – I would add Jesus and the early Church.

The idea of accepting only the elements of one's tradition that one finds spiritually significant, of course, is not without its problems. Does this mean we can simply pick and choose the scriptural passages we like, and reject the others? But this takes us on to the question of authority, which is our next topic.

USAMA

As a teenager during the 1980s, it was from videos of the popular Indian/South African Muslim preacher, Ahmed Deedat, that I first heard the argument that the account of Moses' death at the end of the Pentateuch could not have been written by Moses. Decades later, a Masorti rabbi told me that the latter view was that of his movement, and that there had been a huge controversy in the 1960s when his teacher, Rabbi Louis Jacobs, espoused this position.

Contrary to popular misconceptions amongst both Muslims and others, the Qur'an does not accuse Jews and Christians of totally corrupting their texts: in fact, it honours its Abrahamic predecessors with precisely the title *Ahl al-Kitab* or 'People of Scripture', implying the double-edged sword of being both honoured and entrusted with God's previous revelations. It also confirms that Jews and Christians are in possession of the Torah (*Tawrat*), Psalms (*Zabur*) and Gospel (*Injil*), and charges them with following and obeying these scriptures if they are true believers.

However, it does allege that some people have fabricated scripture, claiming it to be from God, whilst other unscrupulous clergy have deceived people by oral interpolations whilst reading scripture or by misrepresenting it and quoting it out of context, although this latter charge may refer to speech in general, and not just scripture.

Furthermore, the Prophet instructed, 'Transmit from the Israelites, without affirming or denying what they say.' The Qur'an retells many biblical stories without detail, focusing on general features and moral lessons: throughout the ages, Qur'an-commentaries referred to 'Israelite traditions', often taken from learned Jewish and Christian converts to Islam, to provide detail.

Islamic scholarship for the past 14 centuries, in its occasional engagement with Jewish and Christian scriptures, bears out the above paragraphs: only a handful of texts in the entire Bible are alleged to have been corrupted, although the implications are sometimes serious. For example:

1. The command to Abraham in the Old Testament to sacrifice his 'only son Isaac' (Genesis 22.2). Some Islamic scholars allege that the name of Isaac has been interpolated here, and that Ishmael was actually meant, being the elder. This is relevant to any theories of Israelite (Jewish) or Ishmaelite (Arab) favour, superiority or even supremacy. Note that in early Islamic discourse, it was disputed whether the son involved was Isaac or Ishmael, partly because of the existence of 'Israelite traditions' within Islam.

2. John 3.16, in the King James Version, reads, 'For God so loved the world that He gave His only begotten Son…' However, the Revised Standard Version (RSV) omitted 'begotten' from this verse because it was not found in the earliest manuscripts. This has huge theological implications, and tends to support the Qur'anic charge of occasional fabrication of scripture.

3. A similar example is 1 John 5.7, where the enunciation of the Trinity of Father, Son and Holy Spirit is not found in the RSV.

Chapter 2

AUTHORITY

Jewish and Christian scriptures are anthologies, the canon of which was agreed in their early history, and Muslims traditionally hold that the Qur'an is a single discrete text, although conveyed successively at various times to Muhammad. These sets of scriptures are designated as being somehow more important than any other religious writings, but on what grounds? There are many inspiring religious books, but our respective faiths claim that their scriptures are more than merely inspirational. Some believers claim infallibility for their texts, but if they are not infallible, in what sense are they authoritative?

GEORGE

Christians hold that their scriptures have authority, which other writings do not. Particularly in the Protestant tradition, considerable importance has been attached to bringing the Bible into the languages of the people, so that it can be readily understood. Bible translation work has therefore assumed considerable importance. As I mentioned in the previous chapter, some translations are closer to the original Hebrew and Greek than others. Much biblical scholarship has been carried out since the King James Version was compiled in 1611, and no self-respecting Christian scholar would now use this translation as the basis for interpreting Scripture.

Examination of the pedigree of the various extant manuscripts has caused scholars to reconsider the correct reading of the Hebrew and Greek texts. Usama mentions 1 John 5.7 as such an example: it is now generally agreed that the verse should read 'the Spirit, the water and the blood', rather than 'Father, Son and Holy Spirit', although this preferred rendering is certainly more puzzling to interpret. Usama also refers to John 3.16: whether Jesus should be described as God's 'only begotten son' or simply 'only son' is not a matter of textual criticism, but rather of how the Greek word *monogenēs* should be translated, and either rendering is possible. There is certainly no 'fabrication' involved here, and one cannot adjudicate on such matters simply by comparing English translations.

However, the difference in meaning may not be as significant as Usama implies, since much of the language of the Bible is metaphorical. Christian fundamentalists are often loosely said to 'take the Bible literally', but they all must acknowledge that the Bible contains symbolism, metaphors and parables. To claim that God has a son is therefore not quite the same as my claim that I have a son – but this is a topic to which we shall return.

For the Christian fundamentalist, authority means inerrancy. This position is problematic, since fundamentalists must reconcile the apparent contradictions in the Bible, as well as explain why we do not continue to observe many of the Old Testament laws – again a topic for later discussion. On the other hand, however, authority must mean more than inspiration, since we can acknowledge that many other books are 'inspired'.

In the course of its early history the Church defined the canon of Scripture. The word 'canon' means a standard or a measuring rod, indicating that one's life and doctrines were to be measured against the Bible rather than any other book. Christians were agreed that the entire Jewish Scripture should be incorporated, signifying their origins in their parent religion, but obviously they had to add the central message relating to Jesus Christ. At first there was some disagreement about the inclusion of certain books – the enigmatic Book of Revelation was one – but in 367 CE Bishop Athanasius of Rome itemised in an encyclical letter the 27 books of the New Testament, which we acknowledge today. Additionally, the Roman Catholic Church accepts the Apocrypha – books compiled during the intertestamental period but which are written in Greek rather than Hebrew.

The special nature of these writings is reflected, inter alia, in their role in public worship: these books are read, to the exclusion of others.

This canon of Christian scripture is closed, and helps to mark the boundaries of acceptability. There is no prospect of its being reopened.

DAN

As I mentioned in the last chapter, the authority of the Torah rests on the transmission of the Five Books of Moses to Moses on Mount Sinai. The Torah is literally the word of God. *Torah mi Sinai* serves as the bedrock of the Jewish faith. On Mount Sinai God revealed the central truths of Judaism: the creation of the universe, the flood that engulfed the world, God's selection of the Jewish nation as his chosen people, the exodus from Egypt, the role of the patriarchs. All these narratives in Scripture have been regarded for thousands of years as a true record of historical events. And, most significantly, the Torah contains 613 commandments which traditionally regulate all aspects of Jewish life.

Alongside the Written Torah, traditional Judaism maintains that the Oral Torah – the interpretation of the Written Torah – is also of divine origin. It too was revealed to Moses and passed down through the ages. The teachings of rabbinic sages recorded in the Mishnah and the Talmud and eventually codified in the *Shulhan Arukh* (Code of Jewish Law) are thus binding on all Jews. Biblical and rabbinic law serve as the foundation of Jewish existence. Its authority is from the mouth of the Almighty who revealed himself in a still, small voice thousands of years ago. Through the centuries, the Written and Oral Torah have sustained and strengthened the Jewish nation. As the liturgy proclaims, 'It is a tree of life to those who hold fast to it.'

But this is not the whole story. Since the time of the Jewish Enlightenment in the eighteenth century, this cardinal belief has undergone a radical transformation. In the early decades of the nineteenth century, Reform Judaism challenged the doctrine of *Torah mi Sinai* as well as the belief in the inerrancy of the rabbinic interpretation of the law. By the end of the nineteenth century, Reform Judaism no longer regarded the Torah as divinely revealed in its entirety. According to the Pittsburgh Platform produced by American Reform rabbis in 1885, biblical and rabbinic law should no longer be regarded as sacrosanct. 'Today,' they declared, 'we accept as binding only the moral laws and maintain only such ceremonies as elevate and sanctify our lives, but reject all such as are not adapted to the views and habits of modern civilisation…we hold that all such Mosaic and rabbinical laws as regulate diet, priestly purity and dress originated in ages and under the influence of ideas altogether foreign to our present mental and spiritual state.'[8]

Such radical views profoundly disturbed the Orthodox establishment which declared that Reform Judaism is an aberration of the faith. Yet, despite such denunciations, the Reform movement – along with other non-Orthodox groups – continued to reject the binding authority of the biblical and rabbinic tradition. In its place, non-Orthodox Jews view the Torah as divinely inspired rather than the revealed word of God. As George noted, there has been a similar shift in Christian thinking about the Hebrew Bible. In this respect the liberal wings of our two faiths have adopted a similar stance. But what of Islam? Has a similar revolution in thought taken place? Or do Muslims as a whole continue to regard the Qur'an as the authoritative word of God?

USAMA

God is the ultimate authority, but who authoritatively interprets the word of God? Since the name Qur'an means 'recitation', it is originally an oral transmission, and the transmission of its text and meanings depends on people. The Qur'an also refers to itself as a written text, but also as 'clear signs in the hearts of those granted knowledge' (*The Spider*, 29:49).

These contrasting aspects led to a spectrum of approaches to scripture amongst various Muslim groups and sects: from the ultra-egalitarian seventh-century CE Khawarij rebels, who insisted on the primacy of the text and the absolute equality of all believers in interpreting it, to elitist sects that grew out of Islam, such as the Alawites and Druze of present-day Turkey, Syria, Lebanon and Israel; in these latter groups, deep religious learning and teaching is reserved for an elite clergy, whilst the masses are exposed only to basic teachings. (Interestingly, the Khawarij survive as a small sect, neither Sunni nor Shia, known as the Ibadis: Ibadism is the official interpretation of Islam in the state of Oman.)

Mainstream Sunni and Shia Islam tried to balance the two ends of this spectrum by promoting the interpretations of learned, holy people who knew the Qur'anic text but also embodied it in their character and conduct. The *'ulama* (learned) and *awliya* (saints) are common to Sunni and Shia Islam, but the latter also has infallible imams: a chain of divinely appointed leaders of Islam, all of whom are direct descendants of the Prophet himself. Mainstream Shias believe that this chain of imams was interrupted a millennium ago, to be restored by the appearance of a Messianic figure, the Mahdi, at the end of times. The Ismaili branch of Shi'ism claims its contemporary imam, HRH The Agha Khan, to be the latest in an unbroken chain from the Prophet.

The nature of the Qur'an has not been discussed in depth for centuries within Islam due to the trauma of a major controversy from the ninth century CE: otherwise-enlightened rationalist caliphs at Baghdad launched a bloody inquisition against traditionalist theologians because of this crucial issue. The traditionalists held that the Arabic Qur'an was the literal, 'uncreated' word of God, whilst the rationalists held that it was created, fearing that a pre-eternal Qur'an was an Islamic equivalent of the divine Christ of the Trinity. ('Uncreated' in this context is very similar to 'not made' in the Nicene Creed, which refers to Christ as 'begotten, not made'. This is why such words have critical theological implications: hence my reference to 'begotten' in the Bible in the previous chapter.)

The later Ash'ari theological school forged a synthesis: the word of God is manifested at different levels, including those of the Arabic Qur'an and its meaning 'beyond language' known to God within himself, a sort of divine 'mentalese' or 'the mind's language of thought', to borrow a term popularised by modern linguists. By the way, those caliphs felt they could intervene because the Qur'anic command to 'obey authority' (*Women*, 4:59) is traditionally held to cover both religious and political authority.

Since the twentieth century CE, a handful of Sunni and Shia thinkers have argued that the rationalist view of a 'created' Qur'an implies that it is also human – in other words, composed by the Prophet Muhammad, peace be upon him, after divine inspiration. But this interpretation remains a minority one.

GEORGE

The Gospels portray the Pharisees as nit-picking legalists who wanted to obey the Jewish law to the letter, and it is popularly assumed that Muslims hold that the Qur'an is the direct and infallible word of Allah. So it is useful that Dan and Usama should correct these misconceptions. It is probably more obvious that Christians have a range of opinion about the Bible's authority. Some Christian fundamentalists have claimed to take the Bible 'literally', but they cannot really mean that, since the Bible contains symbolism, metaphor, figurative language and parable. When Jesus said that his followers were the salt of the earth (Matthew 5.13), he clearly was not talking about cooking ingredients!

For the Christian fundamentalist, authority means inerrancy. This may seem a firm position that is easy to grasp, until one remembers that the Old Testament advocates washing one's clothes if one touches a menstruating woman (Leviticus 15.22), the need to inform a priest if one discovers mildew (Leviticus 14.35), and the avoidance of garments that mix linen and cotton (Deuteronomy 22.11). The fundamentalist might claim that in some sense the New Testament supersedes the Old, but this suggestion has its problems too. The New Testament still recommends avoiding blood products (Acts 15.20), Paul appears to condone slavery when he advises Onesimus to return to his master (Philemon 12), and his views on homosexuality do not seem very positive (Romans 1.26–27).

For the more liberal Christians such as myself, a looser concept of authority enables us to acknowledge that religious and moral insights can develop, but it leaves open the question of what we mean by authority. Dan stated earlier that the liberal Jews 'accept only those elements of the tradition which they regard as personally spiritually significant', but this suggests that we simply pick and choose those parts of Scripture that we find personally beneficial.

For many Christians, the solution is to acknowledge other sources of authority, namely the Church, conscience and human reason. Protestants have argued that the Bible is the primordial source of authority, since it recounts the formation and character of the early Church, while Catholic scholars point out that it was the Church that defined the canon of Scripture. All traditions, however, have deliberated and delivered decisions on doctrines and ethics, and the individual Christian should be guided by such judgements rather than giving one's own 'private interpretation' – something the Church has often viewed as potentially dangerous.

Paul identified conscience as a further source of authority. Speaking of the Jewish law, he argued that the Gentiles had 'the requirements of the law...written on their hearts, their consciences also bearing witness' (Romans 2.14–15). Although the voice of conscience may tell different people different things, the *Catechism of the Catholic Church* states that the training of conscience is a lifelong task involving education, study of the word of God, prayer and the use of reason.[9]

The concept of the Bible's authority lies between inerrancy and mere inspiration. There are many inspired pieces of Christian writing, but the Church has not defined them as having the status of Scripture. Steering a course between viewing the Bible as inerrant, and subjectively selecting the parts that appeal, is no easy matter. However, the individual Christian would be ill-advised to interpret the Bible unaided by the Church and its scholarly tradition. Many strange beliefs and actions have stemmed from interpretations – or misinterpretations – of scripture that lie outside one's Christian community.

DAN

I think I need to stress the radical break that has occurred in Jewish life between the Orthodox and non-Orthodox understanding of scriptural authority. As I mentioned previously, strictly Orthodox Jews (including the Hasidim) believe that the Pentateuch in its entirety was given by God to Moses on Mount Sinai. As a consequence, all the narratives in the Five Books of Moses are true. Every word is from the Almighty. Over the centuries rabbinic scholars developed various methods of interpreting the text, ranging from a literal to a metaphorical understanding. What this means in effect is that all the narratives in Genesis, Exodus, Leviticus, Numbers and Deuteronomy are true either in a literal or figurative sense.

The doctrine of *Torah mi Sinai* also served as the basis for the legal system. There are 613 commandments in the Torah. Orthodox Jews believe that they are all binding on the Jewish community. Over the centuries rabbinic scholars developed a highly complex method-ology of legal interpretation of these laws (rabbinic hermeneutics) resulting in the development of an extensive corpus of legislation based on Scripture. The rabbinic expansion of the legal code has thus resulted in the formulation of a vast compendium of law. There are literally tens of thousands of prescriptions that must be followed by the Orthodox.

However, non-Orthodox Jews like me no longer regard many of the narrative portions of Scripture as true, nor view the elaborate code of law as binding. Thus, for example, I do not think the universe was created in six days, nor that Noah and his family and two creatures of every kind escaped the flood in an ark, nor that Moses freed the Jewish people from slavery, nor that Joshua and a Hebrew army defeated the Canaanites. Instead I believe (as do non-Orthodox Jews in general) that the Torah was written by the ancient Israelites as a record of their history. Most is myth; some may be true.

George is critical of a subjective approach to the biblical text. But this is precisely the way in which non-Orthodox Jews deal with biblical law and its rabbinic expansion: they choose for themselves which laws they wish to keep. Let me give you a recent example. In the Reform movement, homosexuality is universally accepted, although it is vehemently condemned in the Bible. A number of Reform rabbis will conduct lesbian and gay weddings, but they insist that both partners are Jewish. They will not conduct interfaith marriages of either gay or straight couples. Such a stance has nothing to do with Scripture or rabbinic law – it is a personal decision made on subjective grounds.

Here is a final personal example of the kind of subjective thinking that is universal in the non-Orthodox community. Some years ago I went out with a rabbinic friend for dinner at a Chinese restaurant. Both of us refused to eat pork (forbidden in the Torah); instead we chose prawns (also forbidden in the Torah) on fried rice. But when the prawns arrived, the fried rice was mixed with pieces of pork. Both of us attempted to remove the pork with chopsticks. It was exceedingly difficult. Exasperated, I finally said: 'Look, this is ridiculous. Prawns are forbidden just as is pork. The food is getting cold. I'm going to eat the whole thing!'

USAMA

I should reiterate that the overwhelming majority of Muslims hold that the Qur'an is the direct word of God. However, the interpretation of what this means is contested: for example, the Ash'ari school of theology argued that the word of God exists on many levels.

Regarding authority, George's and Dan's comments remind me that there is a creative tension between tradition on the one hand, and reason on the other. Some verses of the Qur'an apparently teach that both tradition and reason are valid paths to truth and salvation. However, the Qur'an repeatedly condemns people who follow their forefathers without thinking: thus, tradition must be tempered by reason.

This tension was evident in early Islam, when some scholars insisted that authority derived from unbroken chains of righteous people, whilst others insisted that the intrinsic truth of a teaching was paramount, irrespective of who did or did not subscribe to it. The eleventh-century theologian, al-Ghazzali, lamented in his intellectual/ spiritual autobiography, *Deliverance from Error*, that most people of his time did not judge a statement by its intrinsic truth, but by the perceived authority of its author.

The verses of the Qur'an are known as *ayat Allah*, which means 'Signs of God'. Natural phenomena, including the workings of our internal psyches, are also called *ayat Allah* or 'signs of God' in the Qur'an. This supports the notion that the 'authority of experience', and hence of personal, subjective reflection, is also important, for experience consists of 'God's signs' in one's own life.

Furthermore, applying the 'signs of God', manifested as words of the Qur'an, to our lives involves reflecting them against the 'signs of God' in the workings of the natural world. For example, any religious judgement on homosexuality must involve an understanding of its nature scientifically. From my reading of science, homosexuality is neither absent from the animal world, nor is it entirely determined genetically: there is no such thing as a 'gay gene'. In fact, homosexuality, along with many aspects of the human condition and behaviour, appears to arise from a complex interaction between nature and nurture. Any Islamic discussion of homosexuality must therefore reflect this complex situation.

In practice, devout Muslims find their own balance of tradition and reason. For example, Muslim clerics continue to dispute whether or not the veiling of women and traditional gender roles are religious obligations, and to what extent organ transplants and abortion are allowed under Islam. Some Muslims facing these issues will often follow clerics whom they trust most, and thus appeal to authority, whilst others will follow what they consider to be most sensible, based on an appeal to reason and conscience. In an ideal world, both approaches would give a similar answer.

The situation is analogous to other aspects of life such as medical emergencies. Most people are not medical experts, but people occasionally have to make critical decisions such as whether or not to approve an organ transplant or switch off a life-support machine. Although people will respect the expertise of doctors, medics themselves may disagree, with second opinions being sought. The final decision in life-critical situations is often left to people and their consciences, or even gut feelings. The same is often true for religious matters, and rightly so, due to our individual responsibility before God.

Chapter 3

HOW ARE OUR SCRIPTURES USED?

This chapter explores how religious texts are used in practice – in worship, preaching and private devotion. Their importance is typically underlined by accompanying rituals, such as the Torah being brought out of the Ark in procession, or the Bible being carried ceremonially into the congregation at the beginning of worship – at least in some Christian denominations. Some uses of Scripture are discouraged, however – the Christian tradition, for example, has disapproved of 'private interpretation' and of bibliomancy. Which uses are acceptable, and which are unacceptable?

USAMA

The most obvious use of the Qur'an in Muslim life is during daily prayers: devout Muslims perform ritual prayers (*salat*) consisting of a number of units or cycles, each involving standing, bowing, prostration on the ground and sitting. (There are five obligatory daily prayers: their timings are dawn, afternoon, late afternoon, sunset and night. The number of cycles in each prayer are, respectively: two, four, four, three and four, giving a total of 17 cycles of prayer, a daily minimum for the devout.)

The standing part of each unit of prayer includes recitation from the Qur'an: the opening chapter (*Fatiha*), consisting of seven short verses, is recited in every unit of prayer, followed by other verses or chapters selected by the worshipper. Thus, for devout Muslims, the *Fatiha* is recited a minimum of 17 times daily. Muslims who are not devout will perform the occasional prayer: perhaps the Friday prayer sometimes at mosque, or at least the two annual *Eid* (festival) prayers. They will also join funeral prayers.

Recitation and study of the Qur'an is also recommended at all times, but especially during Ramadan, the month of fasting, and the Hajj, the annual pilgrimage to Mecca that lasts several days. During the 29 or 30 nights of Ramadan, a lunar month, extra prayers are held at home or mosque, in which the entire Qur'an is traditionally recited from beginning to end over the course of the month.

Children are often taught to read and recite the Qur'an from a young age, as soon as they are able to, and 'Amen' (Arabic: *Aameen*) parties are held by Indian-origin Muslims to celebrate a child's completion of the recitation of the Qur'an from cover to cover. I can remember vividly my own *Aameen* party aged around seven, when my parents gave me my first wristwatch, a Timex piece. They threw an even bigger party when I completed my memorisation of the Qur'an aged 11, and gave me a Sinclair ZX Spectrum personal computer – very fashionable in those days.

Imams and scholars are required to memorise and study the Qur'an in depth, including associated disciplines such as classical Arabic, commentary, tradition, law and ethics.

Foretelling the future based on the Qur'an is frowned upon, although some people occasionally indulge in this. Arabic letters also have numerical equivalents: the 28 letters of the Arabic alphabet have the numerical values 1–10, then 20–100 in multiples of 10, then 200–1000 in multiples of 100. This means that people can look for number patterns in the Qur'an, especially numerical dates to pin to prophecies.

Prayers from the Qur'an are also recited for spiritual healing, to complement other forms of medicine. These prayers are sometimes written on paper which is then dipped in water so that the ink runs off, with the resulting mixture of very dilute 'sacred ink' fed to the patient as medicine.

The Qur'an is thus recited over the sick, dying and deceased, but also over new lives: newborn babies. A common cultural practice is to randomly select a word from the Qur'an to determine a baby's name. This results in exotic names such as Saqlain, meaning 'the two weighty worlds of humans and genies' and Mantasha, meaning 'whom You [God] will'. I always worry that this practice will, one day, result in a baby named *Shaytan* (Satan)!

DAN

So far I have focused on the Torah (Genesis, Exodus, Leviticus, Numbers and Deuteronomy). But it is not only the Five Books of Moses that are regarded as of divine origin. The prophetic books as well as the other books in the Hebrew canon (which I listed in Chapter 1) are also viewed as divinely inspired. Hence, the entire Hebrew Scriptures are designated holy books, and they play a central role in the life of the Jewish nation. Orthodox as well as non-Orthodox Jews read a section of the Torah in the synagogue every week. The Torah reading is accompanied by a reading from the prophetic books (*Haftarah*) on the Sabbath. In addition, various texts from the Bible appear in the liturgy, and there are readings from other books in the Bible on various festivals. In these various ways the Hebrew Bible is deeply integrated into the religious life of the community.

Many Jewish festivals are also based on Scripture. For example, Sabbath observance is prescribed in Deuteronomy: 'Observe the Sabbath day, to keep it holy, as the Lord your God commanded you. Six days you shall labour, and do all your work; but the seventh day is a Sabbath to the Lord your God; in it you shall not do any work' (Deuteronomy 5.12–14). Similarly, Deuteronomy declares that Jews are to celebrate the three pilgrim festivals (Passover, Shavuot and Sukkot): 'Three times each year shall all your males appear before the Lord your God at the place which He will choose, at the feast of unleavened bread, at the feast of weeks, and at the feast of booths' (Deuteronomy 16.16). Similarly the Jewish New Year (*Rosh Hashanah*) and the Day of Atonement (*Yom Kippur*) are prescribed in Scripture.

In addition, the Hebrew Bible provides the framework for understanding Jewish history. The Book of Genesis describes the creation of the cosmos, and continues with an account of the flood and the patriarchal period. The Book of Exodus depicts the exodus from Egypt, and the revelation to Moses on Mount Sinai. The narrative of Israel's history continues with the Book of Joshua, which portrays the conquest of the land of Canaan. Later books depict the history of ancient Israel under various kings in Israel and Judah. For Jews the Hebrew Scriptures is thus a record of their heroes and history.

For strictly Orthodox Jews, the Hebrew Bible also provides a framework for daily life. The 613 commandments in the Torah are regarded as inerrant; supplemented by rabbinic interpretation, they constitute the basis for living in accordance with God's will. For non-Orthodox Jews like me, however, the Hebrew Bible does not play as critical a role. Because I do not accept the doctrine of *Torah mi Sinai*, I do not feel obliged to follow all the teachings contained in Scripture. Instead, I am at liberty to choose to observe only those commandments which I regard as spiritually meaningful.

In this regard I should stress that because non-Orthodox Jews do not regard the Torah as the word of God, they do not feel obliged to accept the biblical narrative as an accurate account of the history of ancient Israel. Instead, most view the Bible as a human (though possibly inspired) record of the history of the Jewish people. For many non-Orthodox Jews, the biblical figures of the past such as Noah, Abraham, Isaac, Jacob, Moses, Joshua and others should be perceived as pious mythological figures passed on from generation to generation.

GEORGE

When I was a Sunday School pupil many years ago, we had to learn a weekly 'motto text' – a single verse from Scripture. Reciting motto texts has now largely died out, and the prospect of memorising the entire Bible is too daunting: it is substantially longer than the Qur'an, and only a small handful of Christians have read it all, let alone memorised it.

Christians appropriated the Jewish practice of reading Scripture during worship, and it is usual to read from both the Old and the New Testaments. A Gospel reading is especially important, since the Gospels proclaim Jesus Christ's mission. The principal sacraments – baptism and the Eucharist – are enjoined in the Bible (Matthew 28.24; Luke 22.19), and the key festivals of Christmas, Easter and Pentecost commemorate important biblical events. Although the Jewish pilgrim festivals are prescribed in the Bible, most Christians believe that they are superseded by Christ's 'new covenant', although a very few minor sects continue to observe them.

Christians are encouraged to read the Bible, and the devout will use it in their private devotions. Particularly in the Protestant tradition, importance is attached to making the Bible available in the language of the people, rather than in the original languages of Hebrew and Greek, or in Latin – the historic language of the Western Church.

Setting biblical verses to music has been an effective way of transmitting Christian teaching, and many songs and hymns used in Church are scriptural paraphrases or quotations. Outside the churches, several popular songs have biblical themes or allusions – for example, Sam Smith's 'The Writing's on the Wall' (Daniel 5), Leonard Cohen's 'Hallelujah' (Judges 16.19), the Byrds' 'Turn, turn, turn' (Ecclesiastes 3.1–8).

There are many allusions to the Bible in English literature: Shakespeare refers to the Bible well over a thousand times, and many popular expressions come from the Bible, such as the 'skin of one's teeth' (Job 19.20), 'rise and shine' (Isaiah 60.1), or 'the leopard can't change its spots' (Jeremiah 13.23), although probably most people are unaware of their origin.

The Bible can help in times of need. Hotel guests will be familiar with Bibles placed in their bedrooms by the Gideons – a practice that began in 1908. The Gideons offer no commentary on the text, but suggest passages that might be read to meet particular situations, such as grief, anxiety or discouragement.

Usama refers to the use of the Qur'an for naming children and for healing rituals. Many of our children have biblical names such as Ruth, Sarah, John and Peter. Understandably, Judas is not used, nor is Jesus (except in Spanish-speaking communities), since his name is regarded as too sacred.

The use of the Bible in quasi-magical ways tends to be discouraged. It should be studied rather than opened at random. The practice of 'bibliomancy' (using a book for divination) can be dangerous. Readers may have heard the story of the man who sought urgent guidance. Opening the Bible randomly, he found 'He went away and hanged himself' (Matthew 27.5). Thinking that such a course of action was somewhat excessive, he tried again; this time he came on 'Go and do likewise' (Luke 10.37). He tried a third time, and found the verse, 'What you are about to do, do quickly' (John 13.27).

The Bible must be used responsibly, with due regard to its true meaning and purpose. It is not an oracle, a fortune-telling device, or (as writers such as Michael Drosnin have suggested)[10] an encoded document to be deciphered.

USAMA

I referred earlier to Arabic numerology, and I know that this exists in the Hebrew tradition as well. An Orthodox Jewish friend at school used to bring in a book called *Mathematical Byways in the Torah*, which attempted to prove the Torah's divine origin through Hebrew numerology. I remember a liberal Jewish classmate reprimanding him for reducing the Torah to mathematical patterns and demeaning what should be regarded as the word of God.

This discussion intrigued me because we were having parallel discussions in the Muslim world at the time. An Egyptian-American physician had published his theory of a 'mathematical miracle' in the Qur'an based on the number 19, itself referred to in the Qur'an as having some significance (*One Wrapped Up In A Blanket*, 74:30). Although the theory was later discredited, I had taken a huge interest in it, being a keen mathematician myself.

There are cases of interaction amongst the Jewish, Christian and Islamic worlds through numerology. Ibn Kathir of Damascus, a major fourteenth-century CE Qur'an-commentator, recounted a story of early Jews in Medina predicting the length of Muslim rule based on Qur'anic numerology: perhaps they really did so, or the Muslims were aware of Jewish numerology and imagined that they applied it to predicting Islam's political fortunes. The method mentioned by Ibn Kathir gives the following alternative number of years of Muslim rule: 734, 1757 or 3385. None of these numbers bear much resemblance to actual history.

Ibn Kathir also mentions an alleged prophecy by a twelfth-century CE mystic, who is said to have predicted Saladin's reconquest of Jerusalem from the Crusaders in 1187 CE, based on Qur'anic numerology. I have looked into this and concluded that the prophecy was probably interpolated into an earlier text after the reconquest.

The five pillars of Islam are, for all except the most esoteric Muslims, faith (*shahada*), prayer (*salat*), charity or alms (*zakat*), fasting (*sawm*) and pilgrimage (*hajj*). The detailed practices relating to these are often drawn out from Qur'anic passages. For examples, the timings of the five daily prayers (dawn, afternoon, late afternoon, sunset, night) are derived from various verses, and explicitly stated in many hadiths. Similarly, for the alms-rate and the kinds of wealth on which it is payable. Rules for fasting, especially the month of Ramadan, are based on a concise Qur'anic passage, the only one mentioning that month (*The Heifer*, 2:183). The Ramadan passage is followed by another focusing on the pilgrimage (*The Heifer*, 2:196–203), and there is also an entire chapter named *Pilgrimage* (*Hajj*), due to its extensive treatment of the topic (*Pilgrimage*, 22:25–37). Pilgrimage rites are based on these passages, and on the hadith traditions that are said to capture the practice of the Prophet himself.

The variations amongst the Islamic schools of law and jurisprudence in terms of Islamic practice arise from the diverse and even conflicting interpretations of the above passages, and of the multitude of hadith traditions on every topic.

And of course, Muslims refer to the Qur'an and its numerous commentaries for wider questions of ethics, philosophy, the origins of the universe and of life, and even of the possibility and religious permissibility of space travel! Some of these questions are correctly the domain of science and other disciplines, and not of Qur'an commentary: the main job of the latter is to provide moral, ethical and spiritual guidance.

DAN

Earlier in this chapter, I sketched the ways in which the Bible functions in traditional Judaism. Usama pointed out that the Qur'an guides Muslims morally, spiritually and ethically. The same is true of the Hebrew Bible for strictly Orthodox Jews. But as I noted, within the non-Orthodox world the Bible is viewed very differently. Yet, despite the chasm that exists between strictly Orthodox and non-Orthodox Jews, there is commonality as far as memory is concerned.

For Orthodox Jews, the Five Books of Moses contain truths about the nature of the universe, God's selection of the Jewish nation as his special people, the Exodus, and the revelation of the Law on Mount Sinai. The Hebrew Bible thus serves as the framework for living an authentically religious life. Non-Orthodox Jews, like me, however, do not view Scripture in this way. For example, I do not believe that the universe was created in six days. Possibly the events recorded in the Torah did not actually take place. Were Abraham, Isaac and Jacob historical persons? I have no idea. Did the Jewish people escape from Egyptian bondage under Moses' leadership? Who knows? What about the conquest of Canaanites? Archaeology findings do not support the events recorded in the Hebrew Bible. Who can tell?

But is it important? Not really. In Reform synagogues, on the Sabbath we read aloud the Torah portion containing these stories about Noah, Abraham, Moses. It is taken for granted that these narratives record the history of our people. But no one stands up and says: 'Hey, but is it true? Did Abraham really live? Did Moses?' These figures of the past are alive for all Jews in the present even if they are no more than myths.

At Passover, we Jews gather together for the Passover *seder* which commemorates the liberation by Moses of our ancestors who were in Egyptian bondage. My family in Denver, where I grew up, was composed of believers and non-believers. At the Passover *seder* we sat together and recounted the *Haggadah* (Passover prayer book), which recalls the story of the first-born Egyptians who were killed whereas God passed over the houses of the Israelites and spared them. We ate *matzohs*, which symbolise the unleavened bread that the ancient Hebrews baked prior to their escape.

Did the Exodus really take place as described in the Bible? Who knows? Perhaps it is no more than legend. It makes little difference. Did Moses really part the Red Sea? Did God deliver the Jews? These historical questions are set aside as we gather together to remember who we are. Memory and identity are fused as we recite the narrative of our freedom and celebrate our liberation. At the deepest levels of the Jewish psyche, we remind ourselves that we were despised and threatened with death, yet we prevailed.

Whether we are Orthodox or non-Orthodox Jews, or unaffiliated to any particular denomination, the Bible provides a framework for understanding who we are. Full of heroes and heroines, of warriors and prophets, the Bible binds us together. It guides us in worship, in prayer, and in service to the Jewish nation. Biblical memory calls us from the deep. It is the invisible thread that draws us together as one people.

GEORGE

I should like to backtrack to Usama's comments on scriptural numbers and numerology. During my church training, one of my fellow students – I'll call him Darren – was an extreme fundamentalist, who was attracted to biblical numerology. This seemed to involve reading Hebrew and Greek characters as numbers rather than letters, which supposedly revealed a remarkable numeric pattern in Scripture. Darren's numerology revealed that the world would end in 1995. When we confronted him with Jesus' caution that only God the Father knows the day and the hour (Mark 13.32), he responded, 'You don't know the day nor the hour – but you can calculate the year!' Of course, the fact that we are still around is ample demonstration of the futility of using the Bible in this way.

One bestselling book that aroused public attention was Michael Drosnin's *The Bible Code.*[11] The author claimed that, if the letters of the biblical text were placed on a grid, rather like a word search, one could find allusions to modern-day events. The Bible apparently foretold that Shakespeare would write Macbeth – although why the Bible should mention this is far from obvious.

Some Christians have made calculations based on times and dates that the Bible mentions, which purportedly show that certain key events in world history were predicted in biblical prophecy. References to the rise of the papacy, Napoleon, Hitler, and more recently 9/11 and Donald Trump have been apparently identified. Tellingly, such 'predictions' are only recognised after the events, making them of little use as predictions.

Occasionally, the Bible has been used as a good luck charm. There are stories of soldiers whose breast pockets carried a small Bible, which sustained the impact of a bullet and saved their lives. I don't know how authentic such stories are, or whether Bibles are any more effective in such situations than cigarette packets or diaries.

However, the Bible is not an amulet, a fortune-telling device, or a book of word search or number puzzles. It is for devotion, study and use in public worship, and its central message is intended to be understood by all, and not merely a handful of clever codebreakers. Although there are certainly passages that are difficult to understand, their meaning is to be determined by serious scholarship. As Dan rightly suggests, it is for prayer, worship and guidance for life.

Like Dan, I would question whether the Bible can be used as an accurate history or science textbook – issues to which we shall return. The students in my year were equally divided between conservative/fundamentalist Christians and liberal/radical ones. I clearly recall a sermon that the Professor of Theology preached in the university chapel at the end of term. He warned the more radical students not to throw out the essentials of the Christian message, but equally he urged the fundamentalists not to believe the biblical narrative but lose sight of its meaning.

Faith and reason are not to be regarded as enemies. The Christian tradition has always welcomed scholarly enquiry and criticism. I concur with Dan that the Bible does not present history in the sense a twenty-first-century academic historian would write it, but that is not its purpose. Christian scholars have used the term 'salvation history', indicating that the prime purpose of Scripture is to demonstrate how God offers salvation to humankind, and reconciliation through Jesus Christ. I shall explore what this means as our discussion continues.

Chapter 4

METHODS OF INTERPRETATION

Jews interpret their writings through the Talmud, which rabbis have studied extensively. Christianity places the authority of the Church in parallel with the authority of Scripture, and the various traditions have defined means of interpreting the Bible (such as Roman Catholic canon law). Muslims employ Sharia as a means of interpreting the Qur'an. This chapter examines methods of interpretation, and identifies common misunderstandings.

DAN

In the last chapter, George and Usama were discussing the ways in which the Hebrew text can be understood. This is the key issue for this chapter. Such activity has traditionally been a central occupation of rabbinic scholars. During the Tannaitic and Amoraic period (between the second and sixth centuries CE), Jewish sages – referred to as Tannaim and Amoraim respectively – actively engaged in the interpretation of the Hebrew Bible.

Frequently rabbinic scholars sought to clear up a possible mis-understanding. Such exegesis takes place when the biblical text is commented on or accompanied by an explanation. For example, in a *midrash* (rabbinic exegesis) on Psalms, the third-century scholar Rabbi Simlai explained that the fact that Psalm 50 begins with the words, 'The Mighty One, God, the Lord speaks', does not signify that God has a trinitarian nature. Rather all three appellations are only one name, even as one person can be called a workman, builder and architect.

Alongside such explanations of the narrative parts of Scripture, the rabbis developed a complex method for interpreting biblical law. Hillel, who lived about a century before the destruction of the Second Temple in 70 CE, is reputed to have been the first to lay down these interpretative principles. Hillel's seven rules were expanded in the second century CE by Rabbi Ishmael ben Elisha into 13 hermeneutical principles.

Let me give you an example of the way in which these rules were applied. The first of Hillel's principles states that if a certain restriction applies to a matter of minor importance, it also applies to a more important situation. Traditionally, a minor holiday is regarded as of less importance than the Sabbath. Hence, according to this principle, if an action is forbidden on a minor holiday, then it is also forbidden on the Sabbath. In Hebrew, this principle is referred to as a *kal vachomer* (an inference from a minor to a major case).

Through the centuries, rabbinic sages engaged in fervent discussion about the meaning of biblical law, and their views (which were subsequently recorded in the Mishnah and the Palestinian and Babylonian Talmuds) are regarded as binding for all time. In ensuing centuries subsequent rabbinic scholars continued the discussion of biblical law, and their opinions (*responsa*) were recorded along with Mishnaic and Talmudic law in various legal codes, the most famous of which is the *Shulhan Arukh*. Today – as in previous centuries – strictly Orthodox Jews are anxious to follow the *Shulhan Arukh* in all spheres of their lives. In rabbinic seminaries (*yeshivot*), the study of Jewish law is of primary importance. Traditionally those who are ordained as rabbis are experts in rabbinic jurisprudence.

There is an important distinction I should mention regarding the Jewish legal system. Biblical law is referred to as the Written Law. These 613 commandments are understood as having been revealed to Moses on Mount Sinai. They, along with all those regulations contained in rabbinic sources (referred to as the Oral Law) are binding on all Jews. In other words, the rabbinic interpretation of biblical law must be rigorously adhered to.

But this does not apply to the rabbinic interpretation of the rest of Scripture. Through the centuries, rabbinic sages expressed their opinions over a wide range of topics contained in the *Tanakh* (Hebrew Bible). Their opinions were eventually recorded in rabbinic sources (*midrashim*). Frequently their views conflict with one another.

But unlike rabbinic law, such interpretations are viewed as personal opinions – Jews are free to accept or reject them.

USAMA

Over the past 14 centuries, thousands of commentaries on the Qur'an have been written. These commentaries employ one or more of the following, sometimes inter-related, methods of interpretation: (1) interpretation of some verses or passages via other Qur'anic verses or passages; (2) interpretation via an authority such as the Prophet, peace be upon him, his Companions or their followers; (3) interpretation via the many levels of meaning inherent in classical Arabic; (4) interpretation via logic and reason; (5) interpretation via the context of the revelation of the verses – remember that the Qur'an was revealed piecemeal to the Prophet; and (6) interpretation via inner or spiritual meanings. Examples now follow.

First, interpretation of some verses via other verses: many verses of the Qur'an enjoin or recommend 'feeding the poor' generally and in regard to specific legal situations such as to make up for a broken oath, or as a substitute for not being able to fast during the month of Ramadan. But what quality or quantity of food is appropriate for giving to the poor? Most of the verses remain silent on this, but one provides details: 'the average (or best) food with which you feed your families'. Thus, the details in this verse apply to all verses mentioning feeding the poor.

The above case is also an example of the third type of interpretation mentioned above: invoking different meanings from classical Arabic. In this example, the same word could mean the 'average' or 'best' quality of food: individual scholars and believers will choose one of these meanings when feeding the poor. (Just like rabbis, all imams must know their jurisprudence in order to guide their communities.) This is also an example of the fourth and fifth types of interpretation (logic and context): in seventh-century Arabia, people generally ate only two meals per day, so later jurists ruled that if you had to feed the poor to make up for a broken oath or in lieu of fasting Ramadan, you had to provide two meals per day. Nowadays, in societies where people eat three meals a day, logic and reason dictate that they would have to feed the poor similarly.

A famous case of interpretation via authority is in the *Fatiha*, the opening chapter of the Qur'an that is recited multiple times in the five daily prayers. The *Fatiha* ends with the following prayer: 'Show us the Straight Path: the path of those whom You favoured; who neither received anger nor went astray.' In a famous tradition ascribed to the Prophet and his Companions, Jews and Christians are respectively meant by those implied to have 'received anger' and 'gone astray'. This interpretation is a bedrock as to how the other Abrahamic communities are seen as examples and mirrors for Muslims to reflect on their own paths: broadly speaking, Jews are criticised for sometimes focusing on law without spirit, whilst Christians are criticised for affirming spirit without law. But note that the verse is general, simply speaking about ways that people may depart from God's path; furthermore, the Qur'an itself confirms that many Jews and Christians are rightly guided, faithful believers.

Inner interpretations refer to spiritual realities: in the commandment to Moses and Aaron to 'Go to Pharaoh, for he has transgressed', the Pharaoh also symbolises the intransigence of the heart, so this is also a command to approach one's own heart and purify it from its own arrogance.

GEORGE

Dan and Usama's approaches to Scripture sound like lawyers interpreting pieces of legislation, and this is precisely what Christians want to avoid. Scripture is for spiritual guidance, not codified law requiring meticulous interpretation.

One set of approaches to the Bible is sometimes called the Quadriga, which identifies four broad ways in which the Bible can be used. A *quadriga* was a Roman chariot, drawn by four horses, working together. Applied to the Bible, it highlights four hermeneutical approaches, which work together with each other.

The first of these is historical/critical method (sometimes misleadingly called the 'literal' approach). This method is used by post-Enlightenment scholars, who ask questions about the authenticity of the events that the Bible describes, who the authors of Scripture were, what we can know about key figures such as Abraham, Moses, Jesus and Paul, and so on. Most congregations are not seminarians, however, and the scholar's historical/critical approach can sometimes seem arid and uninspiring. Some of the laity think that scholars ask too many critical questions, cutting the ground from under their faith; hence the need to go beyond biblical scholarship.

The word 'anagogic' comes from two Greek words – *ana* ('up') and *agō* ('I lead'), signifying that the Bible leads us up from the earthly to the spiritual. The Bible speaks of God's coming kingdom, and the signs that herald it. It contains the hope of the New Jerusalem (Revelation 22), and describes earthly signs of the approaching eschaton, such as wars, natural disasters, false prophets and persecution (Mark 13.1–31). Some Christians believe that such phenomena herald a literal return of Christ on the clouds of heaven (Mark 13.26–27), while others believe that such evils have always been with us, but will be transcended in Christ's heavenly rule, which has already begun within ourselves (Luke 17.21).

Typological interpretation finds incidents in the Old Testament which are believed to foreshadow others in the New. For example, the Book of Genesis records that Melchizedek, king of Salem, produced bread and wine for Abraham (Genesis 14.18). Since the purpose of this incident is unclear, Christians have sometimes taken this to prefigure Christ's sharing of bread and wine at the Last Supper. The New Testament itself uses typological interpretation: Jesus likens Jonah's three days in the whale's belly to his own period in the tomb (Matthew 12.40). Moses struck a rock at Rephidim, Paul asserts that 'the rock was Christ' (Numbers 20.11; 1 Corinthians 10.4). Such interpretations may seem fanciful and contrived, but Christians needed to make sense of the Hebrew Scriptures, and this was one way of doing it.

The fourth method is tropological (from the Greek *tropos*, meaning manner of life, or character) or – more simply – moral. Not only does the Bible offer explicit moral teaching, but many of its stories make us reflect on our own lives and decisions. The story of Esau selling his birthright to his younger brother Jacob in exchange for a mere plate of soup (Genesis 25.29–34) might make us reflect on comparable bad choices that we make. People have been known to exchange their entire careers for short-term sexual gratification, or swap family life for long working hours, in order to gain a high salary. For the Christian, the Bible gives colour and illustration to its moral teaching, rather than arid regulations to be interpreted by legal experts. People remember the parable of the Good Samaritan (Luke 10.25–37), not because of Jesus' skills in jurisprudence, but because the story captured the imagination and inspired its hearers.

DAN

George thinks that both Usama and I sound like lawyers. As far as the Jewish approach is concerned, he is right. Rabbi means 'my teacher', and traditionally rabbinic students were trained in Jewish law. That is why rabbinic ordination states that the newly ordinated rabbi is qualified to make legal decisions. This was a critical role through the centuries. It was the responsibility of the rabbi to know both biblical and rabbinic law. Rabbinic instruction consisted of years of intense study of the Mishnah and the Talmud in connection with the Code of Jewish Law (*Shulhan Arukh*).

Through the centuries rabbinic sages continued to give legal decisions based on their understanding of these texts. Continually it was necessary to update biblical and rabbinic law so that it could be applied to contemporary circumstances. For example, in the modern world Jews do not turn on electric lights or drive cars on the Sabbath. Neither the Bible nor ancient rabbinic sources dealt with such issues; therefore it has been the responsibility of rabbis to make decisions about such topics.

In the strictly Orthodox world, rabbis still fulfil this role. Continually they are looked to for rabbinic rulings about a wide range of issues. Not all Jews are familiar with the corpus of rabbinic legislation. So it is the rabbi's role to provide guidance about Jewish law. In traditional *yeshivot*, Jewish scholars study the Talmud with its commentaries in the quest to understand the reasoning behind the legislation in the *Shulhan Arukh*. Some of those who engage in such intense study spend their entire lives in a *yeshivah* studying these ancient sources. You might be intrigued by the sight. Jewish learning is not a silent pursuit. Talmud study is done with a partner: the text is read aloud along with talmudic commentaries. *Yeshivot* are noisy places!

So far I have referred to the interpretation of rabbinic legal sources (referred to as *halakhah*). Alongside such study, rabbinic scholars have engaged in the interpretation of narrative sections of Scripture (referred to as *aggadah*). All the books of the Bible have undergone such a process of interpretation using many of the techniques George referred to. Alongside the quest to understand the literal meaning of the text, sages sought to interpret the Bible figuratively, analogically and typologically. These hermeneutical methods are referred to as Pardes. According to the Pardes approach to exegesis, the interpretation of biblical texts is realised through: (1) *peshat* (literal or plain meaning); (2) *remez* (deep meaning); (3) *derash* (comparative meaning); and (4) *sod* (hidden or secret meaning).

It is important to realise, however, that in the modern Jewish world, only the Orthodox adhere to the strict hermeneutical approach to both *halakhah* and *aggadah* that I have outlined. For Orthodox Jews including the Hasidim, the 613 commandments in the Torah are binding as are the rabbinic decisions contained in the *Shulhan Arukh*. The Code of Jewish Law as well as later rabbinic *responsa* concerning the law constitute a rigid framework for Jewish living. Although the opinions of rabbinic sages in the *midrashim* are not binding in the same way, they nonetheless constitute a sacred heritage from the past worthy of study and reflection. For non-Orthodox Jews, like me, however, this heritage of biblical interpretation has a different significance. It is a rich resource of Jewish learning and culture rather than a blueprint for Jewish existence in the modern age.

USAMA

George thinks that Dan and I sound like lawyers interpreting a legal text. If that is how we sound to him, then he is not listening carefully: the second half of my piece earlier in this chapter is entirely devoted to spiritual realities and guidance. If I were to caricature and misrepresent George's position in return, I could say that he sounds like a platitudinous mystic disconnected from the real world, as though we don't live our spiritual lives rooted in human society on earth.

To reiterate: the Qur'an, being God's Word in some sense, has many levels of meaning, as one would expect from scripture of divine origin. Somewhat confusingly, the 'literal' meaning alone has many levels, because Arabic is a polysemic language, that is to say, having multiple meanings at different levels. These levels include the rational, legal, metaphorical, moral and spiritual. Life and reality are complex, and we have to navigate multiple levels together at times. In the simplest terms, the meanings of the Qur'an are 'outer and apparent' and 'inner or hidden'.

For further examples, there is a Qur'anic story about an Israelite fishing village that God tested by causing its local fish to only approach on the Sabbath. Some of the villagers fished indirectly on the Sabbath and thus circumvented the law by sticking to its letter whilst violating its spirit. They were punished by 'becoming apes and pigs' (*The Heifer*, 2:65; *The Last Supper*, 5:60; *The Heights*, 7:163–167). The traditional, literalist commentary is that they were literally transformed and metamorphosed into lower mammals. However, the traditional, rationalist commentators have them becoming *like* apes and pigs: losing their intellectual capacities and becoming dominated by greed and lust.

There is certainly a need for mystical and spiritual commentaries of the Qur'an to be made more widely available, especially as contemporary Islam is often dominated by dry, legalistic interpretations. As another example of inner, spiritual meanings, Moses asks his followers to enter the Sanctified (Holy) Land, but they lack the ambition and courage to fight the tyrants who rule there, instead telling Moses to 'go and fight them with your Lord' (*The Last Supper*, 5:20–26). An inner meaning of this passage is that we are supposed to find and enter the holiest precincts of our hearts, but that most people are too lazy to combat the tyrannical qualities, such as selfishness and envy, that prevent us from doing so.

I appreciate hearing about the four-fold approaches to scripture outlined by both Dan and George. These exist in the Islamic tradition also, as I have indicated. One particular version of this four-fold classification is from Abdullah Ibn Abbas, the Prophet's cousin who specialised in Qur'an-commentary. Ibn Abbas taught that the Qur'an had four types of meanings: (1) 'those known to all Muslims', or basic religious truths; (2) 'those known only to the Arabs', or linguistic understanding of the multiple meanings of Arabic phrases; (3) 'those known only to people of knowledge', or arrived at by deep study, reflection and piety, since the latter is inner knowledge of God; and (4) 'those known only to God'. This last aspect should be remembered to help retain humility, and indeed is implied by Dan and George's mentions of secret or hidden meaning.

Over the centuries, the Qur'an has inspired great rationality, philosophy, science, law, poetry, metaphysics and spirituality, and continues to do so. A multidimensional approach to interpreting scripture is regarded in the Islamic tradition as being inherited from the way of Moses with the Torah, Jesus with the Torah and Gospel, and Muhammad with the Qur'an.

GEORGE

Well, I don't think I've ever been called a mystic before, and I certainly don't feel like one! As for platitudes, I certainly can't find them – although maybe these are inner hidden meanings in my text, which only Usama has penetrated! My comments on legalism were directed mainly at the last couple of exchanges: having listened to both Dan and Usama, I think we agree that our respective scriptures have different levels of meaning. We might agree, too, that there are abuses as well as uses of our scriptures, and that not all methods of interpretation are legitimate or profitable.

I think the main point of difference between the Christians on the one hand, and Jews and Muslims on the other, is that Christians have never used their Bible as a detailed law code. Jews and Muslims have had their own nation states at various points in their history, and their scriptures have served as their law codes. States governed by Christian leaders, such as John Calvin's Geneva, drew on the Bible, but did not use the Bible itself as a law code to be interpreted by legal experts.

Legislation often requires interpretation for new situations. Some time ago, I stayed at a hotel in Nof Ginosar in North Israel, which was run by a strict Jewish management. A notice in one of the toilets read, 'Dear Guests, This facility causes a desecration of the Sabbath. Have a pleasant stay. The Hotel Management.' Some of our party wondered what this curious sign meant. Apparently, the facility had an automatic flushing device that was activated by an electronic sensor, which is the modern equivalent of kindling a flame, prohibited in Exodus 35.3. If the toilet had been programmed to flush automatically at ten-minute intervals, it would have been acceptable to use it, but activating a sensor completed an electrical circuit – hence the violation of Sabbath law.

I know that Dan does not go along with this kind of legalism, but this approach to Jewish law has caused the Pharisees and their successors to earn a bad reputation among Christians. This is unfortunate, since the Pharisees were reformers who secured the survival of the Jewish faith, by championing legal observance above Temple worship. This paid great dividends when the Romans destroyed the Jerusalem Temple in 70 CE. A temple can be destroyed, but not loyalty to the Torah.

When Paul wrote, 'Christ redeemed us from the curse of the law' (Galatians 3.13), he meant that we do not have to engage in over-meticulous probing into the fine detail of God's requirements. I worked for some time within a business school, whose students were often sent out on placements. One frequent criticism by their line managers was that some of them kept asking for clarification about insignificant detail. Asked to design a brochure, one student kept returning to ask about the intended colour of the text and the background, what type and size of font should be used, and other points of detail, when the manager wanted her to use her creativity, and simply get the task done. A good subordinate intuitively grasps what is needed, and gets on with it.

Usama mentions the criticism that Christians affirm the spirit but not the law. This is almost correct. Paul did not mean that Christians have a *carte blanche* to do as they please, but that their reason and conscience should guide them into what is right, drawing on the Bible's teaching, and its concrete illustrations of how to behave.

PART 2

GOD

Chapter 5

THE NATURE OF GOD

The Hebrew Bible presupposes the existence of God, who is the creator and sustainer of the universe. Although concerned with all people, he established a special relationship with Israel. The Hebrew view of God is endorsed in the New Testament, but Christians add that God is made manifest in the life and death of Jesus Christ. Muslims hold the Qur'an to be the word of God, revealed to Muhammad by the same God who revealed the Torah and the Gospels, but believe that Jews and Christians have misinterpreted and falsified the previous revelations; so God sent the final prophet Muhammad with the authentic, true revelation. Can these differences be resolved?

GEORGE

Jesus spoke of the God of Abraham, Isaac and Jacob (Matthew 22.32), and so it follows that all our three faiths share the same God. There have been extreme Christian fundamentalists who have averred that Muslims do not worship the same deity, but such a suggestion is absurd, implying that there is more than one God. The Christian faith is committed to monotheism.

The Bible portrays God as the world's creator, in common with Jews and Muslims, and the Book of Genesis states that the universe was created by God's Word: each time God spoke, something new was created. Jewish thought developed the concept of the Word, identifying it with divine wisdom (Proverbs 3.19) and John's Gospel goes further to speak of Jesus Christ as the divine Word (John 1.1).

Writing somewhat earlier than John, Paul affirms the doctrine of the Incarnation, when he writes to the Philippians that Jesus:

> being in very nature God, did not consider equality with God something to be used to his own advantage; rather, he made himself nothing by taking the very nature of a servant, being made in human likeness. And being found in appearance as a man, he humbled himself by becoming obedient to death – even death on a cross! (Philippians 2.6–8)

In Christ, God gave up his divine qualities to be a human being, in order to redeem the world.

The doctrine of the Incarnation forms part of the Christian belief in the Trinity – an issue that separates Christians from Jews and Muslims. While the Bible does not explicitly state that the Father, Son and Holy Spirit are three persons in one godhead, it identifies God's Spirit as having a role in creation: the Book of Genesis recounts that the Spirit of God hovered over the formless watery chaos before God spoke the divine words that brought the universe into being (Genesis 1.2).

There are some statements in the New Testament that suggest Trinitarian theology. Paul – writing around 55–56 CE – formulated the benediction or 'grace', which is frequently said at the close of Christian gatherings:

> May the grace of the Lord Jesus Christ, and the love of God, and the fellowship of the Holy Spirit be with you all. (2 Corinthians 13.14)

The three persons of the Trinity are also mentioned in Jesus' 'Great Commission' at the end of Matthew's Gospel, when he exhorts his disciples to:

> Go and make disciples of all nations, baptising them in the name of the Father and of the Son and of the Holy Spirit. (Matthew 28.19)

The fact that Matthew attributes the trinitarian formula to Jesus in the context of baptism is significant. When John the Baptist baptises Jesus, Mark and Matthew record that the Holy Spirit descends on Jesus like a dove, and that a voice from heaven (which can only be God the Father) is heard, saying, 'You are my Son, whom I love; with you I am well pleased' (Mark 1.9–11). All three persons of the Trinity are seen in action here.

The *Catechism of the Catholic Church* applies the term 'mystery' to the doctrine of the Trinity, asserting that, 'It is the most fundamental and essential teaching in the hierarchy of the truths of faith',[12] and the phrase 'Father, Son and Holy Spirit' has an important role in Christian writing, and in Christian worship.

Is it mystery, or is it mumbo-jumbo? No doubt Dan and Usama will express their views.

USAMA

When the Prophet, peace be upon him, began his mission, he would walk the streets of polytheist and idolatrous Mecca, saying, 'People, affirm that there is no god except God, and you will be successful.' The certainty expressed by the Shahada phrase of bearing witness that *la ilaha ill'Allah* ('There is no god but God') is the universal key to salvation. In Islamic tradition, a dying person is prompted and reminded to repeat the Shahada, for if it comprises your last words, you are guaranteed heaven because this is a mark of sincerity and faith.

The Shahada, and another version of it: *huw 'Allahu ahad* ('He, God, is One'), echo the First Commandment given to Moses, 'You shall have no other gods before Me' (Exodus 20.3). Indeed, the Prophet taught that all the previous divinely inspired prophets had taught this belief as the fundamental one.

The practical manifestation of this key to salvation is to, as much as possible, dedicate your entire life to God, including prayer and ritual worship but also all other walks of life, which thus become infused with a sense of the sacred and with religious ethics. You thus develop a relationship with God, and since everything is by the will of God, you see your experiences as God's way of talking to you and giving you feedback about how well you are doing as a true worshipper of God.

The most important, and most difficult, aspect of a monotheistic life is that of the heart: to ultimately believe in, fear, hope in, worship and love God alone.

The spanner in the works of this all-embracing monotheism (*tawhid*) is *shirk*, giving anything or anyone a 'share' as a partner in what belongs to God. The term *shirk* covers polytheism, idolatry and atheism. *Shirk* is 'a great injustice'. Jesus is quoted in the Qur'an: 'Christ said, "O Children of Israel! Worship God, my Lord and your Lord. Whoever associates partners with God, God has prohibited the Garden [heaven] for him: his refuge is the Fire".'

However, God has also created an incredibly (and possibly, infinitely) complex world, so how does a solitary, unique being relate to such a diverse world? The Islamic answer is via the Most Beautiful Names of God, of which there are 99 in the Qur'an and an infinite number in reality. These include the Knower of the Hidden and the Witnessed, Merciful, Compassionate, King, Holy, Peace, Guardian of Faith and Mighty. They also include Truth and Beauty.

The Sufis or esoteric Islamic mystics teach that all of existence is a manifestation or reflection of the divine names, a cosmic drama and interplay amongst them. The Sufis are often accused of being pantheist, of believing that 'God is All'.

With regard to the Christian Trinity, orthodox theologians generally regard it as polytheistic, since it appears to give non-divine entities, Jesus and the Holy Spirit, a 'share' of the Divine. On the other hand, the esoteric Sufis oppose it because they say it does not go far enough and limits God to three aspects only, whereas the Most Beautiful Names mean that God has an infinite number of aspects! As a young man, I did regard the Trinity as mumbo-jumbo, but as I've learnt more, I've learnt to appreciate it as a mystery, overlapping with teachings from the Islamic mystical tradition about the ultimately unknowable nature of God.

DAN

Unlike Usama, I am inclined to think that the doctrine of the Trinity is mumbo-jumbo. Or if not that, it is certainly misguided. This is because Jews are strict monotheists. For most Jews the central difference between Judaism and Christianity concerns the doctrine of God. For over two thousand years Jews have daily recited the *Shema*: 'Hear O Israel: The Lord our God is one Lord' (Deuteronomy 6.4). Jewish martyrs proclaimed these words as they gave up their lives. Throughout the ages it has been the most important declaration in the Jewish faith.

In making this statement Jews attest to their belief that there is only one God and that he is indivisible. God is an absolute unity who cannot be linked with other gods. In addition, since the word 'one' in Hebrew also means 'unique', Jews imply that God is different from anything else that is worshipped. Only God possesses divinity. Nothing can be compared to him: 'To whom will you compare me? Or who is my equal?' (Isaiah 40.25). Thus Jewish monotheism denies the existence of any other divine being. There is only one supreme being who is Lord of all.

Among medieval Jewish theologians the doctrine of God's unity embraced the idea that there is no plurality in God's being. God is absolute simplicity. The doctrine of God's unity meant for many medieval Jewish theologians the purification of the concept of God so as to remove any notion of multiplicity. A classic formulation of this view is contained in 'The Kingly Crown' by the medieval poet Solomon Ibn Gabirol:

> Thou art One, the beginning of all computation, the base of all construction.
> Thou art One, and in the mystery of Thy Oneness the wise of heart are astonished, for they know not what it is.
> Thou art One, but not as the one that is counted or owned, for number and chance cannot reach thee, nor attribute, nor form.
> Thou art One, but my mind is too feeble to set Thee a law or a limit, and therefore I say: 'I will take heed to my ways, that I sin not with my tongue.'
> Thou art One and Thou art exalted above abasement and falling – not like a man, who falls when he is alone.[13]

Given this understanding of God it is not surprising that in the early rabbinic period Christianity was attacked for its doctrine of the Incarnation. According to rabbinic sources, the belief that God is in Christ is heretical. The doctrine that God is both Father and Son was viewed as a form of dualism. In the Middle Ages the doctrine of the Trinity was bitterly denounced as well.

Christian exegetes in this period interpreted the Shema, with its three references to God, as referring to the Trinity. Jewish exegetes, however, maintained that in this prayer there is reference only to one

God and not three persons in the Godhead. Christians often asserted that Jewish polemics against the Trinity were based on an inadequate understanding. Although it is true that some of these criticisms were uninformed, all Jewish thinkers were adamant that trinitarianism is incompatible with monotheism. Modern Jewish thought is equally critical of any attempt to harmonise the belief in God's unity with the doctrine of a triune God. Contemporary Jewish theologians of all degrees of observance affirm that Judaism is fundamentally incompatible with Christian belief.

GEORGE

Usama seems much more amenable to the doctrine of the Trinity than I anticipated. This surprises me, since the Qur'an states quite clearly, 'Do not say "Three"…Allah is but one God' (*Women*, 4:171).

It might be useful, though, to clarify a few points about the Trinity doctrine. Theologically, two main heresies have been associated with the Trinity: 'dividing the substance' and 'confounding the essence'. So 'Father, Son and Holy Spirit' are not three different names of God: such a claim would confound the essence, implying that all three 'persons' were identical. Conversely, we do not claim that each member is a 'share' of the Divine: the Father, the Son and the Holy Spirit are not like three pieces of a jigsaw puzzle – which would imply that each member was incomplete. The three persons are not simply three manifestations of God – a heresy known as 'modalism', which implies that God is only one person appearing in three different guises. Each person of the Trinity is equally real and equally and completely divine.

Usama is right to agree that this is a mystery, and few Christians claim fully to understand it. Even clergy whom I have known have expressed apprehension when they have had to preach on Trinity Sunday. One way of explaining the Trinity is a diagram which is sometimes found in churches, usually as an altar fall (a cloth overhanging an altar); the words are usually in Latin but, expressed in English, read as shown in Figure 5.1.

The diagram's import is that each of the three persons is not the other, yet all are equally and fully God.

Dan says that Christians have seen the Trinity expressed in the *Shema* (Deuteronomy 6.4): this is because it has sometimes been alleged that the word *echad* (one) can sometimes refer to a cluster or fusion (such as a bunch of grapes) (see Numbers 13:23), while some have seen other trinitarian allusions in the three visitors who call on Abraham (Genesis 18.2) or the co-creative role of the Word and the Spirit (Genesis 1.1–3). But such allusions are questionable.

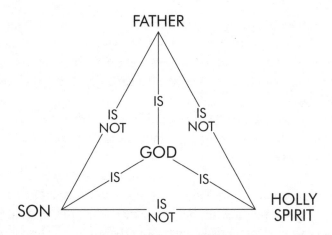

Figure 5.1: Diagrammatic representation of Christianity's Trinity doctrine

To the average believer, human interaction is more important than abstract trinitarian speculation. My uncle was a minister in a village in West Lothian in Scotland, and the front wall of his church bore two texts – one on each side of the pulpit – 'God is Light' and 'God is Love'. Both are from the Bible (1 John 1.5; 1 John 4.8), and are much more within the average believer's grasp. Each encapsulates important characteristics of God. Light signifies illumination for true understanding of the spiritual and physical world, for guidance on one's path, and for highlighting areas in our lives which we might want to keep dark. Love is the key virtue which Jesus identified as the essence of the Jewish law (Matthew 22.34–40).

Usama says that God would be solitary without the 99 names or aspects. For Christians, God is not a solitary being, for love requires that there are others to love, and one important aspect of the Trinity is that it presents the Divine as a social entity. Being in the image of God (Genesis 1.26), humans are not isolated individuals, but interact, and thus the Gospel of John indicates an important intertwining of the Father, Son and Holy Spirit (John 16:5–16).

While we may disagree on the Trinity, perhaps we can agree on God's characteristics of light and love. Indeed, Allah's 99 names include 'the Loving' and 'the Light'.

USAMA

La ilaha ill'Allah, 'There is no god but God'. In Islamic teaching, this is the fundamental truth that is the key to salvation, and was taught by all the divinely inspired prophets before Prophet Muhammad, including the founders of Judaism, Christianity and other major world religions.

'God is One…neither begetting nor begotten: there is no one like God, or equal to God.' In Arabic, similarly to Hebrew, *Ahad* means 'One' as well as 'Unique'.

Muslims too are strict monotheists, and the Trinity as expressed in George's diagram is incoherent and illogical. Christian belief may sometimes appear polytheistic, but a holistic reading of Christian texts and history shows that Christianity is monotheistic; it may be confused monotheism, but it is monotheism nonetheless, and to hold otherwise is extremely uncharitable. Martyrs from all three (!) Abrahamic faiths have died for the sake of the One God.

Muslim theologians generally agree with a strict monotheism like that of Judaism and regard the Trinity as polytheistic whilst Muslim mystics, the Sufis, criticise the Trinity for limiting God to three aspects. The word 'mystic' is related to the word 'mystery', so the Trinity is a mystical teaching, to be handled carefully. Orthodox Sufis uphold the Arabic or Islamic version of the Shema, and frown upon teaching mystical ideas such as the Trinity to the masses, given the immense scope for misunderstanding.

George quotes the Qur'an: 'Do not say "Three"…Allah is but one God.' Does this refer to the Trinity, a triune God, or to tri-theism – that is, a belief in three gods, which would be explicitly polytheistic? I agree with those Muslim theologians who hold the latter view, supported by another Qur'anic verse that refers clearly to tri-theism: 'God will ask Jesus, son of Mary: Did you ask people to take you and your mother as two gods besides God?'

A dry understanding of monotheism leaves God utterly transcendent or removed from everyone and everything, and unknowable, with no way of interacting with creation or being known by humanity, let alone being worshipped and loved. It also ignores scripture that repeatedly tells us that God is close to us, 'closer than a human's jugular vein', that God 'comes between a person and his/her heart' and that God 'is with you wherever you are'. The latter teaching may be summarised as the immanence of God, and appears regularly in the Qur'an, intertwined with God's transcendence.

Thus, God is one and unique, but both transcendent and immanent: completely separate from us, yet totally with us and encompassing us. This may seem intellectually paradoxical, but is actually a hint of the spiritual mysteries that are ultimately resolved through purifying the mind, heart and spirit through worship, service to others and reflection. The Qur'an often presents the Most Beautiful Names of God in opposite pairs to remind us of such paradoxes: 'God is the First and the Last, the Apparent (or Outward) and the Hidden (or Inward)'.

The Qur'an teaches that everything and every matter is mediated by the divine word, 'Be!' – 'and it is!' The Prophet taught that we are created in the image of God. The Most Beautiful Names of God, manifested around us and within us, help us to remember, love and worship God, for God is Love; God is Light; God is Beauty; God is Truth; and yet, God is One.

DAN

George contends that the concept of three in one as a theological notion is entirely reasonable. I should say at the outset that Jews are not disturbed by the idea that God has made himself known in various manifestations. It is a fundamental belief that God acts in human history. But this is not the same as saying that God is Father, Son and Holy Spirit.

The traditional doctrine of the Trinity defines God as three divine persons or hypostases. These three persons are distinct, yet are one substance, essence or nature. According to this doctrine, there is only one God in three persons, yet each person is God, whole and entire. They are distinct from one another in their relations of origin, as the Fourth Lateran Council declared: 'It is the Father, who generates, the Son who is begotten, and the Holy Sprit who proceeds.' These three persons are co-equal, co-eternal and consubstantial.

For Jews and Muslims, the most difficult aspect of such a doctrine is the belief that Jesus, a Jew living in Judaea in the first century BCE, is God on earth. The concept of the Incarnation asserts that God became flesh, assumed a human nature, and became man in the form of Jesus Christ. This foundational position holds that the divine nature of the Son of God was perfectly united with human nature in one divine Person, Jesus, making him both truly God and truly man. The theological term for this is the hypostatic union: the Second Person of the Holy Trinity, God the Son, became flesh when he was miraculously conceived in the womb of the Virgin Mary.

Both Judaism and Islam completely reject such ideas. In contrast to Christian exegetes who interpreted the Shema with its three references to God as denoting the Trinity, Jewish scholars maintained that the Shema implies that there is only One God, rather than three persons of the Godhead. For such medieval scholars as Saadiah Gaon, the Divine should be understood as a single incorporeal Being who created the universe out of nothing. In the twelfth century, the Jewish philosopher Abraham Ibn Daud derived God's absolute unity from his necessary existence. In this view, the concept of divine oneness precludes the possibility of any divine attributes of God. Similarly, Moses Maimonides in the same century argued that no positive attributes can be predicated of God since the Divine is an absolute unity.

For the Jew (as for the Muslim as Usama explains), God is one. He is the transcendent creator of all things, immanent in human history. For some Jewish thinkers he is ultimately unknowable. His nature is beyond human understanding. For the Kabbalists (Jewish mystics), he is the *En Sof* (Infinite), beyond comprehension. Maimonides in his *Guide for the Perplexed* argues that the only thing we can know about God is that he is one, and that he exists.[14] It is a mistake, he continues, to ascribe positive attributes to God. We can only say what God is not, not what he is.

This divide between Jews and Christians has been the cause of centuries of suffering. Today organisations such as the Council of Christians and Jews foster positive encounter between our two faiths. This is to be welcomed and encouraged. But at a fundamental level Jews and Christians are deeply divided, even though both faiths share a common scriptural heritage. The doctrine of God separates us from one another in the most radical way.

Chapter 6

CREATION

The Hebrew Scriptures begin with two creation stories. In the first, God created the universe in six days and rested on the seventh (Genesis 1.1–24). In the second (Genesis 2.4–24), Adam is formed from the earth, and Eve is created from his rib. They are then placed in the Garden of Eden, but are banished after disobeying God. The Christian New Testament explains how Adam and Eve's sin is redeemed – through Jesus Christ, who is the culmination of God's plan of salvation. The Qur'an does not provide a chronological account of God's people, but recounts the creation stories in a number of chapters (*suras*). Adam has a special role as a prophet and progenitor of prophets. This chapter discusses humankind's place in creation.

USAMA

In Chapter 5, when we were discussing God, I emphasised the importance of the 99 'Most Beautiful Names of God' in the Qur'an. The 99 names explain how God, who is utterly transcendent, relates in different ways to all that is not God, that is to say, creation.

Several of the divine names refer to different aspects of God's ways in creating: God is *al-Khaliq* (Creator), *al-Bari* (Evolver), *al-Musawwir* (Fashioner). Further, God is *al-Khallaq*, or 'Creator Supreme'. The phrase, 'God created the heavens and the earth and everything between them' occurs numerous times in the Qur'an.

In medieval times, atheist 'materialists' or 'naturalists' denied any existence of God, and held that 'matter' or 'nature' was eternal, and that everything derived from this primeval substance via material or natural laws. Islamic theist responses to this thesis included two major arguments based on the Qur'an.

The first argument against materialist or naturalist atheism was that it was effectively belief in God 'by another name', since eternity, omnipotence and being the source of everything are all divine attributes. The second argument was that the very existence of eternal matter, nature or primeval substance could not be explained by material or natural laws, and therefore this atheist position was self-contradictory. The monotheist belief in God as being, and having a divine name of, 'Uncaused First Cause' of creation is a religious tenet that also answers philosophical objections to theism. From my understanding as a scientist as well as imam, some of the modern scientific arguments for atheism are essentially the same as the medieval ones, and therefore, so are Islamic responses.

Medieval Islamic theologians disagreed over the notion of eternal substance, whilst agreeing that God was the Ultimate Mover: some believed that God must have created the ultimate substance underlying all creation, which therefore must have come into being at some moment in time; others argued that God as Creator must have always been creating, and so the primeval substance must have always existed. The latter group was wrongly accused of dualist polytheism for believing in matter that was co-eternal with God. This medieval dispute is also relevant today: some monotheists reject the idea of a 'multiverse', or a possibly infinite multiplicity of universes that is seen by some atheists as a good answer to theism. As a physicist and Muslim believer in God as 'Creator Supreme' (al-Khallaq), I have no objection to the idea that God might have created a multiverse, although I would insist on scientific evidence before conclusively accepting such a hypothesis.

The creation of humanity in the Qur'an is described in terms of Adam and Eve. As far as physical creation is concerned, humanity is described as having been created from earth, water, dust and clay. These general descriptions do not contradict scientific facts about the evolution of all life forms, including humanity, from the earth. More important is the teaching, implicit in the Qur'an but more explicit in hadith, that we are created in God's image, especially in the image of the divine name, 'Most Merciful'. God taught Adam 'all the names', displaying humanity's superiority over the angels, who did not know them all. For Ibn Arabi and other Sufi mystics of Islam, the names that humanity learnt were especially the Names of God. Our bodies are of the earth: our spirits are of heaven.

GEORGE

There is much in Usama's discussion of Creation with which many Christians would agree. The Book of Genesis depicts God as creating the world out of a pre-existent watery chaos (Genesis 1.2). Later Christian scholars believed in a *creatio ex nihilo*, some contending that such a belief is implicit in the rather terse opening verse, 'In the beginning God created the heavens and the earth' (Genesis 1.1). Thus God may be construed either as existing before the universe's origin, or as sustaining co-eternal matter.

Usama mentions evolution. The relationship between the biblical account of and evolutionary theory continues to divide Christians. While Christian fundamentalists decisively reject Darwinism, others suggest that the biblical ordering of created life forms reflects evolutionary development. More liberal believers prefer to accept the story as myth – meaning not that it should be rejected as false, but rather that it is a narrative whose import is more important than the story line.

Part of that import lies in the statement, 'God saw all that he had made, and it was very good' (Genesis 1.31). The Christian faith holds that the world was created as a fundamentally good place, to be enjoyed. It is neither evil nor unreal, and we should not live in reclusive isolation from it. Christianity is world affirming, and Christians typically involve themselves in the workplace, in political life, and in pleasurable recreation.

Another important implication, as Usama mentions, is that men and women are created in God's image (Genesis 1.27). Orthodox Christian theologians use the term *theosis* – becoming godlike. Humans are enjoined to aspire to God's characteristics – truth, wisdom, benevolence, creativity, and many of the 99 names Usama mentions.

The creation story also places humankind at the pinnacle of creation. God appoints Adam and Eve to 'have dominion' over creation (Genesis 1.28, King James Version). Humans are the dominant species on the planet, but this involves responsibility and not mere domination. The word 'stewardship' is frequently used to describe our responsibility to use the earth's resources wisely, and to care for creation.

In common with Jews and Muslims, Christians reject deism – the view that God created the world and then left it to its own devices. God may not have literally walked in the Garden of Eden (Genesis 3.8), but he maintained a relationship with Adam and Eve, even after they had sinned, and the Bible portrays God as speaking to the patriarchs and prophets, giving the Law to his people, and finally delivering humankind from sin through Jesus Christ his Son (Hebrews 1.1).

I mentioned earlier that all three members of the Trinity are bound up with the world's creation. The Spirit of God moves over the watery chaos (Genesis 1.2), and God's Word brings order into the world (Genesis 1.3). Our existence as interactive social beings is part of humanity's mirror image of the Trinity: God is not a solitary detached entity who sits on an eternal heavenly throne, but consists of three interacting 'persons'. If this is difficult to comprehend, so are many scientific theories about the universe – Usama mentions multiverses, for example. God is greater than the universe: the theologian and philosopher Anselm of Canterbury (1033–1109) defined God as 'that than which nothing greater can be conceived'. Because of its vastness and complexity, scientists make statements about the universe that are difficult to grasp. We do not reject them simply because they are too difficult to comprehend, so why should we reject theological concepts that may not be totally within the grasp of human understanding?

DAN

Much of what both Usama and George have written about the doctrine of creation in Islam and Christianity is parallelled in the Jewish faith. According to Genesis 1, God created Heaven and Earth. This belief is a central feature of the synagogue service – in the synagogue hymn before the reading from the Psalms, for example, God is depicted as the creator of everything:

> Blessed be He who spoke, and the world existed:
> Blessed be He;
> Blessed be He who was the Master of the world in the beginning.

In the *Ani Maamin* ('I believe') prayer, the first principle of the Jewish faith is formulated as follows:

I believe with perfect faith that the Creator, blessed be His name, is the Author and Guide of everything that has been created, and that He alone has made, does make, and will make all things.

In rabbinic literature, scholars speculated about the nature of the creative process. In Genesis Rabbah (*midrash* on Genesis), for example, the idea of the world as a pattern in the mind of God is expressed in relation to the belief that God looked into the Torah and created the world. Here the Torah is conceived as a type of blueprint. With respect to the order of creation, the School of Shammai stated: 'The heavens were created first, and then the earth.' The School of Hillel, in contrast, argued that Heaven and Earth were created simultaneously.

In the Middle Ages, a number of Jewish theologians believed that God created the universe *ex nihilo*. The Kabbalists, however, interpreted the doctrine of *ex nihilo* in a special sense. God, they maintained, should be understood as the Divine Nothing because as he is in and of himself, nothing can be predicated. The Divine is beyond human understanding. Creation *ex nihilo* thus refers to the creation of the universe out of God, the Divine Nothing. This occurred, they argued, through a series of divine emanations. For the Kabbalists the first verse of Genesis alludes to the process within the Godhead prior to the creation of the universe.

Regarding the question whether in the process of creating the cosmos, God also created intelligent beings on other planets, the Bible offers no information. Although rabbinic sources attest to the creation of other worlds, they similarly contain no reference to the existence of other sentient creatures. The belief in extra-terrestrial beings, however, raises problems for all three of our faiths. In *The Fall and Rise of Man*, the modern writer Jerome Eckstein explores the religious implications of such a possibility:

Let our imaginations roam, and let us speculate about the possible conflicts between future discoveries of space exploration and our old religious beliefs if these religious beliefs are understood as offering knowledge of the kind given by science. Suppose a strangely figured race of creatures with the approximate intelligence of humans and a culture and ethics radically different from ours was discovered on some distant star, would not this pose serious problems to the dogmatic and authoritarian interpretations of the Judaeo-Christian religions [and Islam]. Would these creatures, who obviously were not descended from Adam and Eve, be tainted with original sin? Would they too have souls? Would they be in need of grace and salvation? Did Jesus absorb their sins? Would they be in need of the Messiah? Would they be subject to the laws and traditions of these earth-centred religions? Would they be eligible to life in the hereafter?[15]

USAMA

Dan points out that intelligent, extra-terrestrial life may cause problems for the Abrahamic faiths. This is in part because of the centrality of the Israelite people, Christ and Muhammad respectively in our theologies.

However, just as I have no problem with a multiverse, I also have no theological problem with intelligent, extra-terrestrial life, due to my universalist approach to Islam. But to be more specific, there is an intriguing verse where the Qur'an teaches that God created 'seven earths' as well as the widely repeated 'seven heavens'. Many commentators have historically taken 'seven' to be a literal number, imagining the 'seven heavens' to refer to the orbits or 'spheres' of the visible heavenly objects, in order: moon, Venus, Mercury, sun, Mars, Jupiter and Saturn.

However, I take 'seven' to be metaphorical, signifying 'many' – this is common in classical Arabic, and is especially found in the Qur'an with regard to 70 and 700. Thus, the 'seven heavens' signify all higher aspects of reality, whilst the 'seven earths' refer to the immense variety of physical creation around us, including extra-terrestrial planets, or 'exo-planets' in contemporary scientific terminology, that support intelligent life. In mystical commentaries on the Qur'an, 'heavens' refer to higher realities whilst 'earth' refers to parallel existence.

Regarding the specific 'seven earths', the great early commentator, Abdullah Ibn 'Abbas, taught the mysterious and controversial notion that 'on each earth there is an Adam, a Moses, a Jesus and a Muhammad'. In other words, there is life on other planets and possibly in parallel universes, and since all creation is there to glorify God, other forms of intelligent life may also reach the heights of spirituality amongst their species. Furthermore, since the Qur'an repeatedly teaches that a divinely inspired prophet or messenger of God was sent to every nation on earth, and that intelligent, spiritual life was created to worship God, it seems to me to be an obvious extrapolation that if there is intelligent, and therefore spiritual, life on other planets, God must have sent appropriate divinely inspired guidance to those creatures as well: if aliens exist, so must alien prophets!

Returning to the topic of science and Scripture, I argue that science can help us to choose between differing scriptural interpretations. For example, take the question that Dan mentions: which was created first, the heavens or the earth, or were they created simultaneously? Since most Qur'anic verses mention the creation of the 'heavens and the earth' in that order, this would appear to give us a chronology. However, the great twentieth-century Mauritanian commentator al-Shanqiti, one of my father's teachers, argues at length that the earth was created before the heavens, based on a literal reading of *Surah al-Baqarah*. I am clear that his view is utterly incompatible with modern science, and so I prefer opposing scriptural interpretations that have the heavens created before the earth.

Another example of science applied to scriptural interpretations is with the 'Garden of Eden' story of Adam and Eve. The Qur'an states clearly that Adam, and hence humanity, was created from the earth itself, but the 'Fall' of Adam, Eve and Satan is traditionally understood to have occurred in a heavenly paradise. However, the Qur'anic word for a heavenly paradise is exactly the same as that for an earthly, enclosed garden: *jannah*. A minority of early commentators held that the 'Fall' story happened on our earth, and this fits better with the scientific fact that biologically, we evolved here.

GEORGE

Dan and Usama's comments about extra-terrestrial life are interesting, but we are in the realms of speculation. I can certainly imagine theologians from all three faiths having to take their work back to the drawing board if other life forms made themselves known.

God created all life, terrestrial and extra-terrestrial. The Psalmist reminds us that, however high we might go into the heavens, no one can escape from God's presence:

Where can I go from your Spirit?
Where can I flee from your presence?
If I go up to the heavens, you are there;
if I make my bed in the depths, you are there. (Psalm 139.7–8)

As Usama says, God's creation may not necessarily have occurred in seven literal days. Since the sun was not created until the fourth day (Genesis 1.14–19), and our days are defined by the sun's motion, the author cannot be referring to 24-hour periods. Seven is the number of perfection, and so God's completion of creation on the seventh day highlights creation's original excellence (Genesis 1.31–2.3).

Such perfection did not last long, however, as Dan and Usama agree. Regarding an angelic Fall, biblical support is ambiguous, although certainly the serpent's existence predates Adam and Eve in the biblical story. Luke mentions Satan falling like lightning from heaven (Luke 10.18), but it is unclear whether it is Satan or lightning that is falling. Peter mentions sinful angels awaiting judgement (2 Peter 2.4), and the Book of Revelation describes Satan being cast out of heaven, but neither author indicates when such events occurred. It was John Milton's *Paradise Lost* which interpreted Lucifer's fall from heaven (Isaiah 14.12, King James Version) as an angelic fall: the name 'Lucifer' only occurs once in the Bible, and most modern translations render it as 'morning star'.

The Bible unambiguously affirms the human Fall, however. Although Christian fundamentalists believe that Adam and Eve were real historical characters whom God placed in a paradisiacal garden, the story is best understood as highlighting humanity's sinful condition, and the consequences that ensue. The Bible affirms that the Fall not only affected humans, but the whole of creation. God curses the ground, condemning Adam and Eve to intensive labour to cultivate the land and maintain it (Genesis 3.19). Thus when Paul writes about redemption, he does not merely speak about humans being redeemed but the whole of creation awaiting renewal:

For the creation waits in eager expectation for the children of God to be revealed... We know that the whole creation has been groaning as in the pains of childbirth right up to the present time. (Romans 8.22)

Paul may be alluding to Jeremiah's vision of Judah's destruction, in which he envisages God 'uncreating' the world in his 'fierce anger' against his people:

> I looked at the earth,
> and it was formless and empty;
> and at the heavens,
> and their light was gone.
> …
> I hear a cry as of a woman in labour, a groan as of one bearing her
> first child… (Jeremiah 4.23, 31)

We do not need to wait for God to destroy creation, though. Human beings are perfectly capable of 'uncreating' the world that God has made, either by environmental disaster, nuclear warfare, genetically engineered viruses, or numerous other possible catastrophes. However, Paul offers hope in contrast to Jeremiah's warning, confident that our faith offers the possibility of complete cosmic redemption.

DAN

In raising the issue of life beyond our universe, I meant to highlight the challenge that our three faiths face from the findings of modern science. When the Hebrew Scriptures were first written, the authors had a pre-scientific understanding of the cosmos. The Bible is a glorious epic. But is it true? Clearly it is now a mistake to think that the universe was created in six days. In the past, some Jewish thinkers understood the creation account in Genesis literally; others interpreted the word *yom* (day) to refer to an epoch rather than a 24-hour period. Some modern Orthodox Jewish scholars have sought to reconcile the Bible with science on this basis.

But I believe the challenge of science goes much deeper. Due to scientific investigation and discovery over the last 200 years, we can no longer accept what the Bible tells us about the origin of the cosmos. As Jewish, Christian and Muslim expositors of our traditions, we should confess that the Hebrew Bible has simply got it wrong. And we should not feel compelled to offer sophistic arguments in defence of our traditions. There is no shame in admitting that our ancestors were ignorant and misguided in their understanding of the universe.

Of course, Orthodox thinkers in our three faiths cannot agree. They are bound by theological assumptions to believe that the Bible is the revealed word of God. As such, the Genesis account of creation is true either in a literal or figurative sense. However, such biblical fundamentalism is a mistake. As the result of over a century of biblical scholarship, it is obvious that the Torah (Five Books of Moses) were not written by Moses. Instead, Genesis (as well as Exodus, Leviticus, Numbers and Deuteronomy) were composed by authors from different periods and reflect different views of God's nature and activity.

In this light, the creation account in Genesis should be understood as reflecting the primitive beliefs of an early stage in the history of the Jewish people. This does not mean, however, that the Bible should be relegated to a shelf in the library. Within the Jewish world, it occupies a central place in the religious life of Jewry. Every week a portion of the Hebrew Bible is read in the synagogue. The Torah scrolls are carried aloft in procession. We recite the ancient formula: 'It is a tree of life to those who hold fast to it.'

But as modern Jews, we must acknowledge that the Hebrew Bible does not provide a true account of the formation of the cosmos. Nor should we rely on the biblical narratives to provide an accurate picture of the history of Israel. Instead, the Bible should be viewed as a glorious record of the religious reflections of previous ages. It is full of marvellous stories which, even if historically untrue, can inspire us today. But it is a mistake to look for a correct picture of how the universe came to be within its pages. Let us glory in the wonderful tales about the heroes of the past. But we should not feel guilty if we confess that the Hebrew Bible is full of myth and misinformation.

Chapter 7

GOD'S PRESENCE

Jews, Christians and Muslims all believe that God is immanent in the world. His presence is manifest throughout creation. Yet, given the Christian belief in the Incarnation and the Trinity, their understanding of God's action is interpreted in dramatically different ways. In what ways is God's presence manifested? What does it mean to say that God is always present? If we claim that he is 'in everything', do we mean we could find him in a cupboard or in a jar? Are there places where we are more likely to find God, and other situations in which God seems to be absent, or where God's presence is unlikely to be discovered?

DAN

For Jews, God is conceived as the transcendent creator of the universe. Throughout Scripture this theme of divine transcendence is repeatedly affirmed. Despite this view of God's remoteness from his creation, he is also viewed as actively involved in the cosmos. In the Bible his omnipresence is repeatedly stressed (as is seen in the Psalm from which George quoted in the last chapter):

> Where can I go from your Spirit?
> Where can I flee from your presence?
> If I go up to the heavens, you are there;
> if I make my bed in the depths, you are there.
> If I rise on the wings of the dawn,
> if I settle on the far side of the sea,
> even there your hand will guide me,
> your right hand will hold me fast. (Psalm 139.7–10)

In the rabbinic period Jewish scholars formulated the doctrine of the *Shekhinah* to denote the divine presence. As the in-dwelling presence of God, the *Shekhinah* is compared to light. Thus the *midrash* paraphrases Numbers 6.25 ('The Lord make his face to shine upon you and be gracious to you'): May he give thee of the light of the *Shekhinah*. In another *midrash* the 'shining' of the *Shekhinah* in the Tent of Meeting is compared to a cave by the sea. When the sea rushes in to fill the cave, it suffers no diminution of its waters. Likewise the divine presence filled the Tent of Meeting, but simultaneously filled the world.

In the medieval period the doctrine of the *Shekhinah* was further elaborated by Jewish scholars. According to Saadiah Gaon, the *Shekhinah* is identical with the glory of God, which serves as an intermediary between God and human beings during the prophetic encounter. For Saadiah the 'Glory of God' is a biblical term whereas the *Shekhinah* is a rabbinic concept which refers to the created splendour of the light which acts as an intermediary between God and human beings. At times this manifestation takes on human form. Thus when Moses asked to see God's glory, he was shown the *Shekhinah*. Similarly, when the prophets in their visions saw God in human form, what they actually perceived was the *Shekhinah*. Such a view avoids compromising God's unity and incorporeality.

With the rise of modern science, the traditional belief in divine immanence became more difficult to sustain. Nonetheless, Jewish thinkers continued to insist on the validity of the biblical and rabbinic view of God's involvement with the universe. Pre-eminent among those who championed the traditional view was Schneur Zalman, the founder of the Habad movement of Hasidism. He wrote:

> Here lies the answer to the heretics and here is uncovered the root of their error, in which they deny God's providence over particular things and the miracles and wonders recorded in Scripture. Their false imagination leads them into error, for they compare the work of the Lord, creator of heaven and earth, to the works of man and his artifices.[16]

Such an argument has been echoed across the modern religious spectrum. Religious believers from within the Orthodox, Reform and Conservative movements have continued to affirm the biblical and rabbinic doctrine of God's presence in the world. Although some thinkers have argued that God limited his own intervention by allowing human beings to exercise free will, there has been a firm rejection of deistic ideas in which the Deity is perceived as an absentee God. Instead, Jews from these main groupings have universally affirmed that the transcendent God is immanent in the universe he has created.

GEORGE

Psalm 139, which Dan quotes, is one of the best-known psalms among Christians also, affirming God's constant and all-pervasive presence. Yet I must confess that I have not myself had a special experience which I could describe as 'seeing God'. I therefore have to turn to the Bible's account of special revelations afforded to others. The Bible recounts that the Israelites, escaping from Egypt, had tangible assurance of God's presence in the pillars of cloud and fire which accompanied them, and they experienced thunder, lightning and smoke, signalling God's presence when Moses received the Law on Mount Sinai (Exodus 13.21; 20.18). Isaiah received a powerful vision of God in the Jerusalem Temple, whose foundations were shaking, and with seraphim flying around (Isaiah 6.1–8), and Ezekiel experienced God's heavenly chariot arriving in Babylon, showing that God's presence was not confined to the Jews' homeland (Ezekiel 1.4–28).

Christians who are part of the Charismatic Movement have claimed personally to experience 'signs and wonders' in the form of modern-day miracles, or 'speaking in tongues' – a phenomenon associated with the early apostles' experience of the Holy Spirit at Pentecost (Acts 2.1–4).

My own form of the Christian faith is more restrained. God's presence is mediated by his three 'persons'. As creator, he is manifested in creation: 'The heavens declare the glory of God and skies proclaim the work of his hands' (Psalm 19.1). Most importantly, God has revealed himself in his son Jesus Christ, who took human form, living among us and who, as the world's redeemer, offers reconciliation with God, and access to him, with the assurance of acceptance (Hebrews 10.22).

The Holy Spirit – the third member of the Trinity – is God's in-dwelling power. Paul taught that our bodies are temples of the Holy Spirit (1 Corinthians 6.19). Although consecrated buildings can

convey God's presence, we need look no further than our own selves
to find God – an idea that is similar to the Qur'anic verse which Usama
cited earlier, affirming that God is closer than one's jugular vein.

For the Christian, one distinctive way in which God's presence
is experienced lies in the Church's sacraments. The Church father
Augustine of Hippo (354–430 CE) defined a sacrament as 'an outward
and visible sign of an inward and invisible grace', and this definition
continues to be widely accepted both in Catholic and Protestant circles.
Because God cannot be physically seen and heard, the Church makes
God known through physical signs, most notably in the sacraments
of baptism and Holy Communion (also known as the Eucharist or the
Mass – the name varies according to tradition). I already mentioned
Jesus' Great Commission, which entailed the three-fold formula
(Father, Son and Holy Spirit) for administering the baptismal water,
and Jesus' own baptism, in which all three persons of the Trinity were
active. The baptismal water symbolises cleansing and repentance,
underlying the idea that Christ reconciles us with God.

Although the theology of the sacraments varies among the
Christian traditions, all Christians agree that in some sense Christ's
real presence is experienced in the eucharistic elements. The bread and
wine signify God's reaching down to humankind in Christ's sacrifice,
in which he offered his own body and blood for the sins of the world.
The communal eating and drinking also heralds the (metaphorical)
heavenly banquet for which Christians hope in God's coming
kingdom, when they will be brought truly into God's presence, which
we will experience directly (1 Corinthians 13.12).

USAMA

Where is God? Does the question even make any sense? Can we
experience God's presence – if so, how?

Many Muslims answer the question, 'Where is God?' with
'Everywhere'. This is based on many Qur'anic teachings such as, 'We
are closer to the human than their jugular vein' (Q., 50:16), 'God
manifests in between a person and their heart' (*Spoils of War*, 8:24),
'He is with you wherever you may be' (*Iron*, 57:4) and 'To God
belongs the East and the West: wherever you turn, there is the Face of
God (*The Cow*, 2:115).

Other Muslims argue that this is a blasphemous answer since God is utterly Transcendent and separate from his creation: the idea of God Immanent is repulsive because it necessitates that he is present in the toilet, faeces and other ignoble things.

I agree with those Muslim theologians and mystics who believe that God is both Transcendent and Immanent. They point out that both teachings co-exist in the Qur'an, sometimes within the same verse: for example, 'He is with you wherever you may be', quoted above, follows in the same verse that mentions that God 'settled above the throne' (*Iron*, 57:4), a phrase referring to Transcendence.

Many theologians argue that God's 'being everywhere' (*ma'iyyah*) is conditioned as referring to his attributes only such as divine knowledge, not his essence: for example, a powerful verse which says that, 'God is the fourth of any group of three, the sixth of any group of five and any smaller or greater number: He is with them wherever they may be.' This verse begins with a reference to God's knowledge: 'Do you not see that God knows whatever is in the heavens and whatever is in the earth…' and ends with a reference to God's knowledge: 'Truly, God is with every thing, All-Knowing' (*She Who Argues*, 58:7).

This is a powerful scriptural argument but implies a distinction between the essence and attributes of God, which is incompatible with monotheism in the sense that God is one, unique and indivisible. A counter-argument based on the same scripture is that 'He' in 'He is with you/them wherever you/they may be' refers to God 'entirely', not just to His attributes.

Dan describes *Shekhina*. The Arabic equivalent is *Sakinah* (Tranquillity), as in verses such as, 'It is He Who sent down Tranquillity into the hearts of the believers to increase their faith' (*The Opening/Conquest*, 48:4). The root of *Sakinah* is S-K-N which also means 'to live'. I once heard a rabbi explaining that *Shekhina* referred to God's living or dwelling in the heart. A similar teaching exists amongst the Sufis (Muslim mystics).

On encountering God's presence, a striking hadith says that God will rebuke people on the Day of Judgement:

> I was ill, but you did not visit Me. I was hungry, but you did not feed Me. I was thirsty, but you did not quench My thirst. I was naked, but you did not clothe Me.

When they protest as to how they could feed, clothe or visit God Himself, He replies:

> So-and-so, My servant, was hungry, naked or ill and you did not care. Had you cared about them, you would have found Me with them.[17]

This hadith is one of my favourite teachings about encountering God's presence, especially since it resonates with a New Testament parable that we sang as schoolchildren in the form of the popular hymn:

> I was cold, I was naked, were you there? Were you there?
> I was cold, I was naked, were you there?

DAN

The Jewish idea that God is present in human life presupposes that he is active in history. Throughout Scripture, God acts in the lives of his chosen people. According to the biblical narrative, he freed them from Egyptian bondage, guided them in their wanderings in the desert, revealed his law to Moses, was with them in the conquest of the Promised Land, sent his prophets to warn them of impending doom if they violated the commandments, and was constantly present in the life of the nation. In the liturgy we give thanks for his abiding love.

Yet modern history has raised searching questions about the nature of such divine presence. In the light of the Holocaust, Jewish thinkers have sought to make sense of God's absence in the death camps. Where was God when six million died? Why did he not rescue the Jewish people from the hands of the Nazis? If God is all-powerful and all-loving as the Bible and rabbinic sources tell us, then why did he abandon his people?

In recent years a number of Jewish thinkers have provided a wide range of responses to these haunting questions. At one extreme such thinkers as the Reform rabbi Sherwin Wine argue that Jews today must abandon their belief in a supernatural Deity. In Wine's opinion all theistic interpretations of God's involvement in history should be replaced by a naturalistic perspective.

At the other end of the theological spectrum other more tradi-tional writers argue that we cannot hope to understand God's ways.

According to the Jewish writer David Ariel, there is simply no way that the Holocaust can be explained. God's will is unfathomable. In this regard he refers to God's response to Job that human beings are unable to fathom the divine plan.

Departing from such traditionalism, a number of other Jewish theologians have posited alternative theories about God's absence during the Holocaust. The Conservative theologian Arthur Cohen contends that it has been a mistake to believe that God acts in human history. According to Cohen, God transcends the cosmos that he created. God, he writes, is not an interruptive agent. Instead Jews should conceive of the Deity as transcendent, and therefore it is a mistake to blame him for the terrible events of the Nazi regime.

Arguing along similar lines, the Reform Jewish scholar Steven Jacobs contends that Jewish theology is inadequate to solve the problems presented by the Holocaust. What is now needed is a thorough re-evaluation of the religious tenets of the Jewish faith. In his view it is no longer possible to believe in a God who intervenes in the world. This concept must be replaced by the notion of a God who is compatible with the reality of radical evil, which admits of human freedom for good, or evil.

These various reflections constitute a dramatic shift from the past. In previous centuries Jews steadfastly affirmed their faith in the God of the Bible. The creator of heaven and earth, he was present in their trials and tribulations. Confident of his abiding love, they were convinced of their ultimate destiny. As God's suffering servant, the faithful would eventually be rewarded with eternal life. In contemporary times, all this has changed, and as a community we are deeply divided over the essential tenets of the Jewish tradition.

GEORGE

Are there places or situations in which God is not present? Dan and Usama raise some important questions here. If he is all-present in the world, can we find him in the restroom? Amazon currently advertises 'God in a sealed glass jar' – a clear glass vessel containing God (since God is everywhere), and the product description assures the purchaser that 'As long as the jar is not opened, your God will never leave you.'[18] Much more seriously, Dan raises the question of whether

God can be present amidst great evil, for example with the Jews in the Holocaust, where God could not seem to be more distant.

In my college days one of the more conservative students began telling us about how he once experienced God in a public restroom. This conversation opener was met with such ridicule that he was unable to continue, and we never found out exactly what happened to him. However, if we had known more about Church history, we would have known that Martin Luther experienced chronic constipation and spent many long hours sitting on a toilet that has recently been discovered at Wittenberg.

Most of us think of impressive religious buildings, such as cathedrals, as places where we are most likely to find God. However, as Stephen – the first Christian martyr – said:

> the Most High does not live in houses made by human hands…
> 'Heaven is my throne,
> and the earth is my footstool.' (Acts 7.48–50)

God can be experienced in any situation, however strange or seemingly inappropriate, and one can pray to him at any time and in any place – even on a toilet seat! There is nothing particularly problematic or blasphemous about this, for to claim that God is everywhere and in everything is to use analogical language. God does not literally inhabit time and space, and when we claim that God is 'here', we are not asserting a spatial relationship, but are talking of a presence that cannot adequately be encapsulated in ordinary human discourse. His all-pervasive presence does not mean that he is 'in' that jam jar!

Dan refers to the Jews in the death camps experiencing the absence of God. Jesus is recorded as having a not dissimilar experience on the cross, when he uttered the words, 'My God, my God, why have you forsaken me?' (Matthew 27.46). This, of course, is a particularly problematic verse for the Christian, who believes in Christ's deity, and it has perplexed biblical scholars and theologians over the centuries. If Jesus was God, how could God forsake him? Martin Luther spoke of *deus absconditus in passionibus* – the sovereign God who is hidden in human suffering. The gospel writers emphasised that Jesus was not immune from the depths of human suffering but, being fully human, could identify with them. The bystanders at the crucifixion made similar comments to those of the Jewish thinkers whom Dan mentions:

'He trusts in God. Let God rescue him now…for he said, "I am the Son of God."' (Matthew 27.43).

Jesus of course dies without any supernatural rescue. Yet, like Job (whom Dan cites), his sufferings are vindicated. The gospel narrative continues with an account of ensuing cataclysmic events and the parting of the Temple veil, symbolising God's reconciliation with humankind. Christians are very familiar with Job's words, 'I know that my redeemer lives' (Job 19.25), applying them to Christ.

USAMA

George is right to say that God's presence 'everywhere' is not in a spatial or physical sense. In modern physics, energy or matter is located or moves in space and/or time, and as mediaeval Islamic theologians noted, God transcends space and time.

Of the 99 Names of God, those that denote the Divine Presence include *Al-Qareeb* (The Near), *Al-Muheet* (The Surrounder) and *Al-Wasi'* (The Encompassing). Many Qur'anic verses include appropriate Divine Names: the above three occur memorably in the following, respective verses: 'When My servants ask you about Me, then I am Near: I answer the call of the caller when he calls Me' (*The Cow*, 2:186); 'Lo! They are truly in doubt about meeting their Lord: Lo! He is truly the Surrounder of every thing' (*Signs Explained*, 41:54); 'Wherever you turn, there is the Face of God: truly, God is Encompassing, Knowing' (*The Cow*, 2:115).

Dan mentions several Jewish responses to difficult questions about God's presence in the world. I agree with the Muslim theologians and mystics who say that we can only understand that presence in different ways and not speak about God's 'absence', for how can God be absent in any sense?

I can understand why some theologians might argue that God is utterly Transcendent, so that evil in the world cannot be attributed to Him. But this would disconnect God from all goodness in the world too, and so is an unsatisfactory resolution. Furthermore, as I explained earlier, God is both transcendent and immanent, and intimately manifested in the universe and its events, in the dance and rhythms of energy, matter, space and time.

But what of the enormous human suffering in world wars, the Holocaust, the near-genocides in Bosnia, Rwanda and contemporary

Burma, not to mention the appalling, current conflict in Syria that has claimed about half a million lives in six years?

Traditional Islamic understandings of suffering revolve around three intertwined aspects: test, purification and punishment. Reality, itself a Divine Name (*Al-Haqq*) can be harsh and brutal: God is Severe in Punishment (*Shadeed al-'Iqaab*) and Swift in Reckoning (*Saree' al-Hisaab*). For most people, as for Prophet Ayyub (Job), suffering is a test and purification. For example, the following verse about the Israelites is repeated twice with minor variations:

> Remember, when God saved you from the Family of Pharaoh, who used to inflict terrible persecution upon you, killing your sons and sparing your women: in all of that, there was a great test from your Lord. (*The Cow*, 2:49; *Abraham*, 14:6)

The 'divine punishment' aspect of suffering relates to widespread corruption, often instigated by a small number of tyrants but that affect everyone, including the innocent: 'Beware of trials that are not confined to the unjust amongst you, and know that God is severe in punishment' (*Spoils of War*, 8:25).

So, for example, serious structural injustice and corruption in Middle Eastern societies have led to the numerous, current civil wars there with the appalling loss of innocent lives.

The reality of this suffering is softened by the deep Muslim certainty in the Hereafter, when all wrongs will be righted and justice will ultimately be done. God's presence encompasses the eternal life of the Hereafter, and is not limited to the temporary events of this world. The connection between the two realms, of this world and the Hereafter, with God's presence a constant in both, is key to making sense of worldly suffering.

Chapter 8

GUIDANCE

In what sense do our various scriptures provide guidance for life? If they have authority and are God-given, should we not seek to obey them scrupulously in every detail? But what about commandments that now seem obsolete in the twenty-first century? The Christian faith has drawn on that of the Jews, but where does this leave the Christian regarding the observance of Jewish law? Equally, Muhammad was acquainted with both the Jewish and Christian faiths, so to what extent does the Qur'an align with Jewish and Christian ethics? To what extent are we bound by the requirements of our various scriptures, and to what extent does God expect us to use our own consciences and make our own judgements about right and wrong?

GEORGE

I remember once hearing a preacher tell his congregation that the Bible was our instruction manual. Just as a gadget usually comes with a set of instructions, so God has given us the Bible as the maker's handbook to guide our lives.

Even a Christian fundamentalist should have problems with this idea, however. Critics frequently mock the Bible for its commandments to stone disobedient children, to avoid touching a menstruating woman, not to wear garments that mix wool and linen, to tell a priest if we discover mildew (Deuteronomy 21.18, Leviticus 15.19; 19.19; 14.3).

It will not do for the Christian to claim that all this is 'old covenant' and that we are under the new. Most Christians have no problem in accepting the Ten Commandments (although we may have problems in keeping them all), and the New Testament has its difficulties also.

Even Jesus' teaching in the Sermon on the Mount, which is often regarded as the pinnacle of moral guidance, is problematic. Jesus says that I should always turn the other cheek, that I should not judge people, that I should give to anyone who asks and not refuse to lend to someone who wants to borrow from me (Matthew 5.39; 7.1; 5.42). Are these reasonable expectations of the Christian?

In an earlier chapter I mentioned reason and conscience as sources of authority in addition to Scripture. The writer to the Hebrews, quoting Jeremiah, recounts God's words, 'I will put my laws in their minds and write them on their hearts' (Hebrews 8.10; Jeremiah 31.33). God does not demand blind obedience, but common sense and personal integrity.

The Christian still needs the Bible for guidance, however, and I think the Bible guides in a number of ways. It is a record of how God has already guided his people. Christian scholars often talk about 'salvation history', by which they mean that we own a record of how God has dealt with his people through the ages, giving the Law, and sending prophets, culminating in Jesus Christ – God's Word in human form.

The Bible also helps with life's changing circumstances and problems. Hotel guests have probably come across a Gideon Bible, whose opening pages suggest appropriate passages for support for circumstances or moods which he or she may be experiencing – fear, anxiety, discouragement, anger, greed or whatever. Quite a few travellers have found these directives helpful, and have received guidance from them. (They are now accessible online in expanded form.)[19]

The Bible also causes us to reflect on our own actions. Jesus' parable of the rich man who refused to help Lazarus the beggar (Luke 16.19–31) should remind us of our Western affluence: we dine at upmarket restaurants and drive expensive cars, while many people in countries like Ethiopia cannot find clean drinking water. The penalties of Hebrew scripture may seem harsh, but I once had a rabbi preach about the man who was stoned for breaking the Sabbath (Numbers 15.32–36). He explained that it showed the importance that God's people attached to Sabbath observance. We probably should not stone disobedient children, but the Bible has much to teach about the importance of good parenting. I may be old-fashioned in believing that our child-centred households and educational establishments have lost important concepts such as discipline and obedience, which the Bible supports (e.g. Exodus 20.2; Proverbs 3.11–12; 15–20; Ephesians 6.1).

DAN

Orthodox Judaism maintains that God revealed himself to Abraham; it was this divine calling which is the starting point of the Jewish faith. Subsequently God revealed himself to Isaac and Jacob, and later to Moses. After the ancient Israelites escaped from Egyptian bondage, they wandered in the desert for 40 years. During this sojourn Moses ascended to the top of Mount Sinai where God revealed the Torah to him.

It was thus not just the Ten Commandments that Moses received, but the entire corpus of law which is contained in the Pentateuch. Alongside biblical law (referred to as the Written Torah), all the narratives contained in the Five Books of Moses were also revealed to Moses. Hence, through the centuries Jews have regarded Genesis, Exodus, Leviticus, Numbers and Deuteronomy as containing divine truths about the creation of the cosmos, the origin of human life, the Flood, God's disclosure to Abraham, the patriarchal narratives, the exodus from Egypt and the giving of the Law on Mount Sinai.

It is also a cardinal Orthodox belief that God revealed to Moses the interpretation of the Written Torah. This is the Oral Torah that was passed down from generation to generation, and eventually recorded in rabbinic literature. The Oral Torah is referred to as the '*Torah She-Be-Al Peh*' (Torah by word of mouth) and is viewed as being as holy as the Written Torah. What this means in practice is that Jews are obligated to keep not only the 613 commandments in the Pentateuch, but also all the laws which rabbinic scholars have concluded are implicit in these commandments.

Revelation thus embraces both biblical and rabbinic law. The first collection of rabbinic law was compiled in the second century CE by Judah ha-Nasi. This was followed several centuries later by both the Babylonian and Palestinian Talmuds. Subsequently Mishnaic and Talmudic law as well as the legal opinions of later scholars were recorded in a number of codes of law, the most important of which is the *Shulḥan Arukh* (Code of Jewish Law).

The key point is that both the Written and Oral Torah were divinely revealed, and thus Jews are obliged to observe all the law. They are not free to choose which laws they wish to observe. There are literally thousands of laws that must be followed, and through the centuries Jewish study has focused largely on the study of the Mishnah, Talmud and *Shulḥan Arukh*.

So far I have been speaking about Orthodox Judaism. But, as I noted in previous chapters, the various non-Orthodox movements have departed radically from this traditional understanding of revelation. Both Conservative and Reform Judaism have rejected the concept of the Mosaic authorship of the Pentateuch, and as a result discarded those biblical and rabbinic prescriptions that they regard as anachronistic. Other more radical movements, such as Reconstructionist and Humanistic Judaism, have abandoned the idea of a supernatural Deity altogether. As a result the concept of revelation has ceased to play any part in their philosophies of Judaism.

The modern age has thus witnessed the fragmentation of Judaism into a wide range of denominations with radically different and conflicting theologies. As a consequence, Jewry is deeply divided about the nature of God's activity and the role of traditional Jewish law in the lives of their adherents. Not surprisingly this has led to bitter acrimony within the religious community.

USAMA

The *Fatiha* or opening chapter of the Qur'an, traditionally recited dozens of times in daily prayers by every devout Muslim, contains a short prayer, asking God to 'Guide us to the Straight Path: the path of those upon whom You granted gifts, who did not receive anger and did not stray' (*The Opening*, 1:5–7). This prayer implies the following of 'good' people and keeping their company, whilst avoiding the example and company of 'bad' people. The very next chapter, the longest in the Qur'an, begins with a reference to scripture as guidance: 'A.L.M. That is the Book, in which there is no doubt: a guide for the pious' (*The Cow*, 2:1–2).[20] This verse implies, as confirmed by many others, that sincerity, good intentions and righteous character is a precondition for attaining guidance from scripture. In fact, the Qur'an strikingly declares that many are guided by scripture or God's guidance whilst many are misguided by it: the latter are those whose conduct is wicked (*The Cow*, 2:26–27). Thus, God's Word acts as a mirror, reflecting the goodness or otherwise in a person's heart and actions.

The Qur'an repeatedly refers to itself as guidance (*huda*), and to all the prophets and messengers sent by God as guides (*hadi*). It also describes the Torah (*Tawrat*) and Gospel (*Injil*) as containing guidance and light; the Gospel also contains '*guidance and admonition for the pious*' (The Last Supper, 5:44–46). After a striking passage mentioning Abraham, Isaac, Jacob, Noah, David, Solomon, Job, Joseph, Moses, Aaron, Zachariah, John the Baptist, Jesus, Elias, Ishmael, Al-Yasa', Jonah, Lot and their tribes, the Qur'an declares, 'We chose them and guided them to a straight path. Such is the guidance of God, by which He guides those amongst His servants whom He wills… They are the ones whom God has guided, so follow their guidance!' (*Cattle*, 6:87–90. The full passage begins at verse 74).

The command to follow righteous people, and seek guidance in their example, is manifested most obviously in the following of the *Sunnah*, the way of the Prophet Muhammad, peace be upon him. Although in contemporary Islam, much emphasis is placed on outward practices of the Prophet, such as ritual worship, dress and etiquettes of daily life, the hadith texts place greater emphasis on the 'inward *Sunnah*', that is, on good character and the dedication of all the heart's emotions, not just love and worship, to God.

The Qur'anic command to follow the guidance of previous prophets, most of whom are biblical, led to a famous controversy within discussions of Sharia (Islamic law and ethics) as to whether or not 'the law and ethics of previous people is a source of law and ethics for us'. Effectively, the discussion is whether Islam is a self-contained tradition beginning with the Prophet Muhammad, peace be upon him, or whether it is open to influence from other religions, since Islam recognises the founders of pre-Islamic, major religions as divinely inspired prophets.

George describes the analogy of scripture with an instruction manual: this is regularly employed by Muslim preachers, who forget that there is also direct guidance from God for true believers

(*Pilgrimage*, 22:54), as requested in the basic daily prayer of the *Fatiha*. Muslims, like Jews as described by Dan, also struggle to find a balance between numerous commandments developed in jurisprudence and maintaining the spirit of faith.

GEORGE

Usama, interestingly, refers to the Sharia controversy about whether 'the law and ethics of previous people is a source of law and ethics for us'. The early Christians were faced with precisely this question, since Jesus and his first disciples were Jews, as were all the writers of the Christian New Testament. When the Christian faith expanded beyond its immediate Jewish circles, Gentile converts were faced with the question of whether they were converting to a Jewish sect with all its legal obligations, or whether it was an independent faith.

Paul addresses this problem, particularly in his letters to the Romans and the Galatians. He argues that someone who receives over-prescriptive instructions is being treated like a slave. The more commands one receives, the more difficult compliance becomes, and keeping the law becomes a burden, with the prospect of punishment as a consequence (Galatians 5.1). Paul writes, 'Christ redeemed us from the curse of the law' (Galatians 3.13), meaning that no further atoning rituals were required, such as those performed in the Jerusalem Temple, and no system of detailed rabbinic interpretation is needed to ensure detailed compliance.

By contrast, Paul tells us we are no longer slaves but sons of God, and are entitled to address him as 'Abba' – an Aramaic term of intimacy, used by children to address their father, and the name by which Jesus also addressed God (Mark 14.36; Galatians 4.6). The relationship between people and God is not one in which they are enslaved by 613 meticulous rules, but rather a relationship that brings peace and joy (Galatians 5.22). Jesus and Paul consistently taught that outward observance was much less important than an inner desire to please God.

Paul has sometimes been accused of antinomianism, but he does not advocate lawlessness. On the contrary, the Christian must indeed obey the law, and avoid sexual immorality, fraud, greed, idolatry, obscenity and drinking to excess (Romans 13.1; 1 Corinthians 5.11; Galatians 5.3). The Law's commandments are not abolished, but summed up in the single commandment to love one's neighbour (Romans 13.9).

Jesus' teachings too have sometimes been interpreted as super-seding the Mosaic Law, but again this is a misconception. In the Sermon on the Mount he says, 'You have heard… "Do no murder"… But I tell you that anyone who is angry with his brother will be subject to judgement.' (Matthew 5.21–22) This is often construed as a contrast, but no Jewish teacher would have dared to declare that he knew better than Moses. The Greek word *de*, which is translated as 'but' in this sermon is not necessarily adversative: it can equally mean 'and' or 'in addition'.

What Jesus suggests here is that the Torah applies to thoughts as well as actions. Controlling thoughts and emotions may seem as onerous as complying with the meticulous details that some of the Pharisees advocated. However, taming one's mind has a more obvious purpose than observing nitpicking details such as whether one may use an electronically activated restroom on the Sabbath. Murder often begins with anger, adultery with lust, and theft with covetousness.

Does the Christian need the Jewish law? Although we are free from its detailed observance, Paul emphasises that Jewish scripture prepares the ground for Christ (Galatians 3.24). Christian scripture would make little sense without the background of Jewish law, history and prophecy. Some of the Torah's commandments may seem archaic, even unacceptable, and need to be interpreted in the light of reason, conscience and the guidance of the Church.

DAN

George is right about the biblical background to the Christian tradition. Christianity is deeply rooted in the Hebrew Scriptures. Jesus, Paul and the disciples were Jews, and they did not seek to create a new religion. Jesus' conflicts with the Sadducees and the Pharisees took place in the context of ongoing disputes about the interpretation of biblical law. Paul believed that Jesus was the long-awaited Messiah and was the fulfilment of the law. Many of the early Christians were Jews who sought to embrace the tradition in the light of Jesus' words and ministry.

Yet as the Church developed, the Christian community sought to distance itself from Judaism. And in doing so radically departed from biblical and rabbinic law. Although there was deep reverence for biblical personages such as Moses, Abraham, Isaac and Jacob, and the prophets, Christians deliberately abandoned most of the laws in the Torah as well as the rabbinic interpretation of the commandments. Islam too, while revering the prophetic traditions of the Hebrew Bible, has distanced itself from Judaism. For Muslims, as Usama has explained, God's revelation to Mohammed is of primary importance in guiding the lives of the faithful.

But let me return to the key issue facing Jews in the modern world. For the strictly Orthodox, God's revelation to Moses as well as the rabbinic expansion of biblical law provide a framework for daily living. The Code of Jewish Law (*Shulhan Arukh*) functions as a comprehensive compendium of divinely revealed instruction. In Israel and in the diaspora the Haredim (strictly Orthodox Jews) are committed to preserving the ancient traditions of the faith.

Yet most Jews do not subscribe to the central tenets of the Jewish heritage. Millions of Jews have disassociated themselves from synagogue life. Other Jews, also in the millions, are affiliated to the non-Orthodox branches of Judaism. Instead of rigorously following biblical and rabbinic law, they make subjective decisions about which laws are spiritually relevant. In doing this, they appeal to a wide range of criteria. Contemporary Jewish practice is thus frequently inconsistent and incoherent.

Let me conclude with a personal example. A friend of mine is the senior rabbi of a large American Reform synagogue. We were recently discussing the issue of gay couples in his congregation. He announced that he was soon to conduct the marriage of two lesbians.

'You do that?' I asked.

'Of course,' he replied. 'The Reform movement has taken a strong stance in support of gay men and lesbians. They are fully accepted. It's a matter of principle even though the tradition expressly condemns homosexuality.'

'But what if one partner is Jewish, and the other partner isn't? Would you do the marriage then?'

My friend shook his head. 'That would be wrong,' he said. 'Judaism strictly forbids intermarriage. I would never do it!'

Such inconsistency is universal outside the circle of the strictly Orthodox. Some Jews insist on eating only kosher food at home, but eat non-kosher food when they go to restaurants. Others refuse to eat pork and shellfish, but eat non-kosher meat. Some Reform rabbis refuse to conduct a wedding service on the Sabbath, but go shopping on Saturday afternoon. Frequently Conservative Jews drive their cars to Sabbath services (it is forbidden to drive on the Sabbath), but park their cars several streets away so no one will see they have driven there. As far as divine guidance is concerned, we are a perplexed people.

USAMA

As the three of us have agreed, trying to know and follow what is expected of us from God is difficult. A practical solution that I try to use is twofold, in addition of course to study and reflection on the sacred texts or scripture, and on life's experiences: prayer and struggle in the ways of God.

As for prayer, the thirteenth/fourteenth-century scholar Ibn Taymiyyah recommended a prayer of the Prophet, peace be upon him, itself based on Qur'an 39:46 (*Surah al-Zumar* or Chapter: *The Groups*). The prayer is as follows:

> O God, Creator of the heavens and earth, Knower of the unseen and witnessed! You judge amongst Your servants amongst the matters in which they differ: guide me with Your permission about the truth in matters that have been disputed, for truly, You guide whomsoever you wish to a straight path.[21]

This is a prayer that I try to use whenever possible regarding disputed matters, ever since I translated the short treatise by Ibn Taymiyyah in which he recommends this prayer. I have found that it gives me confidence that I have done my best and sought divine guidance in major disputed matters of Islamic theology and jurisprudence, including contemporary matters such as harmonising religion and science, dealing with questions of religion and universal human rights, and dealing with the complex problems within and external to Muslim communities where I live, as well as further afield.

The second way is struggle in the ways of God, based on Qur'an 29:69 (*Surah al-'Ankabut* or Chapter: *The Spider*): 'As for those who struggle in Us, We surely guide them to Our ways, for truly, God is certainly with those who excel.' Several of the early commentators explained this verse thus: 'Whoever acts with goodness upon his existing knowledge, God grants him knowledge of other matters that he did not previously know.' In other words, knowledge is not gained only by study and learning, but also by virtuous action that leads to the blessing of further divinely granted knowledge in return. Again, this is a principle that many devout Muslims will hold to in order to seek guidance in contested or troubling matters: continue with basic kindnesses and acts of virtue, and God will bless us with the clarity of vision to see through difficult matters.

I would like to end with an amusing anecdote: the main Qur'anic Arabic term for 'guidance' is *huda*. *Huda* is also a popular girl's name: indeed, I have two female cousins with that name, one on each side of the family (one of them is also a *hafiza*, i.e. she has memorised the entire Qur'an in Arabic, and leads women in special prayers during Ramadan when the entire Qur'an is traditionally recited). Some years ago, a young Muslim woman named Huda told me an amusing anecdote: she attended Friday prayers and, not uncommonly, was dozing off during a boring sermon, especially since she couldn't see the imam, as women are often sadly screened off or segregated entirely from men in the mosque, if they are allowed in at all. She was woken up by what she thought was someone calling her name: it was actually the imam, ranting about divine guidance: he was exclaiming, 'Huda! Huda!'

PART 3

GUIDANCE FOR LIFE

Chapter 9

LAW

Jewish law is based on the biblical commandments contained in the Five Books of Moses. According to tradition, God revealed the Ten Commandments in addition to 613 other commandments to Moses on Mount Sinai. Christians sought to break away from what they regarded as undue legalism, and so the two traditions have very different interpretations of God's will. Islam, similar to Judaism, is a 'halachic' religion, in which the religious law, the Sharia, encompasses all aspects of life. If God is the supreme lawgiver, then God ought to be obeyed – but are we in danger of excessive legalism? The alternative seems to be picking and choosing those laws that simply appeal to us. So how do we steer a course between rigid legalism and doing as we please?

USAMA

To speak of 'law' in the context of Islam immediately conjures up the word *Sharia*, with all kinds of associated modern connotations, some of them negative. However, in the Qur'an, *Sharia* and its derivations refer to religion and a path to God in general, or what we might call law and ethics or law and spirit combined: ethical or spiritual law, perhaps. This is a holistic 'sacred path', for *Sharia* also means a path, especially to a well, spring or other source of water in the desert. In modern Arabic, a 'road' is *shari'*, which also means 'lawgiver'. The idea of Sharia as a sacred path to God has a strong Qur'anic resonance with Abrahamic and pre-Abrahamic religion. The relevant verse addresses the Prophet thus:

He has made a path for you (sharia) of the religion, as He enjoined upon Noah, in addition to what We have inspired to you, and what We enjoined upon Abraham, Moses and Jesus: to establish the religion, and not divide yourselves up in it. (*Consultation*, 42:13)

In other words, religion as a sacred path to God is not a new idea: it is Noahite, Abrahamic, Mosaic, Jesuit and Muhammadan. (By the way, these five prophets are known as 'strongly willed messengers' *cf. The Winding Sand-Tracts*, 46:35.) The verse also condemns division and sectarianism, as opposed to diversity and respectful disagreement, within religion.

The diversity of sacred paths is also a Qur'anic teaching, addressing the Prophet, peace be upon him:

We sent down to you the Book with Truth, confirming the Scripture that was before it, and as a guardian over it. Thus, judge amongst them [the Jews, Christians and Muslims of Medina] by what God has sent down. Do not follow their desires against what has come to you of Truth. For each of you, We have made a path (*siryah*) and a way. If God had willed, He would certainly have made you one nation, but He did this in order to test you with what He has given you, so vie with each other in goodness. To God is your return together: He will then recount to you about the matters in which you differed. (*The Last Supper*, 5:48)

The distinction between a 'path' (*siryah*, related to *sharia*) and a 'way' (*minhaj*) is understood by commentators to refer to law and ethos respectively, so we are back to religion as ethical law. Furthermore, in the above, long verse, God's judgement upon disputed matters is promised in the Hereafter, but a practical instruction is given to compete in good works, whatever one's religion or sacred path. For me, this is very important today: people of different religions may discuss their differences respectfully and leave them ultimately to God's judgement in the next life, if one believes in that (Muslims overwhelmingly do). In our current world, a more productive approach is to concentrate on doing good.

But to reduce this sacred path to a spiritless and loveless legalism is utter misguidance: the Qur'an rightfully castigates those Jews (and by analogy, Christians and Muslims) who fall into this trap:

The example of those who were given the responsibility of bearing the Torah, but then did not bear it (responsibly), is that of a donkey carrying tomes: how bad is the example of people who belie the signs of God! And God does not guide unjust people. (*The Friday Gathering*, 62:5)

DAN

Divine law is of fundamental importance in Judaism. For nearly 4000 years it has been the basis of Jewish life. The traditional role of the rabbi has been to act as a legal expert. Yet today most Jews regard the Jewish legal system as outmoded legalism. The corpus of Jewish regulations that shaped Jewish life and bound the Jewish people together through the centuries has been largely abandoned. Strictly Orthodox Jews of course scrupulously observe the commandments, but they constitute a small minority within the Jewish community. They are respected for their dedication to the heritage, but their lifestyle is generally viewed as anachronistic.

Accompanying this abandonment of the Code of Jewish Law is a rejection of the theology of divine reward and punishment. In the past, Jews believed that God had given Moses divine commandments for his chosen people to observe, to guide them through their lives. Adherence to these regulations recorded in Scripture and interpreted in rabbinic sources ensure the righteous eternal life. Those who forsake the law, however, will be condemned eternally. In midrashic literature and the Talmud, rabbinic sages described Heaven (*gan eden*) and Hell (*gehinnom*) in graphic detail. Such an eschatological scheme sustained the Jewish people through centuries of persecution and suffering. Assured that they will eventually be saved by their Redeemer and Deliverer, they remained faithful to the legal heritage.

But this is no longer the case. As I have stressed throughout our discussion, Jews today choose for themselves which, if any, laws to apply to their lives. It is as though the Code of Jewish Law is a gigantic smorgasbord laid out before the Jewish community from which each of us takes whatever we like and disregards the rest.

To put the matter a different way: imagine the Jewish heritage as a gigantic supermarket. Spread out on the shelves are the 613 scriptural commandments plus the thousands of regulations formulated by the rabbis through the centuries. All Jews are free to wander through the aisles filling up their shopping trolleys with those items that appeal to them. Those drawn to the tradition will have overstuffed trolleys; others will leave with only a few items. Some shoppers will depart with nothing.

Let me conclude with a personal example. My mother was Chairman of the Ritual Committee of the Reform synagogue where I grew up in Denver, Colorado. This was an enormous congregation with thousands of families. At home we strictly avoided pork, but from time to time my mother served bacon. When I was studying to be a rabbi at the Hebrew Union College in Cincinnati, Ohio, I returned home for the holidays and confronted her.

'Mom,' I said. 'I don't get it. You are Chairman of the Ritual Committee. You are supposed to be an expert in Jewish law. Your committee has the duty to ensure that Jewish ritual is carried out properly. This is a responsible position in the community. But here you are making lunch, and you have prepared bacon sandwiches. You won't have pork in the house, but somehow bacon is OK.'

My mother looked puzzled. 'But it doesn't look like pork,' she said.

'Do you know what bacon is made of?' I said.

'You're making a fuss,' she replied as she handed me a sandwich.

GEORGE

As a child, I had a very fine Sunday School teacher called Miss White. She was a great help to my mother in quite difficult times, and I'm sure she deserves a place in heaven, if anyone does. However, like most of us, she had her misconceptions. She once mentioned a Christian family who lived in a Glasgow tenement, and whose upstairs neighbours were strict Orthodox Jews. On the Sabbath, the father of the household would come down and ask his Gentile neighbour to come and light the gas.

'It's all very well for the Jews to have a day of rest,' she commented, 'but they don't mind the Gentiles doing their work for them.'

Miss White's impression of Jews, which went uncorrected until much later in life, was of the stereotypical Pharisee, burdened with observing 613 detailed regulations. This is a far cry from Dan's type of Jew, who treats the law as a kind of spiritual buffet. As a Christian, of course, I knew which I would prefer – to light someone's gas fire, or to have to observe all the laws prescribed in the Torah. Paul said, 'Christ redeemed us from the curse of the law' (Galatians 3.13).

What Miss White did not take on board, and what I did not understand until much later, is that the Jewish law was given specifically to the Jews, with some occasional provision for foreign residents in their land. Being the chosen people does not mean special privileges, but special obligations.

In the early years of the Christian Church, controversy arose as to whether converts to the Christian faith were required to obey the Jewish law. The early apostles met in Jerusalem, where they convened the first Council, and they decided that a Christian should 'abstain from food polluted by idols, from sexual immorality, from the meat of strangled animals and from blood' (Acts 15.20). The jury is still out on whether this recommendation was intended for all first-century Christians or merely Gentile converts, and its exact requirements are still matters of some debate.

Usama refers to Noachide (or Noachian) Covenant, and this may be what the Council had in mind. This is a set of laws acknowledged by Jews, and believed to have been given by God from the time of Adam up to Noah:

> Do not deny God.
> Do not blaspheme God.
> Do not murder.
> Do not engage in illicit sexual relations.
> Do not steal.
> Do not eat from a live animal.
> Establish courts and a legal system to ensure obedience to these
> laws.[22]

I doubt if many Christians have heard of the Noachide Covenant but, since it precedes the Mosaic Law, it is intended to apply to all people. If it is true that only Noah's family survived the flood, then all humankind are his descendants.

The Mosaic law, by contrast, consists of ceremonial and ritual as well as moral requirements, and only the last of these has relevance for the Christian. However, the Christian does not have to scour the Hebrew Scriptures to check every detail. When asked which was the greatest commandment in the Law, Jesus' response was, 'Love the Lord your God with all your heart and with all your soul and with all your mind,' followed by, 'Love your neighbour as yourself' (Matthew 22.37–39). For the Christian this is quite sufficient. The difficult part, of course, is putting it into practice.

USAMA

As I implied in my earlier section in this chapter, Sharia in early Islam was understood to refer holistically to the totality of Islam as an inner-outer spiritual and legal-ethical tradition and path to God. This did include 'written' or 'enjoined' rules (*kitab*) and 'commandments' (*ahkam*). I am delighted that we all seem to be agreed that God does not wish us to be trapped in soulless legalism. Another problem with the latter is that it naturally leads to 'legal tricks' (*hila*) in order to observe the letter of the law whilst violating its spirit, illustrated by the Qur'anic story of the 'People of the Sabbath' (*The Heights*, 7:163–166). According to Islamic tradition, this Israelite fishing village was tested by God, who sent shoals of fish to them on the Sabbath day only: they set their fishing nets before the Sabbath and hauled in their catch after it, thus technically avoiding work on the Sabbath although in reality they had fished throughout it, for which they were punished.

In similar vein, a hadith declares, 'May God fight those Jews who were forbidden to eat fat, so they sold it and ate from the profit!' (Bukhari).[23] I actually agree with George's Sunday School teacher, and have had a similar experience to her as a child: I, along with my two older brothers, used to regularly accompany our father on Saturday evenings to the East London Mosque in Whitechapel, where he would teach the Qur'an. We would often skip parts of the lesson and play outside with other Muslim children. Once, on a long summer day, Orthodox Jews in the neighbouring Fieldgate Street Synagogue, emerged and asked us to switch on the lights in their building since they were religiously prohibited from doing so.

On the other hand, Prophet Ayyub (Job) is said to have been taught a 'legal trick' by God to circumvent an unwise oath he had made (S, 38:41–44).[24] Throughout Islamic history until now, the jurists have clashed vehemently between those who favoured legal tricks wherever possible to make life easier for the faithful and those who condemned this as being the way of errant Israelites.

Muslims have fallen into the same trap of innovating malevolent legal tricks. For example, on the first of Ramadan, state banks in the Islamic Republic of Pakistan used to annually deduct, from all accounts, 2.5 per cent as *zakat*, the religiously compulsory, yearly alms-tax. Rather than cheerfully donating this amount to the needy, many Pakistani Muslims would form long queues outside state banks on the eve of Ramadan to withdraw their deposits in cash, only to re-deposit these two days later. Technically, the government could not deduct *zakat* because it was withdrawn before the end of the financial charity year. Morally and legally, *zakat* was still due because the wealth was owned by the same people during the trick, but there was no way to prove this.

When, as George mentions, the apostle Paul refers to the 'curse of the law', he surely means its burdensome aspects. However, Jewish and Islamic tradition have an advantage in that ancient forms of prayer, charity, fasting and pilgrimage are preserved along with their deep wisdom and symbolic, metaphysical meaning.

The Prophet's teachings also form the basis of Islamic civic law: for example, the legal principles of 'actions are judged by intention', 'do no harm' and 'innocent until proven guilty' are found in basic hadiths.[25]

DAN

In modern times the issue of law deeply divides the Jewish community. Strictly Orthodox Jews continue to observe the 613 commandments in the Torah, as well as legislation based on rabbinic interpretation. They are adamant that in doing so they are carrying out God's will, and they regard the non-Orthodox movements with contempt. We Reform Jews (as well as Conservative, Reconstructionist and Humanistic Jews) are viewed as despicable violators of God's will. Not only are we disobeying the divine law during our lifetime, we are destined to suffer eternally for such neglect. This is not an academic issue – for the Orthodox it is a matter of the utmost urgency.

Usama and George are right to point out the significance of the Noachide Covenant. These laws preceded the revelation on Mount

Sinai, and they are obligatory for every person. As George pointed out, they are a set of imperatives which were given by God as a binding code for all of humanity. And, significantly, they serve as the basis for determining if a non-Jewish person is worthy to enter into the Hereafter. The paradox is that it is much easier for gentiles to enter into the World to Come than for Jews. Those born of Jewish maternal descent (or those who have converted to Judaism) are traditionally under an obligation to observe all Jewish law. It is not a personal decision whether to live under the yoke of the law – it is a requirement for all Jews. But non-Jews are only required to observe the Noachide commandments.

But as I noted previously, the vast majority of Jews today do not observe Jewish law, are generally ignorant of the requirement to do so, and ignore the dire consequences of such action. Instead, they simply select those observances and customs which they are drawn to. This is legal chaos. But we in the Jewish community are used to it. The vast majority of us live a Jewish life as we see fit, and ignore the legal requirements of the past unless we find them spiritually relevant.

As a consequence of this subjective approach to Jewish life, Judaism is no longer what it was in previous eras. For nearly 2000 years, Jews were bound together by a shared heritage. The Bible and rabbinic sources such as the Mishnah, Talmud and *Shulhan Arukh* (Code of Jewish Law) guided the Jewish nation through centuries of hardship and suffering. Remaining faithful to God and tradition, Jews were united as a people. Yet, the emancipation of Jewry from the eighteenth century to the present day has brought about a fundamental shift in Jewish consciousness.

In essence, there no longer is a unified, coherent body of belief and practice that binds us all together. There is no single system of Judaism that we Jews observe. Instead, there exists a variety of Judaisms with radically distinct and opposing assumptions about the nature of God, revelation, providence and law. Never before in the history of the faith have we been so divided. Yet, beyond such disunity, Jews universally regard the State of Israel as fundamental to Jewish life. Strangely, for many Jews it has taken the place of the covenant between God and the Jewish people. Throughout the Jewish world, we have come to believe that the Holy Land (not the God of Scripture) will ensure our survival.

GEORGE

Dan acknowledges that living the Jewish life 'as we see fit' is a subjective approach to Jewish law. I wonder if that is going somewhat too far. After all, Moses was given the Ten Commandments, not the Ten Suggestions.

I have already mentioned the role of reason and conscience in determining how we act, but most people need firmer direction. The Ten Commandments seem a good place to start when looking for guidance for life. Few would condone murder, adultery, theft or false testimony. No doubt in the twenty-first century, we may have trouble with the commandments about worshipping other gods, misusing God's name, and observing the Sabbath. Some Christians still take these commandments literally but, like Dan, I think we need to look at their spiritual relevance. Most of us have our 'false gods', such as wealth or ambition, and we misuse God's name when we invoke divine authority for our own personal ideas. As for Sabbath observance, working hours have increased, and taking time off has become more necessary than ever.

I once shared an office with a colleague who was not at all religious. He had some knowledge of the Bible, however, and found some of the ancient Hebrew laws somewhat bizarre. One such verse was, 'Do not curse the deaf or put a stumbling-block in front of the blind' (Leviticus 19.14). He found it hilariously funny to imagine ancient Israelites going around digging holes for blind people to fall into. However, if one considers the spiritual relevance of the verse, we find advice considering the disabled. The twenty-first-century equivalent might be occupying a disabled parking space if we are able-bodied, or taking advantage of people's ignorance or credulity, as often happens in advertising or in politics.

I think we all agree about excessive legalism. For the strictly Orthodox Jew, it would actually be easier to light the gas for oneself than to trek downstairs to ask a neighbour. At the very Orthodox hotel in Nof Ginosar mentioned in Chapter 4, the entrance had two doors: one was automatically activated by an electronic sensor, while the other was a very stiff traditional door, which had to be pushed hard. Paradoxically, this second door was the 'sabbath door' – more difficult to use, but did not involve 'kindling a flame' (Exodus 35.3), which includes completing an electrical circuit. Sabbath observance, originally established as a day of rest, has thus become a means for observant Jews to express their Jewish identity, rather than for physical and spiritual renewal.

Difficult rules, as Usama points out, invite us to find ways of circumventing them. Interestingly, he refers to the Islamic notion of *hila* – ruses to avoid compliance. This is nothing new: the Jews and Christians got there before the Muslims! Mark's gospel records an exchange between Jesus and the Pharisees, in which he accuses them of avoiding observance of the fourth commandment ('Honour your father and your mother'), by declaring that money, which should be used to support them, is 'corban' (Mark 7.11), meaning a gift for the Temple. The ruse was to hold the gift back for an unspecified period, thus enabling the son or daughter to continue to enjoy their wealth.

We often look for ways of avoiding obligations, whether it is helping someone in need or donating to a good cause, persuading ourselves that it is not our responsibility, or that others will step in, or that we have already done enough. Perhaps we need to revisit Jesus' summary of the law – loving God and loving one's neighbour.

Chapter 10

SIN

'Sin' is not a word that is used in common parlance, and people do not like being reminded of their misdeeds and failings – which is what our faiths often do. Yet none of us is perfect, and religions typically offer ways by which we can overcome our shortcomings. Christians in particular – especially those in the Calvinist tradition – are often accused of dwelling too much on sin. Do our faiths dwell too much on sin, and should we not give more emphasis to human virtues? How does God regard sin, and how does God deal with it within our respective traditions? What are the just penalties for sin, and how is it dealt with, both by God, and within our various spiritual organisations? In this chapter we explore the question of what sin is, the different types of sin that are distinguished theologically and institutionally, and the means by which our faiths offer repentance and forgiveness.

DAN

In the Bible, sin is understood as a transgression of God's decree. In Biblical Hebrew the word *het* means 'to miss' or 'to fail'. Here sin is conceived as a failing, a lack of perfection in carrying out one's duty. The term *peshah* means a 'breach'; it indicates a broken relationship between human beings and God. The word *avon* expresses the idea of crookedness. Thus, according to biblical terminology, a sin is characterised by failure, waywardness and illicit action. A sinner is one who has not fulfilled his or her obligation to God.

According to rabbinic Judaism, sins can be classified according to their gravity as indicated by the punishments prescribed by biblical law.

The more serious the punishment, the more serious the offence. A distinction is also drawn in rabbinic texts between sins against other human beings, and offences against God alone. Sins against God can be atoned for by repentance, prayer and giving charity. In cases of offence against others, however, such acts require restitution and placation as a condition of atonement.

Rabbinic texts teach that there are two tendencies in every person: the good inclination and the evil inclination. The former urges individuals to do what is right, whereas the latter encourages sinful acts. At all times, a person is to be on guard against assaults of the evil inclination. It is not possible to hide one's sins from God, since he knows all things. Thus, God is aware of all sinful deeds, yet through repentance and prayer it is possible to achieve reconciliation with him.

In the Bible, the concept of repentance is of fundamental importance. Throughout the prophetic books sinners are admonished to give up their evil ways and return to God. According to Jewish teaching, atonement can only be attained after a process of repentance involving the recognition of sin. It requires remorse, restitution and a determination not to commit a similar offence. Both the Bible and rabbinic sources emphasise that God does not want the death of sinners, but declares that they return from their evil ways. Unlike in Christianity, God does not instigate this process though prevenient grace; rather, atonement depends on the sinner's sincere act of repentance. Only at this stage does God grant forgiveness and pardon.

With regard to unwitting offences against ritual law, a sin offering was required in the biblical period as a sacramental act that restores the relationship between God and the transgressor. Following the destruction of the Second Temple in 70 CE, prayer took the place of sacrifice. In addition, fasting, kindly acts, and the giving of charity were also viewed as a means of atonement. In the Jewish yearly cycle, a ten-day period is set aside commencing with *Rosh Hashanah* (New Year) and ending with *Yom Kippur* (Day of Atonement), which is devoted to prayer and fasting. The Day of Atonement, however, only brings forgiveness for sins committed against God; for sins against others, atonement is granted only after the sinner has made final restitution and sought forgiveness from the offended party.

In the modern world, religious Jews of all persuasions view themselves as responsible for their actions and must repent of their sins.

Such action is fundamental to the faith. Although non-Orthodox Judaism does not accept biblical and rabbinic precepts as binding, it nevertheless affirms that all Jews are required to search their ways and make atonement for transgression. *Yom Kippur* is designed to remind the Jewish people of this divinely sanctioned task.

USAMA

Islamic teaching on 'sin' largely overlaps with Jewish teaching as presented by Dan, with some differences, and the commonalities extend to similar scriptural words in Arabic and Hebrew respectively: the Arabic equivalent of *Yom Kippur* would be *Yawm al-Kaffara*.

Het sounds very similar to the Arabic, Islamic equivalent *khat'*, that also means to miss a target (as in archery) and 'mistake', but is used for major crimes: for example, killing children out of fear of poverty is 'a great sin'. In my occasional sermons or Qur'an translations, I sometimes use 'mistake' in English, because 'sin' has some negative connotations for the modern ear, reminiscent of past over-emphasis on guilt in religious teaching.

A more common Qur'anic word for 'sin' is *dhanb*, related to *dhanab*, a 'tail'. (Incidentally, this is the origin of the star name Deneb: the tail of Cygnus the Swan; most major star names are of Arabic origin, from the medieval, golden period of Arabic-Islamic astronomy.) Islamic theologians give a compelling explanation of the relationship between 'sin' and 'tail': we tend to see the sins of others and not our own, as animals with tails will tend to see other's tails, and not their own.

As in Judaism, sins are categorised according to gravity, especially 'major' and 'minor' (*The Star*, 53:32). However, there is no agreement on the distinction between these. Many theologians, such as Imam Dhahabi of Syria (eighth/fourteenth century),[26] wrote books detailing the major sins (*kaba'ir*): some limited these to seven, possibly influenced by the Christian idea of the seven deadly sins, whilst others said there were 70 or 700. Still others argued that it all depended on one's intention and frequency of sin, so that a repeated minor sin would become major because it had become a habit that a person was not bothered about correcting.

The rabbinic teaching about good and evil within ourselves is exactly the same in Islam. Repentance (*tawba*), too, is of fundamental importance: the word means to turn back, so that repentance is literally a U-turn away from evil towards good. The ninth chapter (*sura*) of the Qur'an, well known for its verses about military jihad in self-defence, is actually and ultimately about spirituality, and is named 'Repentance' (*Tawba*). Furthermore, one of the Most Beautiful Names of God is *al-Tawwab*, the Oft-Returning in accepting the repentance. The root verb *taba* applies to both the human and God: the human turns away from evil towards God, and God reciprocates by turning in acceptance to the human. For Sufis such as Ibn 'Arabi, the fact that the same verb is involved is powerful, signifying a mystical union of humanity and God through repentance.

Qur'an and hadith teachings indicate concurrent temporal cycles of sin alongside opportunities for repentance or divine forgiveness: daily (morning/evening), weekly (Friday to Friday) and annually (from one Ramadan or Hajj until the next).

On the issue of whether salvation is achieved through divine grace or human effort, Islamic scripture tends to emphasise both and tries to combine them, perhaps paradoxically.

Although Islam rejects 'original sin', according to canonical hadiths, sin is an essential aspect of the flawed human condition: 'Every human constantly makes mistakes, but the best of you are those who constantly repent' and 'If you did not sin, God would replace you with creatures who did, for He loves to forgive.'

Dan says that God does not want sinners to die. What, then, is meant by the biblical verse, 'The soul that sins, shall die' (Ezekiel 18.20)?

GEORGE

There is much in what Dan and Usama have said that Christians would agree with. I have heard many sermons explain that sin is like the marksman missing the target, and that we must make a U-turn, showing repentance. The word used in the New Testament is *metanoia* – meaning a change of mind.

Usama says that sin has negative connotations to the modern ear, but I think that is precisely the point. People often accuse Christians of over-emphasising sin. However, I would challenge anyone to look at any set of news headlines, and count the number that report human wrongdoing. It is usually the majority.

Sin's prevalence relates to the Christian doctrine of original sin. Sin is not just a 'mistake', as Usama suggests. It is an inbuilt propensity, as old as the human race. Whether or not Adam and Eve were real people, the Genesis story highlights God's intention that men and women should not die, but enjoy God's presence eternally. Adam and Eve's disobedience prevented them from accessing the Tree of Life and living eternally (Genesis 3.22), and thus, as Paul says, 'the wages of sin is death' (Romans 6.23).

Augustine of Hippo explained the notion of original sin by noting that in Adam the entire human race was seminally present, and hence original sin was transmitted from one generation to the next through sexual activity, entering the unborn child at the moment of conception. Few Christians today would accept Augustine's quasi-biological account of sin, although probably few are familiar with it. However, Augustine highlights the point that sin is more than a series of mistakes that humans make, but an inbuilt propensity. The seven deadly sins, which Usama mentions – typically listed as pride, covetousness, lust, envy, gluttony, anger and sloth – are not actually sins in the sense of deeds like murder and theft, but propensities that manifest themselves frequently in our thoughts and actions. Such tendencies are there from birth: we do not need to teach children how to be selfish and how to throw temper tantrums, but we do have to teach them how to behave well. Misbehaviour comes only too naturally.

Christians would agree with Dan that repentance is needed, but traditional Christian teaching is that forgiveness comes through grace, rather than by elaborate acts of contrition. Christians parted company with the Jewish faith, at least partly because the early Church taught that observance of the Jewish law and its system of ritual sacrifices were of little or no value in putting one's heart right with God. Of course, grace does not mean that we need not make an effort to behave well. On the contrary, Jesus' standard was 'Be perfect, therefore, as your heavenly Father is perfect' (Matthew 5.48). If sin is missing the mark, none of us have a good aim!

Usama mentions major and minor sins. The Roman Catholic Church classified sins into 'venial' and 'mortal'. The latter were grave sins which required confession to a priest, followed by any prescribed penances, before one could be readmitted to receive the sacrament at the Mass. Venial sins merely required personal repentance. While Protestant Christians would agree that some sins are more serious than others, they do not accept the Roman Catholic distinction, which is not found in the Bible, preferring to leave the individual believer to put his or her heart right with God.

DAN

There is much in common in our three faiths about the concept of sin and repentance. Although non-Jews are not obligated to keep Jewish law, the Hebrew Bible has served as a basis for the understanding of human sinfulness and repentance in Judaism, Christianity and Islam. Yet, I should stress (as I have repeatedly in other chapters) that most modern Jews in general no longer view biblical commandments (and the rabbinic expansion of these laws) as binding. Thus, to use the analogy of shooting and missing a target, for most Jews there is no longer a target to shoot at.

The situation is a bit like the caucus race in Alice in Wonderland. You will remember that the Dodo marks out a course, sets everyone in place and yells, '1, 2, 3 and away!' The animals run around haphazardly until the Dodo declares half an hour later that the race is over. The Dodo says that everyone has won and all must have prizes. Alice passes mints to all the animals, leaving herself without a prize. But finding a thimble, she hands it to the Dodo who in turn presents it back to her as her prize.

Law and sin is rather like this in the non-Orthodox Jewish world. No one is sure what sin is, certainly with regard to regulations concerning ritual. And there is considerable uncertainty concerning a wide range of ethical issues as well. For example, homosexuality and lesbianism are viewed as unethical in Orthodox circles, whereas Conservative, Reform and Humanistic Judaism embrace gay people and regard censure of homosexuality as a serious ethical violation.

In other words, the situation is a general shambles. Most Jews do not know when they have done something wrong, and therefore aren't sure if they should repent. We are all running off in different directions, and are not certain where exactly where we are going. This is most obvious with regard to ritual law. The Orthodox view us as violators of God's law when we fail to observe the 613 commandments. But we do so unhesitatingly nonetheless.

Let me give you an example. A rabbinic friend of mine refuses to conduct weddings on the Sabbath. This has caused considerable inconvenience to his congregation because it rules out marriage ceremonies on Saturday when most congregants would like weddings to take place since it would free up the weekend. He has adopted such a policy since he believes the Sabbath should be regarded as sacred. Yet, despite such determination, he drives his car and goes shopping on the Sabbath (which is expressly forbidden according to Jewish law).

Matters are, as I suggested, more complicated in the moral sphere. Most of us regard the Ten Commandments as valid moral guidelines. There is general agreement, for example, that stealing is wrong. But beyond the Decalogue, there is widespread ignorance and confusion about the myriad commandments dealing with morality in the Hebrew Bible and rabbinic sources. The Orthodox regard non-Orthodox Jews as wayward sinners. But we non-Orthodox Jews feel no sense of guilt when we violate the complex moral code elaborated in the Code of Jewish Law. And, because we are free of guilt, we feel no obligation to repent. While it is true that we pray in synagogue for God to forgive us our sins on the Day of Atonement, for many Jews this is a matter of rote rather than true repentance.

USAMA

A measure of the seriousness of sins is needed, it seems to me, if 'the soul that sins, must die' and 'the wages of sin are death'. Presumably, this would only apply strictly to serious sins, or what Muslims might call 'major sins' (kaba'ir). Alternatively, perhaps different parts of the soul die depending on the type of sin being committed.

The latter idea resonates with a principle of Islamic law and ethics: 'Punishment or reward is of the same nature as the original action.' Many Muslims believe that this applies to morality, so that sins against other people will be repaid by reality in a commensurate way: if we cheat others, we will be cheated by others; if we are unkind to someone, another person will be unkind to us, and so on. 'Evil plots only rebound and surround their authors.' The opposite is true also: good deeds and kindnesses attract others in like measure.

Dan says that many Jews do not know if they are sinning or not. This is where our consciences come in: according to a celebrated hadith, the Prophet, peace be upon him, advised someone unsure about these matters to, 'Consult your heart...for righteousness finds satisfaction in the heart whereas sin unsettles the heart.' Another version states, 'Righteousness is good character, whilst sin is unsettled in the heart, and you dislike that people learn of it.'

This teaching underscores the importance of our moral consciences and the judgement of our peers in deciding whether or not our actions are sinful and unethical, or righteous and ethical.

Despite the theological and jurisprudential arguments about whether or not an action is sinful, the issue of sin is a very practical one in the sense that sin has a subjective impact. Another famous hadith says that sins cause 'black marks' or 'dark stains' on the heart: good deeds polish the heart again, so it shines with light. But if a person continues doing bad deeds, the dark stains cover the heart and it becomes incapable of knowing and doing good. Many Muslims will use this as a subjective test for self-reflection: if we feel our heart and character is taking a turn for the worse, there may be sins from which we need to desist and repent. If, on the other hand, we feel that our heart and character is improving, we need to continue doing the positive things that are inspiring this.

Another practical aspect related to sins is that of confession: although the Qur'an emphatically declares, 'Who can forgive sins except God?!' it is true that practically, many believers would like the reassurance from others more advanced on the spiritual path that their sins are indeed forgivable. Although Muslims do not have weekly confessionals with imams as a regular practice, many will indeed confess their sins to an imam or spiritual guide whom they trust. In one hadith, one of the Prophet's Companions in Medina was overcome by lust and kissed a beautiful woman, who was a complete stranger to him, in the marketplace. He came, plagued by guilt, to the mosque and confessed to the Prophet, who reminded him that 'Good deeds replace bad ones' and told him that his sin was forgiven, since he had offered congregational prayers. (The above verse begins with encouraging prayers at 'both ends of the day, and during the darkness of night'.)

GEORGE

Dan and Usama's contributions seem to focus on sins rather than sin. In Dan's case, the lack of distinction is surprising, since Jewish scriptures refer to a state of sin, which exists independent of disobedience to the Law. The Psalmist writes: 'Surely I was sinful at birth, sinful from the time my mother conceived me' (Psalm 51.5).

As I mentioned previously, Christians hold that the state of sin exists right from the moment of birth, even before we think of sins to commit. The Christian faith teaches that the only remedy for sin is God's grace, shown in Christ's atonement by his death on the cross. Humans cannot achieve forgiveness of sin by their own efforts, but only by God's grace, since all of our acts are insufficient to atone, and stem from our sinful nature.

If we look at the enormity of wrongdoing in the world, it seems obvious that centuries of political action, philanthropy, humanitarian organisations, social and health care have proved insufficient to return humankind to its original state of perfection. Something much greater than human action must be needed. While politicians, social workers, conflict mediators and the like have their place, they are rather like someone who witnesses a major accident and offers a small piece of Elastoplast to help the victims.

Our inability to remedy sin, on account of our sinful nature, has caused some theologians – John Calvin is the most renowned – to teach the doctrine of 'the total depravity of man'.[27] This teaching entails that, however good our actions, they still count as sins because they stem from our sinful nature. Whatever we do, good or bad, is sinful.

While some Christians still espouse this doctrine, probably most would regard it as somewhat extreme, although it does have some biblical support. In my youth, our minister, who had strong Calvinist leanings, was very fond of quoting the text in Isaiah: 'All our righteousnesses are like filthy rags' (Isaiah 64.6, King James Version). Article 13 of the Church of England's *Thirty-Nine Articles* (its traditional statement of faith), entitled 'Of Works before Justification', reads:

> Works done before the grace of Christ, and the Inspiration of his Spirit, are not pleasant to God, forasmuch as they spring not of faith in Jesus Christ; neither do they make men meet [fit] to receive grace,...yea rather, for that they are not done as God hath willed and commanded them to be done, we doubt not but they have the nature of sin.[28]

'Justification' is a word used by the apostle Paul, meaning the state in which the believer is put right with God (literally, 'made straight'), having repented of sin, and accepted God's grace, which comes through faith in Christ and not good works (Romans 5.1). This does not entail that good deeds are unimportant, but rather that they follow through a process of 'sanctification', which is the work of the Holy Spirit (1 Peter 1.2).

It is sometimes said that Christians talk too much about sin, and that our religion is gloomy and pessimistic. Should we not have more to say about 'original virtue' – the state of perfection that Adam and Eve enjoyed before the Fall? This is a bit like criticising doctors for focusing unduly on illness, or the police for targeting crime. We need to diagnose the condition in order to find the remedy – which Christians find in Christ.

Chapter 11

FOOD

Much of the Torah relates to diet and food preparation. Although historically some of these may have been connected with hygiene, Christians cannot help wondering whether these are really relevant in today's world. Christianity, by contrast, has no food restrictions, allowing individual Christians to exercise their conscience to decide what to eat and drink. Islam takes an interesting middle position. It acknowledges the validity of Jewish dietary law, but only as applicable to the Jews. At the same time, Islam also has specific dietary laws, some of them quite close to the ones prescribed by the Torah and Jewish law, such as the impurity of pigs. In what follows we discuss our dietary practices and the rationale for them.

GEORGE

The apostle Peter had a vision in which he saw a net descending from heaven, containing all kinds of animals, reptiles and birds, and he heard a voice saying, 'Get up, Peter, kill and eat' (Acts 10.13). Peter was about to be visited by Cornelius, a Roman centurion and therefore a Gentile, who had also received a vision, encouraging him to seek out Peter, who would introduce him to the Christian faith. Peter was a traditionalist, who observed the Jewish dietary laws, and the vision indicated that he should be more liberal, and not require Gentile seekers to observe the food laws as a precondition of accepting Christianity.

With few exceptions, Christians do not have dietary restrictions, although Seventh-day Adventists continue to observe the Old Testament dietary laws, but not kosher, since kosher laws are extra-biblical. Christians have permission to eat anything, with the proviso that one should keep one's body healthy, since it is a 'temple of the Holy Spirit' (1 Corinthians 6.19). The Seventh-day Adventists have been particularly keen to promote healthful eating, and the Kellogg family, well known for their breakfast cereals, came from this tradition.

I am personally a vegetarian, but this is a matter of choice, and I know that I am in a minority. However, there is some biblical authority for vegetarianism. When God creates Adam and Eve, he gives them permission to eat 'every seed-bearing plant...and every tree that has fruit with seed in it' (Genesis 1.29). It is only after the Fall that God permits Noah to eat 'everything that lives and moves', adding, 'Just as I gave you the green plants, I now give you everything' (Genesis 9.3), the word 'now' indicating a change in God's laws. Some Jewish vegetarians share this observation, arguing that vegetarianism is the diet of humankind's perfect state, and that meat-eating was a concession to human weakness.

Jesus said, 'What goes into someone's mouth does not defile them, but what comes out of their mouth, that is what defiles them' (Matthew 15.11), meaning that our speech and actions are more important than dietary laws. Food is frequently used in the New Testament as a metaphor for spiritual nourishment, which is more important than what we physically eat. On one occasion Jesus says to his disciples, 'I have food to eat that you know nothing about.' The disciples, as they often do, construe this statement as referring to physical food, and respond, 'Could someone have brought him food?' So Jesus has to explain, 'My food...is to do the will of him who sent me and to finish his work' (John 4.32–34).

Three items of food and drink have particular symbolic importance to Christians: fish, bread and wine. When Jesus miraculously feeds large crowds of people, bread and fish are multiplied to satisfy their hunger (Matthew 14.13–21). Four of his disciples are fishermen, and after the disciples miraculously catch shoals of fish in the Sea of Galilee, Jesus prepares a breakfast of bread and fish on the shore (John 21.1–14). At the Last Supper, Jesus shares bread and wine, which have become the symbolic elements of the Christian Eucharist (Mark 14.22–24).

The fish is a significant Christian symbol, the Greek word for fish (*ichthus*) being an acronym in Greek for 'Jesus Christ, Son of God, Saviour'.[29] The Eucharistic bread and wine, consumed as a symbolic meal, herald the celestial banquet, which will be the culmination of the Christian life in God's kingdom of heaven.

USAMA

Food is a particularly apt theme for Muslims at the moment: I write these words on the twenty-sixth day of Ramadan, the month of fasting: I am feeling hungry, but must wait another five hours until sunset, when we break the day-long fast. The goal of fasting, which involves giving up food, drink, sex and idle thoughts, words and actions, is to increase one's awareness and consciousness of God (*The Cow*, 2:183).

In a lovely hadith, the Prophet, peace be upon him, taught that, 'One who eats gratefully is like one who fasts patiently.'[30] Thus, fasting and eating represent patience and gratitude, complementary qualities of faith, that are often mentioned together in the Qur'an (*Abraham*, 14:5; *Sheba*, 34:19; *Consultation*, 42:33). The Qur'an removes some of the dietary restrictions that were placed on the Israelites (*The Heights*, 7:155–157), but retains the prohibition of swine-flesh and adds the prohibition of wine.

Abraham's hospitality serves as the traditional basis for the very important tradition of Arab and Islamic hospitality towards guests, something that devout Muslims take very seriously, and of which I have experienced extraordinary examples during my travels (*Winds That Scatter*, 51:24–28). In contrast, denying a stranger food or hospitality, especially when it is requested, is considered extremely bad manners. Moses and his mystical friend Khidr ('the green one') are denied food and hospitality by ill-mannered people during their travels (*The Cave*, 18:77–78, 82).

Abraham is known as the Friend (*Khalil*) of God (*Women*, 4:125). (From this derives the Arabic name of Hebron, where Abraham is traditionally said to be buried: *Al-Khalil*.) A related word is *khall*, which means a sauce such as vinegar. For Islamic mystics such as Ibn Arabi, this is significant: Abraham's spirit was permeated by the Divine, just as sauce permeates bread. Furthermore, this permeation is related to divine immanence: it is important that Abraham honours his guests by swiftly and personally serving them food, because he is a divine instrument amongst people. In this, he is the human equivalent of the Angel Michael (Arabic: *Mika'il*) (*The Cow*, 2:98), who is traditionally understood to be in charge of rain and crops, the bases of our food cycle.

George mentions vegetarianism and healthy living: many Muslim nutritionists point out that the Qur'an refers to many foods that would contribute to a healthy, balanced diet – water, milk, honey, dates, fruit, grains, figs, olives, olive oil and others. There is a hadith that seems to discourage vegetarianism, but the Prophet's diet was mainly vegetarian, often consisting of no more than dates, water and barley bread. Some of my devout Muslim friends are vegetarian: my head tells me that I should become vegetarian, whilst my heart and stomach are too addicted to meat. In India, the land of my ancestors, meat-eating often represents a major demarcation between Muslims and Hindus.

No discussion of food in the Qur'an would be complete without a mention of the food of Paradise in the afterlife: the righteous are promised rivers of water, milk, wine and honey (*Muhammad*, 47:15); any food that they like, and low-hanging fruit. The fruit of heaven resembles earthly fruit but tastes much better, a reference to higher, spiritual realities (*The Cow*, 2:25). The theologian Ghazzali recommended serving guests fruit before meat, based on the order of service in Paradise (*The Inevitable Event*, 56:10–26); however, he remained silent about the previous and next items: respectively, wine and beautiful, young virgins!

DAN

According to the Jewish tradition, food must be ritual fit (*kosher*) if it is to be eaten. The Bible declares that laws of *kashrut* (dietary laws) were given by God to Moses on Mount Sinai. Thus Jews are obligated to follow this legislation because of its divine origin. Nonetheless, various reasons have been adduced for observing these prescriptions. Allegedly forbidden foods are unhealthy: that is why they are forbidden. Another justification is that those who refrain from eating particular kinds of food serve God even while eating, and thereby attain an elevated spiritual state. Indeed, some of these laws – such as refraining from eating pork – have gained such symbolic significance that Jews were prepared to sacrifice their lives rather than violate God's decree. In this way these martyrs demonstrated their devotion to the Jewish faith.

The laws concerning animals, birds and fish that may be eaten are contained in Leviticus 11 and Deuteronomy 14.3–21. According to Scripture, only those animals which both chew the cud and have split hooves may be eaten. Such animals include domestic animals like cows and sheep. No similar formula is stated concerning which birds may be consumed. Rather, a list is given of forbidden birds such as the eagle, the owl and the raven. Although no reasons are given to explain these choices, it has been suggested that forbidden birds are in fact birds of prey: by not eating them human beings are able to express their abhorrence of cruelty as well as the exploitation of the weak over the strong. Regarding fish, the law states that only fish which have both fins and scales are allowed. Again, no reason is given to support this distinction: however, various explanations have been proposed such as the argument that fish that do not have fins and scales frequently live in the depths of the sea, which was regarded as the abode of the gods of chaos. On this basis the law constitutes a protest against idolatry.

A further category of *kashrut* deals with the method of killing animals for food (*shehitah*). Although the Torah does not offer details of this procedure, the Talmud states that this method has divine authority because it was explained by God to Moses on Mount Sinai. According to tradition, the act of slaughter must be done with a sharpened knife without a single notch since that might tear the animal's food pipe or windpipe.

Another restriction concerning ritual food is the prohibition against eating milk and meat together. This stipulation is based on Exodus 23.19: 'Do not cook a young goat in its mother's milk.' According to the rabbis, this rule refers not only to the act of boiling a kid in its mother's milk, but to any combination of meat and milk. Tradition stipulates that it is forbidden to cook meat and milk together. Later, this prohibition was expanded to eating milk and meat products at the same time. Eventually the law was introduced that dairy dishes should not be eaten after a meal until a stipulated period of time had passed.

Until modern times the rules of *kashrut* were universally practised by Jewry. Yet in the nineteenth century the Reform movement broke with tradition, decreeing that the dietary laws were connected with Temple ritual and thus not integral to the Jewish tradition. Conservative

Judaism, however, adheres to the laws of *kashrut*, although allowance is made for personal selectivity. Orthodox Judaism, on the other hand, strictly follows the tradition.

GEORGE

As I write this exchange, our Muslim friends are almost at the festival of Eid, on the cusp between fasting and feasting. At the small computer shop I patronise, the Muslim owner recommended that I should join them in observing these four weeks of fasting. Maybe one year I will try it, but I am not so keen on the idea of going without drink as well as food.

As Christians, many of us observe the season of Lent, which marks the period in which Jesus fasted in the desert and was tempted by the Devil (Matthew 4.1–11). Lent is not as stringent as Ramadan, since it is not obligatory to observe it, and those who do so usually decide to forego some small luxury, like alcohol or chocolate. (I normally use Lent to help control my weight.) The down side is that it lasts longer than Ramadan. The Bible mentions 'forty days and forty nights' (Matthew 4.2), but the period between Ash Wednesday and Easter Sunday is actually 46. Most Christians probably do not notice this discrepancy, but one way of keeping it to 40 days is to exclude Sundays, when one might be a little less strict with oneself.

Some Christians now regard Lenten fasting as unduly negative, and have tried to promote spiritual nourishment instead. Many churches now promote Lent programmes of devotional activities, Bible study, and Lent groups where some aspect of the Christian faith is discussed.

Some Christian communities have viewed abstinence from meat as a way of fasting. Traditionally Eastern Orthodox Christians observe the liturgical calendar that alternates periods of fasting and feasting, the former involving abstinence from animal products. Perhaps my father's side of the family (who are Greek Orthodox) are not very pious, since I have never noticed any change in their dietary habits during the year. On the other hand, when we were children, my mother, who was a Protestant, always instructed us never to order fish in restaurants on Fridays, lest anyone should think we were Roman Catholics! However, it is unfair that foregoing meat should be regarded as a spiritual hardship, although there are occasional biblical passages that seem to imply that a vegetable diet is inferior (Proverbs 15.17; Romans 14.2).

The opposite side of fasting is feasting, and food is invariably associated with festivals and celebrations in most faiths. According to some traditions, religious significance can be found in some of the foods associated with the Easter and Christmas season. Hot cross buns, traditionally associated with Good Friday, bear the sign of the cross; the spices connote those that were used for Jesus' burial (Luke 23.56), and the yeast purportedly symbolises rising and resurrection. It has also been suggested that Christmas puddings traditionally contain 13 ingredients, signifying Jesus and his 12 disciples.

Most Christians are probably unaware of such explanations, and simply enjoy having a good time. When we do so, we are following Jesus' example. He appears to have loved celebrations and eating out. The disciples of John the Baptist, who had somewhat different eating habits (Mark 1.6), seemed surprised that Jesus and his disciples did not fast, in reply to which Jesus compared his presence to that of a bridegroom at a wedding feast (Matthew 9.14–15). This imagery prefigures life after death, which Jesus frequently compares with a wedding banquet (Matthew 22.1–14; 25.1–13).

While being concerned with world hunger – a topic to which we shall return – those Christians who have food may enjoy it and be thankful for it.

USAMA

Dan has explained in great detail some of the dietary restrictions that God placed on the Israelites. The Qur'an declares that, updating the Torah and Gospel, the Prophet Muhammad, peace be upon him, 'legalises pure things and prohibits impure things, and removes their heavy burden and the yokes that were upon them'. The mention of pure and impure here resonates with one of Dan's explanations for dietary laws: the promotion of healthy food.

In the previous *surah*, forbidden (*haram*, as opposed to lawful: *halal*) foods are summarised as follows: (1) carrion, that is, meat from animals that die by themselves, without being slaughtered according to the halal method that is very similar to the Jewish *shehita*; (2) flowing blood; (3) swine-flesh; (4) meat from animals slaughtered in the name of idols or false gods.

There are some other contested dietary rules found in various hadiths, such as a prohibition on eating all animals of prey, including birds and possibly fish. One hadith states that water-carrion, or animals found or pulled out dead from seas, rivers and lakes, is *halal*. This includes all fish and seafood, although shellfish are controversial, in a dispute that was probably influenced by Jewish tradition. The jurists have very interesting discussions about whether an animal is *halal* or *haram* to eat. Amphibians, such as frogs, are controversial because if they are regarded as water-animals, they are halal without slaughter.

Horses are disputed (I once ate horsemeat – it was very tasty), whilst donkey-meat is generally regarded as *haram*. For those who regarded horsemeat as *halal* and donkey-meat as *haram*, mules presented a problem: some jurists regarded them as *halal*, arguing that food in general is *halal* unless specifically prohibited, whilst others were more cautious and classified them as *haram*. This dispute extends to modern, technological innovations: it is now possible to genetically engineer new animals, such as the 'geep' that is a genetic crossover of a goat and sheep. Since both these animals are *halal* to eat, so is eating geep. But what if a *halal* animal was crossed with a pig?

The prohibition on eating animals of prey leads to a dispute about sharks: are they simple seafood, and hence *halal*, or *haram* because they are predators? Another hadith defines predators as those with long, sharp teeth: this led to various views on eating elephants, since many jurists did not know that these are herbivores and mistook their tusks for hunting-teeth. The Andalusian theologian and jurist, Ibn Hazm, quipped, 'If you actually manage to fell an elephant and slaughter it, you may eat it!'

Dietary rules aside, the patience and gratitude that come respectively with fasting and feasting are paramount. I would encourage George to try a few days at least of Ramadan-style fasting: I know Christians and Jews, including a rabbi, who have fasted some or all of Ramadan in recent years. There are also Muslims in the West fasting Lent to follow Jesus: in Islamic tradition, Moses spent 40 days and nights on Mount Sinai, as did Jesus in the wilderness, resisting Satan's temptations.

There are other patterns of Islamic optional fasting outside Ramadan: the middle three days of the lunar month, twice a week (Monday and Thursday), or the 'most excellent fasting: that of Prophet Dawud (King David), who would alternate between days of fasting and eating'. The latter is the ultimate balance of fasting and feasting, of patience and gratitude before God.

DAN

I should point out that, although Jews are permitted to eat meat, Jewish vegetarianism is an important element of the tradition. Such a practice is based on the belief that following a vegetarian diet is implied in the Torah. Although Scripture gives precise details of how animals are to be slaughtered, various rabbis such as Abraham Isaac Kook, formerly the Chief Rabbi of Israel, have argued that the complexity of these laws was intended to discourage eating meat. A modern writer, Richard H. Schwartz, the author of *Judaism and Vegetarianism*,[31] maintains that God's original plan was for humanity to be vegetarian; it was only later that God gave permission for human beings to eat meat in a covenant with Noah (Genesis 9.1–17). This was a concession because of humankind's weak nature.

Some writers maintain that the Jewish prophet Isaiah was a vegetarian, and on the basis of passages in the Book of Isaiah that extol non-violence and reverence for life, these writers refer to the 'vegetarian Isaiah', or 'the notorious vegetarian Isaiah', or 'the vegetarian prophet'. In Daniel 1.8–16, Daniel, Shadrach, Meshach and Abednego became vegan – at Daniel's request they were subjected to a test of being fed vegetables and water for ten days. At the end of this period, they were in better condition than those who ate a non-vegan diet. As a consequence, they remained vegan.

Jewish vegetarians deploy a number of arguments in defence of their practices. One *mitzvah* cited by vegetarians is the concept of *tza'ar ba'alei hayyim* (the injunction not to cause pain to living creatures). They argue that the laws of *shehitah* were meant to prevent the suffering of animals. However, factory farming and various high-speed mechanised kosher slaughterhouses arguably fail to meet this standard. Hence, vegetarianism should now be followed because it is in accord with

Jewish law. Another *mitzvah* cited by Jewish vegetarians is *bal tashchit* (the law which prohibits waste). The argument is that an omnivorous diet is wasteful since it uses much more grain, water, land and general resources as compared to a vegetarian diet.

Another argument stresses the importance of maintaining health and not harming oneself. Jewish vegetarians contend that a diet high in animal products is detrimental to health. In this connection, they maintain that global warming, hunger and the depletion of natural resources would be lessened by a shift to a vegetarian diet. Finally, Jewish vegetarians argue that vegetarianism is consistent with the highest ideals of Judaism such as compassion, health, life, conservation of resources, charity, peace and justice. By contrast the mass production and consumption of meat and other animal products contradicts Jewish teaching. It gravely harms people, animals and communities, as well as the environment.

Most Jews, however, are not persuaded by these arguments and continue to eat meat. Strictly Orthodox Jews scrupulously follow biblical and rabbinic injunctions regarding *kashrut*. Other Jews are less strict, and avoid eating pork and shellfish. As is the case generally, the vast majority of modern Jews select from the tradition those features they find spiritually meaningful. This means in practice that, with regard to Jewish food laws, they freely interpret the tradition to suit their own personal needs.

Chapter 12

MARRIAGE AND FAMILY

Jews follow a world-affirming religion, in which marriage and family life are valued. Its founding leaders – Abraham, Jacob, Moses – had wives and children. Similarly, Islam, too, promotes the marriage institution, and the Prophet Muhammad, peace be upon him, is known to have been married to many wives. By contrast, Christian founder-leaders – Jesus and Paul most notably – appear to have been unmarried. Although family life tends to be the norm within Christianity, many Christians have viewed celibacy, monasticism and holy orders as an alternative to marriage. Which lifestyle is preferable, and which makes for greater spirituality?

USAMA

On my first visit to Jerusalem in 2013, I bought a wooden hanging made of Palestinian olive, inscribed with the Ten Commandments of the Torah. According to its text, 'Honour thy parents' is the Fourth Commandment. However, in the Qur'an, including the passages recounting the injunctions given to the Israelites, kindness to parents is the second commandment (*The Cow*, 2:83; *Cattle*, 6:151; *Children of Israel* or *The Night Journey*, 17:23; *The Spider*, 29:8; *Luqman*, 31:14; *The Winding Sand-Tracts*, 46:15). Both scriptures agree, of course, that worshipping the One God is the primary commandment.

Children and grandchildren are a blessing and favour from God (*The Honey-Bee*, 16:72). This blessing especially emanates from the primary Divine attribute of mercy: family relations are *arham*, or literally, 'wombs'. The womb (*rahm*) is related directly to mercy (*rahma*). 'Cutting off family relations' is regarded as a major sin

(*Muḥammad*, 47:22–23), and one hadith explicitly states that, 'A person who cuts off family ties will not enter the heavenly Garden' (Bukhari and Muslim (no. 2556)). The opposite of 'cutting off' family ties is to 'join' or 'connect' them, hence traditional Islamic family values, that are obviously also rooted in human nature. In the Islamic culture of South Asia, the land of my ancestors, one always speaks respectfully to elders, especially family members: I have never addressed my elder brothers and sister by name, although there is not a huge age gap; we refer to them respectfully as 'brother' or 'sister', even if we are yelling at them!

Another hadith explains that 'joining' family ties is not simply to reciprocate good behaviour, since that is easy. The real test is to repay bad behaviour with goodness, or in Qur'anic terms, 'Repel evil with what is better' (*The Believers*, 23:96; *Signs Explained*, 41:34). This teaching is thus similar to 'love thine enemy'.

Parents, siblings, children and wider family are indeed a great blessing, but also a great test, especially when it comes to family squabbles and politics. The Qur'an declares, 'We have made you tests for each other: will you have patience?' (*The Criterion*, 25:20). This applies to all human relationships.

Children, along with wealth, are an adornment of life (*The Cave*, 18:46) but also a test and responsibility (*Spoils of War*, 8:28): spouses and children may even become one's spiritual enemy if this test is not handled carefully (*Mutual Loss and Gain*, 64:14). This is why the twelfth-century CE theologian Imam Ghazzali said that towards the end of time, a person might be better off spiritually without a spouse and children.

The exemplars of humanity are the prophets and messengers of God, and they generally had spouses and descendants (*Thunder*, 13:38). Two notable exceptions to this rule in the Islamic tradition are Prophets Yahya (John the Baptist) and Isa (Jesus). John the Baptist's chastity (*The Family of Imran*, 3:39) is understood by mainstream commentators to mean that he never married, and renounced women and sex. Jesus' chastity is similar, although many Muslims believe, based on some hadiths, that he will return for a Second Coming, when he will marry and have children.

In Islam, we have a concept of sacred sex: sexual intercourse between husband and wife is regarded as something sacred; indeed, one hadith describes it as an act of worship. This resonates with those Qur'an-commentaries that regard Adam and Eve's forbidden fruit as being the sexual act.

About the topic of homosexuality, there is a raging debate in contemporary Islam.

GEORGE

In the Garden of Eden, God creates a man and a woman and instructs them to 'be fruitful and increase in number' (Genesis 1.27–28). The story suggests a binary division between male and female, and has been taken to mean that marriage and family life are the norm, as Usama has suggested, with the further assumption that extra-marital sexual relationships are sinful.

Attitudes are changing, however. Today, couples who have not officially married can be found in Christian congregations, and do not incur disapproval, and if they decide to have a church wedding, their children are often present. In 2009 the Church of England promoted a (somewhat controversial) 'two for one' ceremony, at which their children were baptised at the end of the marriage rite.

In biblical times, marriage was not performed in the context of religion. Jesus' parable of the wise and foolish bridesmaids depicts the social custom of his time, in which the bridegroom came to his bride's home, taking her back to his own, where the celebrations began (Matthew 25.1–13).

Although churches still advertise 'family services', family attendance is the exception rather than the norm in every church I have recently visited. Congregations often consist of widows, divorcees and single people. Those who are childless, either through choice or through infertility, can often feel excluded – especially since the Bible tends to stigmatise 'barrenness' (Genesis 11.30; 1 Samuel 1.2).

As Usama points out, Jesus was not a family man. Despite speculations about a possible liaison with Mary Magdalene, there is not a shred of evidence to suggest that Jesus either married or planned to do so. When his family try to contact him, he seems to regard his itinerant teaching ministry as more important than family ties (Matthew 12.46–50).

Many churches now accept gay marriages, and conduct same-sex ceremonies. As for the male/female binary, we are increasingly familiar with the phenomenon of genital abnormality and trans-sexuality, recognising that these conditions and lifestyles are not chosen and have often been misunderstood and treated unsympathetically. One Christian denomination – the Metropolitan Community Church – was set up specifically for LGBT people.

Paul has often been interpreted as denouncing homosexual relationships (Romans 1.27). However, some modern interpreters of the Bible have suggested that Paul's catalogue of presumed sexual malpractices is a rhetorical device, culminating in his statement, 'You, therefore have no excuse, who pass judgement on someone else' (Romans 2.1). Paul, like Jesus, may have meant that we should be slow to judge other people (Matthew 7.1).

The Christian view of divorce deserves mention. The Roman Catholic Church condemns it unequivocally, and in the past divorcees were not permitted to receive the sacrament at the Mass. While most married Christians would hope that their relationship is 'till death us do part', Christians increasingly accept that marriages do not always work out. In 2016, however, Pope Francis expressed a more lenient attitude, suggesting that those in 'irregular family situations' might benefit from the Church's sacraments.[32]

Jesus himself did not regard divorce as ideal, but he did allow that it was permissible in the case of adultery (Matthew 5.31–32). Christians have always regarded marital fidelity as important: as Jesus taught, 'What God has joined together, let no one separate' (Matthew 19.6). However, where Christian missionaries have worked in polygamous societies, this has caused much soul searching, with the issues still unresolved.

For the Christian, the principle of love should be paramount amidst all these different lifestyles. Many Christians are overwhelmed by the rapidity of social change, and are struggling to apply Jesus' teaching to these diverse situations and lifestyles.

DAN

Judaism does not have a tradition of celibacy, as does Christianity. According to Genesis, when God created Adam, he pronounced: 'It is not good for the man to be alone.' Thus God created the first woman and he 'brought her to the man. The man said, "This is now bone of my bones and flesh of my flesh"... That is why a man leaves his father and mother and is united to his wife, and they become one flesh' (Genesis 2.18, 22–23). Apart from the Essenes, a first-century desert sect, there have been no Jewish celibate communities.

In strictly Orthodox Jewish communities, early marriage is often the norm. Boys and girls are educated separately, and they are largely kept apart during adolescence. Then, during the young man's final years at *yeshiva* (rabbinical academy), he is expected to get married, and families, friends and teachers are all co-opted to find a suitable bride. In the old days, in the villages of Eastern Europe, there was a recognised matchmaker who organised the brokering between families and made introductions. Today it is more informal. Nonetheless, anxious parents keep a close eye on proceedings.

For the vast majority of Jews, however, the situation is different. Most Jewish children go to secular, co-educational schools. They attend secular universities, and they often travel far from home to complete their education and for their jobs. Parents have far less control. According to Jewish law, certain marriages are prohibited: those that are incestuous (such as between father and daughter or brother and sister), those that are adulterous (when one partner is already married to someone else), and those between a Jew and a gentile. Today it is the latter which is perceived as the greatest threat to the community. In the past when Jews were isolated in their own communities or when there was serious antisemitism, the danger of intermarriage was small. In the State of Israel, Jews are likely to marry Jews. In the diaspora, however, it is a different story.

In biblical and talmudic times weddings took place in two stages. The first element was betrothal. This involved the delivery of an object of monetary value by the bridegroom to the bride in front of two witnesses. The object (which is now invariably a wedding ring) was given with the words, 'Behold, you are consecrated to me with this ring, according to the law of Moses and Israel.' The second stage was the wedding proper. This involved the young couple standing together under the marriage canopy. The marriage contract, the *ketubah*, is then recited. Since the Middle Ages, however, the two stages have been combined, and the betrothal and wedding ceremonies take place one after another.

The Jewish tradition recognises that marriages sometimes break down. This is not to say that divorce is encouraged; rather, it is regarded as a tragedy, and according to the Talmud, the very altar of God weeps when a man divorces his wife. Nonetheless, divorce is regarded as an occasional and sad necessity and formal procedures are laid down in the law. According to tradition, a man who wants to be rid of his wife is required to give her a proper divorce – this is done according to an elaborate procedure. A bill of divorce is written out by a special scribe. The document is then read and signed by two witnesses, and the husband formally delivers it into the wife's hands.

USAMA

Homosexuality has traditionally been regarded as sinful in Islam, with most authorities calling for a death penalty for homosexual acts, as they did for adultery (as opposed to fornication, for which the punishment was flogging). The sinfulness and punishment was based on the story of the people of Lut (Lot), who were destroyed by a rain of stones for their sins.

However, some traditional authorities disputed this, arguing that no case of homosexuality was ever brought to the Prophet, peace be upon him: they said that there is no automatic penalty for homosexuality, and it is up to the community to decide how to deal with this phenomenon. Imam Kisai, an early Qur'an expert, argued that the story of Lot's people was not about homosexuality, but about the practice of gang rape of male visitors by married, heterosexual men. These traditional dissenting voices provide a basis for the opening up of the theoretical discussion about homosexuality in contemporary Islam.

I say, 'theoretical discussion', because in practice, Islamic societies have for long had a tradition of diverse sexuality. Even in the Prophet's time, 'hermaphrodites', or people with both male and female genitals, stood in a separate row for prayer between those of the men and women, indicating that gender and sexuality is a spectrum. Throughout Muslim societies, historically and in contemporary Asia and Africa, hermaphrodites, transvestites and people we now call LGBT, occupied a place in society with their own patron saints and social roles, including prostitution.

A heterosexual, monogamous family is not the only norm in traditional Islam: there are several other models. Polygamy, or to be exact polygyny, has always been present, with a man being limited to four wives maximum: 'If you fear that you will not be able to do justice to orphans, then marry women whom you find to be pure: two, three or four; but if you fear not being able to treat them equally, then marry only one.' Ibn Hazm of Andalusia read 'or' in this verse as 'and' and raised the limit to nine wives, two plus three plus four. The Prophet himself is said to have married about a dozen women, with a maximum of around nine at any one time, so Ibn Hazm's view is consistent with that. However, every other jurist limits polygyny to four wives, with the Prophet's case being exceptional.

A Nigerian Muslim friend of mine told me that his father, a village chief, had almost 30 children by several wives, being married to no more than four at a time. Debate still rages within Islam as to whether monogamy or polygamy is preferable, or whether it depends on people's economic and social circumstances. There are some polygamous families where the co-wives are quite happy with the arrangement, and some working, professional Muslim women prefer being a 'part-time wife' or co-wife. However, polygamy, like monogamy, has its own risks and pitfalls.

Furthermore, although Sunni Islam prohibits them, Shia Islam recognises 'temporary marriages' or those expiring on a predetermined date. This is sometimes practised by people working abroad or in other temporary locations.

Divorce is allowed, although usually discouraged. The schools of jurisprudence range from making divorce very difficult to making it relatively easy if the relationship fails. Hasan, the Prophet's grandson, is said to have married and divorced hundreds of women, although all his ex-wives continued to love him. This may explain the very large number of Muslims who claim to be *sayyids*, or descendants of the Prophet.

GEORGE

It is interesting that Usama mentions polygamy, for it is often popularly supposed that Muslims have many wives while Jews and Christians are confined to one marriage partner. This would be an over-simplification.

The Bible records that Abraham, Isaac and Jacob had plural wives. We are not told exactly how many King David had, but his son Solomon must have had quite an exhausting time with 'seven hundred wives of royal birth and three hundred concubines' (1 Kings 11.3). One passage in the Torah indicates that polygamy could sometimes even be an obligation: if two brothers lived together and one died without a son, the surviving brother should marry the widow, presumably even if he already has a spouse (Deuteronomy 25.5–6).

Polygamy appears to have declined in the intertestamental period, for no New Testament character has more than one spouse. The writer to Timothy states that overseers and deacons should be 'the husband of one wife' (1 Timothy 3.2, 12, King James Version). (The author explicitly uses the Greek word *mias*, meaning 'of one' – which is lost in numerous modern translations.) However, this requirement applies only to office bearers, not to the laity. Jesus and Paul do not mention polygamy, although Jesus quotes God's command to Adam – to which Dan refers – that he must be 'united to his wife [singular], and they become one flesh' (Genesis 2.24; Matthew 19.3–6). Jesus adds, 'So they are no longer two, but one.' These passages suggest, although not explicitly, that the ideal relationship between a husband and a wife is a monogamous one.

Although the Bible does not explicitly prohibit polygamy, it gives the impression that it is not a great idea. Solomon's wives 'led him astray', we are told (1 Kings 11.3). The rivalry between Sarah and Hagar causes Abraham to send Hagar and her young son Ishmael into the desert, homeless (Genesis 21.14). Penninah taunts Hannah because she is infertile (1 Samuel 1.6). Polygamy does not seem to be working well.

The issue is no mere academic matter. Christian missionaries encountered problems in recent times where they converted members of polygamous societies. This caused a dilemma: should they impose Western monogamy – which is not wholly supported by Scripture – demanding that the husband chooses a favourite wife, abandoning the others, or should they accept polygamy as an acceptable but different way of life? Some missionaries compromised by requiring that polygamous husbands acquire no new wives, while others barred polygamous men from holding office, in line with 1 Timothy.

Whatever one thinks of polygamy, the Bible is quite clear about marital fidelity. Adultery is forbidden in the Ten Commandments (Exodus 20.14), and ancient Jewish punishments were harsh: both guilty parties were to be put to death (Leviticus 20.10). Jesus appears to have reservations about this penalty, however: faced with a crowd who were about to stone an adulteress, he stops the execution with the challenge, 'Let any one of you who is without sin be the first to throw a stone at her' (John 8.7). It should be noted, of course, that although Jesus does not condemn, he does not condone the accused woman's sin.

Finally, lest the discussion becomes too serious, here is an irrelevant – and irreverent – joke based on this story. Jesus says, 'Let anyone without sin cast the first stone,' whereupon someone in the crowd throws a piece of rock. Jesus turns to identify the culprit. 'Oh, Mother!' he exclaims, 'You always have to spoil everything!'

DAN

It is true that initially Jews were allowed to have more than one wife, but this was banned in Ashkenazi countries with the decree of Rabbenu Gershom in 1000. In modern society, all Jewish communities – Sephardic and Ashkenazic – follow this ruling. Hence, unlike Christianity and Islam, Jews are united in their adherence to monogamy. However, there is wide divergence with regard to homosexual practice and marriage within the Jewish world. Not surprisingly, the Orthodox condemn any form of homosexual encounter, and marriage between two gay men or lesbians is regarded as totally abhorrent.

Within various non-Orthodox branches, however, this is not the case. Reform Judaism, for example, has a long and proud tradition of working for the full inclusion of lesbian, gay, bisexual and transgender people in Jewish life and for their civil rights. As early as 1965 the Women of Reform Judaism called for the decriminalisation of homosexuality. Resolutions by the Union for Reform Judaism and the Central Conference of American Rabbis (the central body of Reform rabbis) joined in this campaign, and the social justice arm of the Reform movement (the Religious Action Centre) has been at the forefront of the fight for LGBT equality.

In adopting this stance, Reform Jews are guided by the belief that all human beings are created *b'tselem Elohim* (in the divine image), as it states in Genesis 1.27: 'So God created mankind in his own image, in the image of God he created them; male and female he created them.' According to David Saperstein, the Director of the Religious Action Centre, 'regardless of context, discrimination against any person arising from apathy, insensitivity, ignorance, fear or hatred is inconsistent with this fundamental belief. We oppose discrimination against all individuals, including gay men, lesbians, and bisexuals, for the stamp of the Divine is present in each and every one of us.'[33]

Today, in addition to a number of congregations whose primary outreach is to the LGBT communities, LGBT Jews and their families are welcome in all Reform congregations. LGBT Jews may be ordained as rabbis and cantors, and some of these individuals serve throughout the Reform movement. Most Reform rabbis and cantors officiate at same-sex ceremonies. However, such marriages are governed by principles that apply to heterosexual marriages. If the LGBT couple are both Jews, there is no problem about holding a Jewish marriage ceremony. However, this is not the case, if one or the other is a non-Jew.

When it comes to officiating at weddings between Jews and non-Jews, there are a variety of practices. The Central Conference of American Rabbis (CCAR) discourages its members from officiating at interfaith weddings (whether the couple is heterosexual, homosexual, bisexual or transgender). Many rabbis view their ordination as authorising them to officiate only at Jewish weddings where both members of the couple are Jewish. While the CCAR discourages its members from officiating at interfaith weddings, it does not prevent them from doing so. Ultimately rabbis are given authority in such matters and each rabbi interprets the Jewish tradition according to his or her own understanding. Some Reform rabbis reach the decision that a greater good is served by officiating at such weddings. Often they require that the couple or non-Jewish partner take an introduction to Judaism class and commit to creating a Jewish home and raising Jewish children.

Chapter 13

RITES

Christians cannot help wondering why it is necessary to retain the rite of circumcision as a means of entry to the Jewish faith, or as a rite of passage in Islam. Is this not outmoded and cruel? Equally, Jews can find it difficult to understand the Christian sacraments. The Torah prohibits the consumption of blood (Genesis 9.4), yet the Gospel of John speaks shamelessly of eating the flesh and drinking the blood of the Son of Man (John 6.53). Is not this offensive to Jews, and why should Christians find it necessary to drink Christ's blood, even symbolically? Islam also argues for ultimate monotheism, and yet one of its five main pillars, the pilgrimage, involves circumambulations of a stone. How can this rite be contained within the Muslim claim for abstract monotheism?

DAN

For the Jewish people, prayer has served as the vehicle by which they have expressed their joys, sorrows and hopes. It has played a major role in the religious life of the Jewish nation, especially in view of the successive crises and calamities in which they have been involved throughout their history. In such situations Jews continually turned to God for assistance. Thus, in the Torah the patriarchs frequently addressed God through personal prayer.

In addition to personal prayer, Jews have throughout history engaged in communal worship. In ancient times this centred on the Temple in Jerusalem. Twice daily – in the morning and afternoon – the priests offered prescribed sacrifices while the Levites chanted psalms.

On Sabbaths and festivals additional services were added to this daily ritual. At some stage it became customary to include other prayers along with the recitation of the Ten Commandments and the *Shema* (Deuteronomy 6.4–9; 11, 23–21; Numbers 15.37–41) in the Temple service.

With the destruction of the Second Temple in 70 CE, sacrificial offerings were replaced by the prayer service in the synagogue. To enhance uniformity, they introduced fixed periods for daily prayer which corresponded with the times sacrifices had been offered in the Temple. The morning prayer (*shaharit*) and afternoon prayer (*minhah*) correspond with the daily and afternoon sacrifice. Evening prayer (*maariv*) corresponds with the nightly burning of fats and limbs. By the completion of the Talmud in the sixth century, the essential features of the synagogue service were established.

From earliest times the Torah (Five Books of Moses) was read in the public gatherings; subsequently regular readings of the Torah on Sabbaths and festivals were instituted. In Babylonia the entire Torah was read during the yearly cycles; in Palestine it was completed once every three years. The Torah itself is divided into 54 sections, each of which is known as an 'order' or 'section' (*sidrah*). Each section is subdivided into portions (each of which is called a *parashah*).

In surveying Jewish worship, the Sabbath and the pilgrim festivals are of paramount importance in the Jewish yearly calendar. Genesis 2.1–3 declares:

> Thus the heavens and the earth were completed in all their vast array. By the seventh day God had finished the work he had been doing; so on the seventh day he rested from all his work. Then God blessed the seventh day and made it holy, because on it he rested from all the work of creating that he had done.

This passage serves as the basis for the decree that no work should be done on the Sabbath.

Scripture also serves as the basis for the observance of the three pilgrim festivals. According to Deuteronomy, Jews are to celebrate three pilgrim festivals each year:

> Three times a year all your men must appear before the Lord your God at the place he will choose: at the Festival of Unleavened

Bread [*Pesach*], the Festival of Weeks [*Shavuot*] and the Festival of Tabernacles [*Sukkot*]. (Deuteronomy 16.16)

In addition, the New Year (*Rosh Hashanah*) and the Day of Atonement (*Yom Kippur*) are central features of the yearly cycle of public worship.

In addition to personal and public forms of worship, there are a range of life cycle events that are of spiritual significance in the life of Jewry. In ancient times the birth of a child was accompanied by numerous superstitious practices. In modern times, such observances have been abandoned. Instead, the focus is on circumcision for a baby boy, and baby-naming for a girl. The custom of redemption of the first born has been retained in Orthodox circles. At the age of 13 the *bar mitzvah* ceremony is observed in all branches of Judaism as is *bat mitzvah* for a girl at the age of 12. Later the marriage ceremony unites Jewish men and women as husbands and wives.

GEORGE

Only a very small handful of minor Christian sects celebrate the Jewish festivals that Dan describes. Most Christians regard them as being superseded by Christ's coming: as the writer to the Hebrews argues, Christ is the high priest whose sacrifice brings an end to the Jewish ritual obligations associated with the Jerusalem Temple, and who provides access to the heavenly temple (Hebrews 4.14–5.10).

Christians celebrate Pentecost (known to Jews as the Feast of the Weeks), but it bears a different meaning, being associated with the Holy Spirit's descent to the early disciples, marking the birth of the Church (Acts 2.1–41). There are no particular directives about the celebration of festivals in the Christian calendar such as Christmas and Easter, and worship on such dates tends to be themed rather than ritualised, with use of appropriate music and readings from Scripture. However, certain events described in the Bible are often re-enacted: for example, on Palm Sunday many churches recreate Jesus' entry into Jerusalem (Matthew 21.1–11), beginning the service with a procession with palm branches, and the inclusion of a real donkey has become increasingly popular.

Jesus instructed his disciples to perform two rites: baptism and the Eucharist (Matthew 28.19; Luke 22.14–20). These are regarded as sacraments in the major Christian traditions, a sacrament being a rite whereby the physical actions symbolise the receiving of spiritual grace.

Disagreement has arisen as to how to administer the sacraments. Baptists and Pentecostals regard baptism as an affirmation of faith, to be administered to those of sufficient age to understand what Christian commitment involves, and baptism is by immersion. This follows the example of Jesus' baptism by John the Baptist, which involved immersion in the River Jordan, as an accompaniment to repentance and forgiveness (Mark 1.4–11). Other Christians believe that children should be recognised as part of the Christian community, and therefore should be baptised in infancy, and (with the exception of Orthodoxy) by the sprinkling of water. Arguably, there is some biblical support for child baptism: on the day of Pentecost, Peter exhorts his listeners to 'repent and be baptised', adding, 'The promise is for you and your children' (Acts 2.38–39), and there are references to entire households being baptised, such Lydia's family, and that of the Philippian jailer (Acts 16.15, 33). However, those favouring adult baptism contend that children are not explicitly mentioned, and that this is only conjecture.

The Gospel of John does not explicitly mention the sharing of bread and wine at Jesus' final meal, but records that Jesus washes the disciples' feet, saying, 'Now that I, your Lord and Teacher, have washed your feet, you also should wash one another's feet' (John 13.14). Although ritualised foot-washing is not regarded as a 'means of grace', Seventh-day Adventists and Pentecostals have regarded it as an ordinance for many years, and in recent times other denominations have incorporated it into the Maundy Thursday liturgy.

The Roman Catholic and Orthodox churches add five sacraments in addition to baptism and Eucharist: confirmation, penance, anointing the sick, holy orders and marriage. Protestants observe all of these except penance, but argue that there are no explicit biblical instructions to administer them. Jesus was present at the wedding in Cana (John 2.1–11), thus showing his approval of the institution of marriage, but he gives no instruction that men and women must marry, or that marriage should be ceremonially solemnised. In the absence of explicit biblical instruction, Protestants observe such rites, but do not regard them as sacraments.

USAMA

I have always loved the symbolism of Islamic 'rituals', especially at the Hajj or annual pilgrimage to Mecca. The circumambulation (*tawaf*) of the Ka'ba, especially when tens of thousands of people do it simultaneously, affords a magnificent spectacle from the upper floors of the Grand Mosque, or from overhead TV cameras. I've always thought of people in *tawaf* as 'orbiting' the Ka'ba, with its cosmic resonances of electrons 'orbiting' atomic nuclei, the planets orbiting the sun, stars orbiting the centre of their galaxy, spiritual hearts 'orbiting' God, and so on.

Supposedly minor details are important in such symbolism too: the *tawaf* always proceeds 'anti-clockwise' or by walking to the right: this keeps a person's physical heart closest to the Ka'ba, since the heart is located on the left side of the body.

The Ka'ba is a cuboid stone building, with the 'Black Stone' being its holiest part: tradition has it that this descended as a white stone from heaven (a meteor?), but as it helped to purify people by absorbing their sins upon being touched or kissed, it gradually turned black. The early Muslims recognised that it was important to remember the symbolism of one's spiritual heart in *tawaf* around God, otherwise we would descend into idolatry: the rationalist Mu'tazilite school even criticised some forms of *tawaf*, and Caliph Omar famously addressed the Black Stone, saying, 'By God! I know that you are only a stone, with no power to harm or benefit me. Had I not seen the Messenger of God kissing you, I would never have kissed you!' In other words, Caliph Omar would have otherwise regarded this practice as idolatrous, but followed the tradition of the Prophet, trusting in a deeper meaning.

A weak or disputed hadith even says that the Black Stone is God's right hand on earth: this is a disputed hadith because of its implications of idolatry and anthropomorphism of God, or comparing God to a holy man or king whose right hand is to be touched and kissed.

The word 'rites' does not feature prominently in the Qur'an, except in the case of the Hajj (*The Cow*, 2:128, 196; *Pilgrimage*, 22:34), where it includes reference to ritual sacrifice during the pilgrimage and Eid al-Adha festival. But even here, it is not merely a 'sacrament', for the sacrificial meat must be shared with the poor, for whom meat was then, as it is now, an expensive, luxury food (*Pilgrimage*, 22:36).

Furthermore, 'Their flesh and blood will never reach God, but piety from you reaches Him' (*Pilgrimage*, 22:37).

Rituals as symbols imbued with higher meaning and divine grace means that they are sacraments, but not limited to a few, rare events. In fact, all of life is a sacrament if underpinned by faith in, and love of, God.

Daily ablutions before prayer are a regular 'baptism' in Islam, with the water physically purifying the body and spiritually purifying the senses of mistakes and sins. The daily ritual prayer (*salat*) is permeated with symbolism, for example, outwardly facing Mecca and inwardly turning the heart towards God.

The Qur'an castigated those polytheists and 'People of the Book', or Jews and Christians, in Medina who made a big deal out of the Muslim change of direction of prayer from Jerusalem to Mecca, calling them 'fools' who did not understand higher realities (*The Cow*, 2:142–150). Furthermore, it emphatically declared that righteousness does not ultimately lie in which way we face for prayer, but in faith, charity, prayer, integrity, truthfulness and perseverance (*The Cow*, 2:177).

DAN

So far I have been referring to traditional Jewish practices. But I should mention that alongside these observances, Jews in the past engaged in a wide range of superstitious customs. For example, it was a Jewish practice to spit three times in response to something exceptionally evil – this was a prophylactic measure to prevent such a tragedy from happening or reoccurring. Paradoxically, it was also customary to perform the same action in response to something wonderful such as the birth of a child. This was done to ward off the evil eye. Spitting was long considered a potent protector against magic and demons. Ancient and medieval physicians, including the twelfth-century philosopher Moses Maimonides, describe the positive values of saliva and spittle.

Another practice was pulling or tugging one's ears when sneezing. This was especially common among Jews from Galicia and Lithuania. The reason for this practice is unclear. Originally it was performed if the sneeze occurred when speaking about a person who had died. However, tugging has long been extended to all sneezes and was usually accompanied by reciting a Yiddish phrase meaning 'to long, lucky years'.

Alongside these rituals, closing prayer books, Bibles and talmudic tracts that had been left open was a common act in synagogues and study halls. The explanation is related to the medieval fear of the evil power of devils and demons who would take holy knowledge and somehow use it for their own nefarious purposes.

Demons and similar creatures were also perceived as residing in new houses and causing chaos. For this reason people were paid to live in them before the arrival of their intended occupants. Because salt was generally regarded as having powers against evil spirits, it was often placed in the corners of a room where these creatures hid. The same reasoning applied to new clothes, where smaller goblins and elves could secret themselves in pockets. By placing a small amount of salt in the pockets, the owner of the clothing hoped to drive these beings away and foil their designs.

In some communities a safety or straight pin was attached out of sight under a shirt collar or on a sleeve. Metal was thought to be a powerful protective substance. Thus according to the medieval sage Eliezer of Worms, metals were the products of civilisation and thus could successfully attack and repeal the evil spirits of a less sophisticated society.

In addition to these practices it was a custom for Jews to use amulets to ward off the evil eye. One of these objects is a *hamsa*, in the shape of a hand with the palm facing outwards and the fingers spread open. Other amulets have Hebrew verses such as, 'The sun shall not smite thee by day, neither the moon by night' (Psalm 121.6).

Most of these practices have now disappeared. But I do remember that my grandmother who was a Yiddish-speaker used to spit three times under her breath when she heard about anything bad. I don't know if she actually believed that doing this would be effective against the evil eye. But maybe she did. It was also a superstition when giving someone an article of clothing to say: 'Wear it in good health.' It is rumoured that sometimes during the emergency safety demonstration on El Al airplanes when the use of seat belts is explained, the stewardess similarly suggests to the passengers that they should be worn in good health.

GEORGE

Christians are perhaps less sympathetic to superstitions than Dan appears to be. Although many of us touch wood and cross our fingers, I doubt if we really believe that they fend off disaster. Several such folk practices find their way into Christian festivals: we are not averse to pulling the wishbone in the Christmas turkey, kissing under mistletoe, or having a Yule log. It can be hard to determine where religious celebration ends and folk practice begins.

The celebration of Halloween is more controversial. Originally it meant 'Holy Evening' – the Christian festival of All Souls – when churches commemorated the dead. In my childhood, churches sometimes held Halloween parties, and we went around the neighbourhood wearing ridiculous costumes – we called it 'guising' in the days before the American phrase 'trick or treat' gained currency. However, because of its associations with death, many evangelical Christians now warn against celebrating it as a popular festival, regarding it as a form of occultism. King Saul, they point out, had an ill-advised consultation with the 'witch' (or medium) at Endor (1 Samuel 28.3–25) – a cautionary tale that God's people should not attempt to contact the dead. For many years, Christians have disapproved strongly of spiritualism (or 'spiritism', as some prefer to call it).

Other practices that evangelical Christians regard as occult include forms of fortune-telling. In the book of Acts, we read of Paul and his co-worker Silas meeting a clairvoyant slave girl whose owners make a tidy profit from her skills (Acts 16.16–19). Regarding this as incompatible both with the Jewish law (Deuteronomy 18.10–12) and the emergent Christian faith, Paul casts out the evil spirit within her, who purportedly bestowed her powers. Although I know Christians who consult horoscopes, and may regard them simply as a piece of fun, others – particularly those in leadership roles – regard them as contrary to Scripture, and as superstitions, believing that such practices may promote false hopes and fears.

Invoking supernatural aid is more acceptable within the context of the Christian faith. Particularly in Roman Catholic circles, invoking the help of saints is popular: owners of Saint Christopher medallions, for example, may believe that the saint offers added protection to travellers. The notion of patron saints associates these spiritual adepts with specific causes, for which they can be accessed for assistance. I have a Christian acquaintance who firmly believes that Saint Anthony of Padua invariably succeeds in helping her find items that she has lost. Apparently this belief harks back to an incident in Saint Anthony's own life. Saint Anthony had a psalter, which was stolen by a defecting novice. Anthony prayed for its return, and – the story goes – a fierce demon brandishing an axe appeared to the departing novice, threatening to trample him underfoot if he did not return the item. A likely tale indeed! I have tried invoking Saint Anthony when I have lost things, but without success – but perhaps he knows of my Protestant upbringing!

It is interesting that Dan quotes Psalm 121 in connection with amulets. The psalm ends:

> The Lord will keep you from all harm –
> he will watch over your life;
> the Lord will watch over your coming and going
> both now and for evermore. (Psalm 121.7–8)

This does not mean that Christians will never come to any harm, but rather that our lives are in God's hands, rather than protected by amulets, charms or even saints. Prayer and devotion, accompanied by careful driving, are more likely to ensure a safe journey than a Saint Christopher medallion.

USAMA

For Abrahamic monotheistic traditions, superstitions pose a problem since God is the ultimate cause, and prayer to, or reliance upon, anything or anyone other than God may be idolatrous or polytheistic.

Hence, Dan and George's discussions are fascinating since, as usual, we have parallel debates within Islam. In particular, these issues are at the core of the puritan message promoted by the Wahhabi and salafi movements, particularly since the eighteenth century CE, that have had global repercussions, far beyond the world of Islam.

Pre-Islamic Arabian superstitions as opposed to monotheism are vehemently condemned in the Qur'an, especially in the chapter named *Cattle* (*Cattle*, 6:136–140): the pagan Arabs divided tilth and cattle between God and their idols, consecrating some to each. Some crops and cattle were taboo, only edible by an elect. Some cattle were forbidden to yoke or burden, and others were slaughtered without the name of God being invoked. The offspring of some pregnant cattle were reserved as food for men, being prohibited for women; but if the offspring was stillborn, men and women could eat it. These are all condemned as polytheism or false practices in the name of God: the idea is that authentic, divinely revealed, symbolic ritual is fine, but not made-up, superstitious ritual.

Thus, on a daily basis, Muslims recite the opening chapter of the Qur'an, the 'Verse of the Throne' and the final three chapters of the Qur'an, all of which are also short prayers, to invoke goodness and ward off evil. On the day that I'm writing this, I have been invited to bless a Muslim couple's new home: I shall recite these traditional prayers from the Qur'an in each of the major rooms of the house.

The use of amulets or other practices is disputed, often fiercely so between 'puritans' and 'spiritualists' or 'spiritists' within Islam. These disputes have political and social impacts because most Muslims live in South Asia and Africa, where the practice of Islam has been influenced by local spiritual or spiritist traditions. Numerous hadiths speak of astrology, fortune-telling, and the use of amulets as being *shirk*, the cardinal sin of polytheism or associating partners with God. However, many Muslims do follow such practices, arguing that only their unsound aspects are forbidden. For example, some early authorities allowed amulets as long as these consisted only of written verses of the Qur'an. However, many popular amulets use magical formulas: I have seen an amulet containing a parchment, upon which were inscribed verses of the Qur'an, as well as non-Arabic magical formulae and mathematical, 'magic squares'. For puritans, the latter are polytheistic.

Similar arguments rage over holy people or *awliya'*, 'friends of God' and their tombs: do we pray to God via them, or not? The puritans argue that such prayer through intermediaries is polytheism, whereas other Muslims argue that it is within monotheism, by recognising the channels of God's grace. These disputes have often taken violent turns, with the destruction of tombs and shrines by puritans.

George mentions seat belts: strict monotheists, and we Muslims have many, will argue that to put your faith entirely in your seat belt or driving abilities, is idolatrous: our ultimate trust must be in God. The mainstream resolution to this is to recognise God as the ultimate cause and natural laws as divinely created secondary causes: when a man asked the Prophet whether he should tie his camel or simply trust in God to keep his camel from running away, the Prophet replied, 'Tie your camel, and trust in God!'

PART 4

SOCIAL AND POLITICAL ISSUES

Chapter 14

SOCIAL JUSTICE

The prophet Amos preached against the oppression of the poor (Amos 5.11–15), and the New Testament speaks of bringing down the mighty and exalting the poor (Luke 1.51–53). The Qur'an requires the proper treatment of orphans and beggars (*Women*, 4:2; *The Morning Hours*, 9–10). Yet all three religions have experienced gross inequalities of wealth, with little sign of the fortunes of the poor being reversed. How does each religion reconcile its ideals with reality? Conversely, ancient scriptures seem to condone the practices we would now find reprehensible. Is it possible to progress beyond ancient traditions without simply abandoning the faiths of our ancestors?

GEORGE

Having decided to go beyond the Bible stories of Sunday School, I began reading the Bible more systematically. One book that particularly impressed me was the Book of Amos. As I had attended a conservative evangelical church which laid emphasis on the spiritual life, reading Amos came as a welcome change. He was a prophet who was interested in the world in which people lived, rather than in prayer or church attendance, or gaining access to some distant afterlife which, according to Protestants, was made possible through faith rather than works.

Amos' clear message was that the outward trappings of religion were of no value unless the worshippers showed greater concern for social justice. He berated them for oppressing the poor, taking their clothes as equity for unfair loans, using false scales in the marketplace, where the merchants mixed chaff with the wheat to boost their illicit profits, and perverting the course of justice by offering bribes.

Of course, the Book of Amos is not alone in its emphasis on social justice. Isaiah and Jeremiah urge concern for orphans and widows in distress (Isaiah 1.17; 25.40; Jeremiah 22.3). The Book of Leviticus recommends the farmer not to reap the crops right to the edges of the field, but to leave some of the harvest for the poor and for the foreigner. (Presumably the foreigner was at a disadvantage, not being a land-owner.) The prophet Micah sums up one's social responsibilities when he writes:

What does the Lord require of you?
To act justly and to love mercy
and to walk humbly with your God. (Micah 6.8)

When we turn to the New Testament, we find similar sentiments. Mary's famous hymn, The Magnificat, which continues to be sung in churches ('My soul doth magnify the Lord') contains the lines: 'He has brought down rulers from their thrones but has lifted up the humble. He has filled the hungry with good things but has sent the rich away empty' (Luke 1.46–55). The letter of James was disliked by Martin Luther because it emphasises works rather than faith, but it is a necessary reminder that faith is insincere if it is not put into practice, and the early Christian community organised a food distribution service for widows (Acts 6.1–5). And when we turn to the teachings of Jesus, he preaches that people will be judged on whether they have given food to the hungry, provided clothing for the destitute, visited inmates in prison, and shown hospitality to strangers (Matthew 25.31–46).

The Bible not only commands that the oppressed should be treated fairly, but also that we should actively campaign on their behalf: 'Speak up for those who cannot speak for themselves…defend the rights of the poor and needy' (Proverbs 31.8–9). Christians have therefore been actively involved in supporting famine relief, and in organisations such as the Fair Trade movement, which seeks to ensure that farmers in developing countries receive a fair price for their produce, and are not exploited by richer countries who are in a position to impose unfair trading conditions.

One particular practice which the Bible appears to condemn is 'usury' (Exodus 22.25; 15.5; Ezekiel 18.13). The Jewish-Christian scriptures seem to suggest that it is improper to lend money expecting interest in return. Interestingly, the New Testament only mentions the subject in one place: Jesus tells a parable of a landlord who gives three servants money to invest. Two of them show good business acumen, making a profit, while the third merely buries his coin to keep it safe. He is chided for failing at least to put the money in a bank to attract interest.

Of course, it is just a parable, and we should be wary of drawing conclusions about Jesus' views on usury here. However, the main problem with usury was that in ancient times it tended to be exploitative. Modern economies need investors, and business loans that are repayable with interest usually benefit both parties. However, there are situations where borrowers are exploited. One issue that the current Archbishop of Canterbury took up was 'pay-day loans' – monies that are lent at very high rates of interest (one firm demands 229 per cent equivalent per annum interest) to those who have literally no money to tide themselves over until pay day. By way of response, the Church of England has set up a number of credit unions, which offer loans at much fairer rates to those who need them.

Christians have generally had no problem about making loans with interest attached, as long as it is not done by exploiting the vulnerable.

DAN

George quotes the prophet Micah as an exemplar of biblical morality. Perhaps I should tell you about my experiences as a Jewish minister. When I was a congregational rabbi, I served congregation Temple Micah in Denver, Colorado. On the front lawn in front of the synagogue was a sign with TEMPLE MICAH in large, bold type. Underneath was the quotation George refers to:

> What does the Lord require of you?
> To act justly and to love mercy
> And to walk humbly with your God. (Micah 6.8)

All this was highly commendable. Yet several feet away was an even bigger sign advertising bingo every Thursday night. In large red and blue letters it said: 'BIG PRIZES!' As I looked out of my office window, I wondered how far the two sentiments could ever be compatible.

From its inception in the nineteenth century, Reform Judaism –
even more than Orthodoxy with its stress on observing biblical and
rabbinic law – has emphasised the moral dimensions of the Jewish
faith. The prophets George refers to were viewed as exemplars of
the highest ideals of the Jewish heritage. Proudly, Reform Judaism
regarded itself as the preserve of the ethical principles of the faith. The
prophets were seen as the champions of these ideals and models for
the modern Jewish community.

But in my short career as a congregational rabbi, I quickly
discovered that trying to put such high standards into practice is
exceedingly difficult if not impossible. Let me tell you what happened
when I was an interim rabbi in South Africa in the 1970s. Taking
seriously the words of the Hebrew prophets, I preached a *Rosh
Hashanah* (New Year) sermon about apartheid. I began by explaining
that when I arrived in Johannesburg, I was cautioned not to speak
about apartheid. But I believed the time had come for me to face
this issue. As I spoke, I observed that the congregation was becoming
increasingly uncomfortable.

I tried to lighten the theme by teasing the congregation about its
materialism. I said I was blinded by their diamond rings, and amazed
to see many expensive cars in the parking lot. Such a concentration on
materialism, I argued, was misguided given the economic deprivation
I had experienced in the country. It was not enough to be rich Jews
among poor blacks. Our ancestors were slaves in Egypt; in each and
every generation Jews are obliged to struggle for the liberation of those
who are oppressed and persecuted. As Jews, we must not become the
Pharaohs of the modern world. Instead, the Jewish community must
stand shoulder to shoulder with their black brothers and sisters and
oppose all forms of racism and exploitation.

When I finished, there was a stunned silence. I thought I had
followed the noble tradition of the ancient prophets in taking such
a moral stance. But the congregation was outraged. The senior rabbi
was incensed. Eyes blazing, he castigated me for breaking my word
not to speak about apartheid. 'That was the most impolitic sermon I
ever heard,' he said.

'But...' I stammered. 'We are supposed to be the conscience of
our people.'

'Don't be stupid,' he said. 'You've just insulted the entire congregation.'

George, of course, is right about the Judeo-Christian tradition. The Bible is the repository of the highest ethical ideals. It is full of fine words. But trying to put them into practice is full of perils.

USAMA

When the Prophet Muhammad, peace be upon him, received his first revelation from Angel Jibril (Gabriel) on the Mountain of Light outside Mecca at the age of 40 and began his prophetic mission around the year 610 CE, his preaching combined the highest ethics (or 'noblest morals') with strict monotheism. He and his followers were known for freeing slaves, helping widows and orphans, and condemning cheating in the marketplace (e.g. Qur'an, *Those Who Employ Double Standards*, 83:1–6). An entire *sura* or chapter of the Qur'an (no. 83) begins by vehemently condemning those who, literally or metaphorically, employ double standards. Many of the Prophet's earliest and closest Companions (disciples) were slaves who were freed via his efforts: Bilal the Abyssinian, originally an African slave, later became Islam's first muezzin or caller to prayer, and is still revered by Muslims worldwide, especially Africans.

The Prophet was thus following the way of earlier prophets, Biblical and Arabian: in the Qur'anic account, all of them preached monotheism, along with a secondary, intertwined mission: this is especially vivid in *Sura al-Shu'ara* (Chapter: *The Poets*, no. 26), where the stories are each told in similar ways, to emphasise the similarity and resonances amongst the missions of the Prophets. Moses' secondary mission is to liberate the Israelites. The Arabian prophets Hud and Salih preach against corruption by power and material comforts. Lot preaches against homosexuality or male rape (commentators differ), and Shu'ayb, Moses' father-in-law, exhorts fair dealing in the marketplace. Interestingly, Noah and Abraham focus on worshipping God alone.

The Prophet ended his mission as he had started: with an emphasis on our duty to God and our duty to fellow humans. In his 'farewell sermon' delivered during the Hajj at the Mountain of Mercy outside

Mecca in 632 CE, he urged the male-dominated society to look after women, to treat slaves as equals, to abolish the charging and payment of usury, and preached total equality: 'No one has superiority over another, white or black, Arab or non-Arab, except by piety (which is known only to God).' This echoed the Qur'an, 'The most honoured of you with God are those who are most pious' (*The Chambers*, 49:13). This was Islam's 'Martin Luther King moment', except that it occurred 13 centuries before the famous 'I have a dream' speech by the American civil rights activist.

This spirit of social justice and equality has always inspired Muslim communities and leaders, helping to abolish slavery[34] and reduce economic inequality. Additionally, the Prophet, being from a mercantile background himself, promoted free market economics, as is evident from numerous hadiths on the subject. A leading contemporary banker even credits modern capitalism as having its origins in Islamic and pre-Islamic Arabia.[35] The Islamic prohibition on usury inspires thousands of Muslim economists and financiers today to seek reforms and alternatives to modern capitalist and financial systems. Based on this Muslim heritage, I find 'ethical capitalism' an appealing idea, although it is much easier said than done!

Dan's brave stance on apartheid in South Africa is inspiring. Thousands of Muslims also took part in the anti-apartheid struggle, and many were close friends of Nelson Mandela. Israel is a modern, democratic Jewish state within its 1967 borders, but its policies in the Occupied Palestinian territories are often compared to apartheid, including by a leading British rabbi with whom I once shared a platform. We need Abrahamic co-operation to help solve the Israeli-Palestinian conflict justly.

GEORGE

Muhammad's farewell sermon, from which Usama quotes, echoes the sentiments expressed by the apostle Paul centuries before: 'There is neither Jew nor Gentile, neither slave nor free, nor is there male and female, for you are all one in Christ Jesus' (Galatians 3.28).

Each of our three faiths hopes for a world in which there will be perfect justice, and where differences between individuals become irrelevant to the ways in which they are treated. Usama alludes to several areas of injustice: usury (which we have already mentioned), sexual inequality, racial and ethnic prejudice (Arab and non-Arab), and differences in social standing, of which slaves and slave-owners are an example.

We shall discuss the issue of land and the roles of men and women in subsequent exchanges. I would like to develop our discussion here by focusing on slavery, for three reasons. The first is that slavery is an institution which we all deplore, but which is not explicitly condemned in Jewish-Christian scripture, and even appears to be condoned. Key figures in Scripture have their slaves, for example Abraham, King Saul and King Solomon (Genesis 16.3; 2 Samuel 6.20–22; 1 Kings 19.21), and the Torah states that slaves are the owners' property (Exodus 21.21). Paul's letter to Philemon concerns a slave called Onesimus, who has met up with Paul. The exact circumstances of their association are not clear, but Paul sends him back to his owner, not as a free person, but to remain a slave – although Paul requests that he should be treated well. This is in accordance with the Torah, which required that slaves should at least be treated humanely (Exodus 21.20). The absence of any clear biblical prohibition on slavery lent support to the anti-abolitionists in nineteenth-century Britain and America, while other non-biblical considerations (some were ethical while others were political and economic) enabled abolitionism to prevail.

The second reason for focusing on slavery is that it shows how the Bible needs to be revisited for guidance. It is a mistake to view the Bible as a precise rule book and to infer that actions are only acceptable or otherwise, if an explicit prohibitions or permissions can be discovered. When we look at the Bible's overall portrayal of slavery, it is clear that the Bible presents it as undesirable. The Israelites' slavery in Egypt requires escape, and when Paul describes the followers of Jewish law as 'slaves to sin' (Romans 6.6), he is by implication denigrating the institution.

Thirdly, and most importantly, we should recognise modern forms of slavery. Slavery is manifested in prostitution (which is usually a way of life enforced by poverty or drug addiction), and human trafficking, where (mainly) women and children can be lured into enforced labour or sexual exploitation, often through false hopes of economic betterment. But we need also to consider the extent to which we are all complicit in supporting modern slavery. Are we not condoning, even encouraging, the conditions under which people – sometimes young children – work, when we buy clothes that are made in sweatshops, or use electronic equipment? Electronic goods require metals such as cobalt, which are typically mined in countries such as the Congo, where workers – sometimes four-year-old children – are subjected to long hours in filthy conditions? Without their labour, this book might not exist, since we rely heavily on our electronic equipment.

What are we to do? It is all too easy to commend social justice, but to live normal twenty-first-century lives seems to require complicity in the social injustices we condemn.

DAN

George is right that the Hebrew Bible condones a number of practices which modern society regards as abhorrent. Slavery is a striking example. This raises a critical point in our discussion. We need to remember that the Hebrew Bible was composed thousands of years ago by ancient Israelites who had unsophisticated and sometimes primitive ideas about human society and the nature of the universe. This, of course, is not the view of strictly Orthodox Jews who believe that the Torah was revealed by God to Moses on Mount Sinai and that the other books of the Bible were in some sense divinely revealed.

But biblical scholarship has demonstrated that this is a misapprehension. For over a hundred years the vast majority of biblical scholars have argued that the Five Books of Moses is a composite work created by different writers at various times in the history of ancient Israel. In a similar vein they stress that the rest of the Bible was similarly composed by writers whose views reflect the times in which they lived.

In this light it would be a mistake to regard Scripture as an authoritative ethical guide. Rather it is an epic account of the history of the Jewish people. Yet, it is unquestionably moving. There is no doubt that embedded in the biblical narrative are elements which are morally compelling and continue to have relevance for contemporary society. In particular the words of the prophets of ancient Israel continue to inspire modern Jewry.

In my last exchange I pointed out that Reform Judaism has from its inception championed the prophetic tradition. Distancing itself from Orthodoxy, it stressed the contemporary relevance of the words of Amos, Hosea, Isaiah, Jeremiah and the other prophets who saw themselves as the conscience of Israel. In my sermon to my congregation in South Africa, it was their message that I tried (unsuccessfully) to convey.

Yet, there nonetheless remains a critical problem. Given that the Hebrew Bible (as well as the New Testament and the Qur'an) were composed centuries ago by authors whose world views were different from our own, what are we to make of their ideas about morality? In other words, how are we to decide which moral principles and practices we should adopt and which should be abandoned?

From its origin in the early nineteenth century Reform Judaism has struggled with this question. Some of its leading theologians have attempted to isolate key principles in making this decision. The late Rabbi Solomon Freehof, for example, sought to isolate criteria which could be used to distinguish anachronistic practices from those that continue to have spiritual significance. The difficulty, however, is that ultimately such notions as 'equality' or 'justice' or 'the dictates of conscience' which have been advocated by various Reform Jewish thinkers are inevitably subjective in character and lead to different conclusions.

The issue of intermarriage, for example, is bitterly contentious. Some Reform rabbis view intermarriage as a catastrophic threat to Jewish survival. Other Reform rabbis officiate at intermarriage ceremonies and welcome intermarried couples into their congregations. The point is that Scripture should not be seen as an authoritative moral guide. Many of its teachings should be disregarded. Yet there is no question that it contains inspiring ethical ideas. The problem is how to distinguish one from the other.

USAMA

Contemporary Islam is struggling with the same questions that George and Dan raise: how do we understand and apply the Qur'an, and the associated hadiths, that date back to the seventh century CE, in the modern world, especially given its exponential growth in complexity over the past few centuries?

There has always been a 'Reform Islam' movement, or more accurately, a strand of 'Renewed Islam': in a hadith, the Prophet, peace be upon him, is said to have stated that God will send a person or people at the beginning of every century to renew the religion of Islam for the community. A renewer (*mujaddid*) arguably reminds the faithful of the essential principles of the faith and recontextualises them in the changing circumstances.

The view of 'Islamic reformers' on slavery may be summarised as follows: this was a human institution that was prevalent in the seventh century CE, when slaves, including their bodies, were the property of their owners. This meant that male slave-owners were allowed to rape unmarried female slaves, although the reverse-gender case did not apply because of the patriarchal society. The Qur'an contains numerous exhortations to free slaves, and the religious compensation for several crimes involves freeing slaves. The 'highway to heaven' is firstly to free a slave, then to feed the starving, orphans and indigent, with a spirit of faith, patience and mercy (*The City*, 90:11–17). Freeing slaves is also a way to compensate for intentionally breaking vows or oaths (*The Last Supper*, 5:89), and for accidental murder (*Women*, 4:92). One of the reasons that the Prophet was opposed so vehemently by the rich and powerful of Mecca was that he and his followers freed many slaves and taught that slaves were equal as humans to their owners, and whilst slavery persisted, slaves were to be given the same food and dress as their owners. Furthermore, the Prophet's 'farewell sermon' specifically mentioned kind treatment of slaves, and his very last teaching before death was 'God, God, and your slaves', that is, to do your duty to everything in existence, from the Almighty to the lowest in society.

Thus, although some passages of the Qur'an appear to condone slavery, others condemn it. The question is: which passages have precedence? As with the Bible-inspired anti-abolitionists that George mentions, there are Muslims who defend slavery. At the time of writing, there are Mauritanian anti-slavery activists, sons of former slaves, who have been sentenced to death for speaking against pro-slavery attitudes: the religious dimension is clear from the fact that they have been accused of blasphemy and criticising Islam. I and others are very clear that it is the anti-slavery passages that represent the clear spirit of Islam, as evidenced by the examples above.

On modern slavery, it is inspiring that the Catholic-ethos St Mary's University in Twickenham, UK, has a new academic faculty dedicated to this topic. I attended the inaugural conference in 2017, and learnt that millions of people, many of whom are women and children, are modern slaves, mainly for sexual trafficking and forced labour.

I agree with George that much of modern life, especially technology, relies on modern slavery such as Bangladeshi sweatshops for textiles and Chinese factories for smartphone components. This is one reason that I personally keep the same smartphone for years and years. But the underlying causes of this problem are related to modern, usurious capitalism, which brings us to our next chapter on the theme of 'Wealth'.

Chapter 15

WEALTH

The Jewish scriptures forbid 'usury' (Psalm 15.5). Yet, of all people, the Jews have acquired a reputation as wealthy money-lenders. Have they been unfaithful to their own scriptures? Jesus appears to have sanctioned usury (Matthew 25.27), although he warned against the acquisition of riches (Mark 10.21). Islam, too, forbids usury, and Islamic banking tries to run its business in accordance with both religion and market laws. Muhammad himself was a merchant – a man of trade and profits. How do the three faiths reconcile their religious teachings with business acumen and wealth acquisition?

USAMA

Wealth is more than just money: wealth is our tangible possessions of property, furniture, vehicles, livestock, precious minerals and jewellery.

According to the Qur'an, all wealth ultimately belongs to God: we are merely trustees of it, so although we do own the wealth in a relative sense, our sacred duty is to spend the wealth wisely and for real benefit. 'Give them from God's wealth, that He has given you' (*Light*, 24:33).

The Qur'anic word for 'wealth' (*maal*) is related to the verb 'to incline' (*maala, yameelu*). Hence, theologians argue that 'wealth' is so named because human hearts naturally 'incline' towards wealth: we have basic, materialistic desires. Breaking this addiction to wealth is one of the objectives of charity, as well as of course to help the poor.

Money is a sophisticated invention of advanced human civilisation, although barter is not obsolete: even in the modern world of usurious money-lending, Bartercard bills itself as the world's largest exchange network.[36]

Medieval Islamic jurists helped develop modern economic theory, and were well aware of modern financial teaching:

Money is a matter of functions four:
A medium, a measure, a standard, a store.

This rhyming couplet refers to the four classical functions of money: a medium of exchange, a measure of value, a standard for deferred payments and a store of value.

The Qur'anic injunction against usury appears to refute the argument for interest or usury on the basis of 'renting money': usurers may argue that we are used to paying rent for the use of someone else's property or car, so why not for their money. 'They say: "Trade is like usury," but God has allowed trade and prohibited usury… God deprives usury of blessing, and gives usury on charitable payments' (*The Cow*, 2:275–276).

Islamic economic theorists thus argue that because of the critical, neutral, facilitative role of money, it can only be used for its four functions and not used as a commodity, otherwise it would lose its special status as money. Therefore, one cannot rent money as one rents other goods.

The Bible and Hindu scriptures contain warnings against usury; the philosophers Plato and Aristotle also condemned it. Apart from a few exceptions, Islam has tended to regard all interest as usury, unlike say, the Catholic position that only exorbitant interest rates amount to usury. However, the issues are hotly debated within Islam, and some authorities relax the rules on usury to allow low interest rates.

The Qur'anic contrast between usury and charity is striking (*The Romans*, 30:39). An immediate example of this contrast is that under traditional Sharia, excess wealth, defined as that which remains untouched for a calendar year, is liable to compulsory alms (*zakaat*): thus, the amount reduces to help the poor. In modern savings accounts, such money automatically increases via interest rates, even if it has not been invested in ventures that involve the risk of loss as well as the opportunity of profit.

Whilst Islam helped develop modern, free markets and banking systems,[37] the greedy, exploitative aspect of modern, usurious capitalism results in poorer peoples and countries being trapped in an ever-increasing spiral of debt; it leads to a growing gap between rich and poor in every land, and results in a net transfer of wealth from poor to rich. Clearly, we must help to reverse this situation.

DAN

Both George and Usama have raised the issue of usury. There are two biblical passages that deal with this topic:

> If you lend money to one of my people among you who is needy, do not treat it like a business deal; charge no interest. (Exodus 22.25)

> Do not charge a fellow Israelite interest, whether on money or food or anything else that may earn interest. You may charge a foreigner interest, but not a fellow Israelite, so that the Lord your God may bless you in everything you put your hand to in the land you are entering to possess. (Deuteronomy 23.19–20)

The meaning of these verses is clear: in an agrarian society a loan to a poor man to tide him over until the harvest or to help him buy farming instruments is understood as an act of kindness. This should be done freely without demanding any return. If the lender takes interest on the loan, this would impoverish the borrower further. However, this does not apply to a foreigner. A person who travels to the land of Israel is in a different category and is not bound by the same restriction. He is permitted to take interest on loans made to Israelites. Conversely if an Israelite lends to a foreigner, he too may take interest. In the Middle Ages, the Christian Church adapted this biblical law: 'your brother' was interpreted as referring to other Christians, and the 'foreigner' to non-Christians. Thus Jews were allowed to become money-lenders to Christians.

Rabbinic sages maintained that the terms 'usury' and 'interest' were synonymous. As a result, they extended the biblical laws so as to prohibit any benefit the borrower bestows on the lender, even to greet him if it was not his usual practice to do so, or to thank him for the loan. According to talmudic scholars, the prohibition applies to the borrower as well as to the lender. That is, it is not only forbidden to lend on interest but also to borrow on interest. Any witnesses to such a transaction also offend against the law, as does the scribe who draws up the bond of indebtedness. Laws against usury are dealt with in detail in Chapter 5 of the tractate *Bava Metzia* in the Talmud. Here are discussed questions regarding business transactions, some of which may fall under the heading of usury by rabbinic law. The general principle is that any reward for waiting is forbidden – this means it is forbidden for a lender to be rewarded by the borrower for waiting for the return of his money.

Despite such rabbinic legislation, traditional Judaism maintains that the spirit of the law against usury is not violated when money is invested in business in an advanced industrial economy. This is because money is being used to increase profits and there is no reason why A should invest his money in B's business unless he hopes to gain as B hopes to gain.

GEORGE

Our discussion of usury raises the wider question of how we should acquire wealth. I agree with Dan that there is an important difference between investing in a business and lending money. Investing money means buying part of a company, not lending to it, and the investor's financial fortunes are bound up with that company's success or failure. Investors are always reminded that the value of their shares can go down as well as up – unlike the pay-day loan, which must be repaid in full, with very substantial interest.

Managing one's wealth involves risk, but how much risk is acceptable? One area in which many people risk their money is gambling, and it will be interesting to hear Jewish and Islamic comments on this. A recent report suggested that the average British citizen spends £416 a year on scratch cards, and the UK gambling industry nets in £13.8 billion annually. In my youth our minister preached a sermon on the topic, insisting that one's wealth should be earned through work, not through luck. He recalled God telling Adam after he fell from grace that 'By the sweat of your brow you will eat your food' (Genesis 3.19), and the New Testament recommends that 'The one who is unwilling to work shall not eat' (2 Thessalonians 3.10).

Yet the Bible does not explicitly condemn gambling. When casting lots is mentioned, it is usually for the purpose of decision-making, and the only reference to gambling is when the Roman soldiers cast lots for Jesus' clothes at his crucifixion (Mark 15.24). I have heard it suggested that gambling is a means of exploiting the poor and the less intelligent, since the poor might be more easily lured into a false hope for acquiring wealth, and smart people should realise that the gambling industry could not survive unless the average gambler lost out. However, an extensive study of gambling some years ago demonstrated that the profile of gamblers' household incomes and educational qualifications did not differ markedly from those of the British population more widely.[38]

Christians have sometimes argued that gambling involves covetousness, and hence that the desire to win a jackpot is a violation of the Tenth Commandment. Yet when churches organise raffles, tombolas, and beetle drives, prizes are small and unlikely to encourage the deadly sin of greed. They are in a good cause, and provide a good measure of fun. The National Lottery supports good causes, and many churches have benefited from substantial funding for their buildings.

Although the odds against winning the National Lottery are enormous, I once vaguely knew someone who did win £1,000,000. He was not particularly wealthy, and the win ought to have transformed his life. He had needed a hip replacement operation, and was now prepared to have it done privately. Unfortunately he was too heavy to have the operation, and while he was addressing his weight problem, he died of a heart attack. An acrimonious family feud followed about who should inherit his winnings. Scenarios like this are not new. Jesus told a parable about a rich farmer who decided to build enormous barns to store surplus crops to finance a life of leisure. His dream was unfulfilled, since he died that very night (Luke 12.16–21).

A key concept in Jesus' teaching is stewardship. Wealth is all very well, but the crucial question is what we do with our money.

DAN

There are no references to gambling in the Hebrew Bible. This does not mean, however, that gambling was unknown in the ancient world. However, it appears that it was not widespread enough in the biblical period to constitute a social evil – otherwise, the biblical writers would inevitably have condemned it. Although the casting of lots is referred to in Scripture, it appears that this has more to do with divination than gambling *per se*. Lots were cast to determine which of the two goats were to be offered to God and which to Azazel (Leviticus 16.8–10); in the affair of Jonathan (1 Samuel 14.42–43) and to divide up land (Numbers 26.55; Joshua 15).

From the legal point of view, the Mishnah states that two types of gamblers are untrustworthy and therefore disqualified from acting as witnesses in a Jewish court of law. These are the dice-player, and according to one view, the man who bets on pigeon-racing. The reason why the gambler is disqualified is discussed in the Talmud.[39] One opinion is that it is the professional gambler who is disqualified – the reason is because he makes no useful contribution to society. Another view is that the disqualification applies even to the occasional gambler. Jewish law follows the first opinion. As a result, it is permitted to play cards for money, to bet on horses, and to organise and participate in a raffle. In this light, it has become acceptable for Jewish charitable organisations to raise money by holding raffles, but bingo is generally frowned upon even if the proceeds go to charity. Whenever gambling has got out of hand, Jewish moralists condemn it as a frivolous pursuit because it could lead to impoverishment and destroy family life.

A discussion of wealth should include the topic of charity. In the Jewish tradition, alms-giving and care for the poor is referred to as *tzedakah*. In the Bible this term denotes righteousness, but in post-biblical Judaism it is used to refer to charity. The poor are not to be patronised but given the assistance they need because they have a just claim on the wealthy. With its emphasis on action, Judaism developed a system of laws governing the exercise of charity. The twelfth-century philosopher Moses Maimonides specified that there are eight degrees of charity. The lowest degree is where the donor gives but is glum about doing so. Next is when he gives cheerfully but not as much as he can afford. Next is when he gives cheerfully and as much as he can afford but only when his donation is solicited. Next is where he gives without having to be asked. Higher still is where the donor does not know which of the poor he benefits. Higher still is where the poor do not know the identity of their benefactor. Higher still is where the money is given to the charity collectors. Highest of all is where a man is prevented from being poor by being given a job or a loan without interest so that he can adequately support himself.

USAMA

The Qur'anic prohibition of usury is very strong: 'O you who have believed! Be conscious of God, and leave any remaining usury, if you are believers. If you do not do so, then take notice of war from God and His Messenger. But if you repent, you will have your capital wealth: you will not oppress, and you will not be oppressed' (*The Cow*, 2:278–279).

A canonical hadith further states, 'God has cursed the consumer of usury, its payer, its scribe and its two witnesses.' From Dan's explanation, this hadith has a high degree of overlap with the Talmud.

Charging interest is not the same as investing in a business: with investment, there must be the risk of profit or loss. With usury or guaranteed interest payments, poor people are vulnerable to exploitation.

Islamic jurisprudence addressed many such issues by insisting on trade as a series of transactions of exchange: for any payment, there must be an equal *counter-value*, resulting in a fair exchange. Therefore, prices must be fair, so that buying and selling involves the exchange of equal counter-values. Charging interest is usury and not permitted, because one side pays more whilst the other side receives more. But investing in a business is equivalent to buying a share in it, and this is subject to all partners in the business sharing the risk of profit or loss. Islamic commercial practice is based on risk-sharing.

The same theory is extended to gambling: this is prohibited because rewards and losses are not proportional to work done, but involve a large amount of luck and chance, such as a million pounds won from a £1 lottery ticket. The Qur'anic term for gambling is *maysir*, from the root *y-s-r* that denotes 'ease'. Gambling profits are 'too easy' to be admissible under ethics of fair trade and hard work.

The Qur'an recognises that gambling, along with wine, has benefits as well as harms, but the latter outweigh the former (*The Cow*, 2:219). A later verse prohibited both, along with games of chance and polytheistic sacrifice (*The Last Supper*, 5:90–91).

Therefore, although the National Lottery does indeed support many good causes, Muslims will argue that its harms outweigh these benefits in terms of encouraging an addiction to gambling and distorted views of how wealth is gained. I think Islam sets very high standards: no gambling or usury, the latter perhaps being synonymous with interest. A better alternative is charity, for which the Qur'anic words *zakat* and *sadaqa* denote purification, development, growth, truthfulness and sincerity. Thus, whenever there is a temptation to buy a lottery ticket or scratch card, Islam reminds the believer to give that money to charity instead.

A Muslim acquaintance once bought a scratch card with the sole intention of supporting a charity: he found himself in a moral dilemma when the scratch card won him £1,000! Based on general Islamic principles and a particular story found in the hadith literature, the religious advice to him was to donate the entire amount to charity. The story runs as follows: before the Qur'anic prohibition of gambling had been revealed, the Prophet's companion and future caliph, Abu Bakr, had placed a bet with Meccan polytheists that the Byzantines would soon defeat the Persians. This was based on a Qur'anic prophecy (*The Romans (Byzantines)*, 30:1–7). When Abu Bakr won the bet, he brought the winnings to the Prophet, who advised, 'This is unlawfully acquired wealth (*suht*): give it away in charity.'

GEORGE

Usama and Dan mention giving wealth to charity, but charitable organisations can themselves become wealthy. The year 2017, in which I am writing, is the five-hundredth anniversary of the Protestant Reformation, and one of Martin Luther's principal criticisms of the Roman Catholic Church was its acquisition of wealth.

Jesus encouraged giving to the poor, yet John's Gospel recounts an incident towards the end of Jesus' ministry, where Jesus attends a dinner party in Bethany, at which Mary – one of Jesus' devotees – produces an outsize jar of perfume, which she pours on Jesus' feet (John 12.1–10). John tells us it cost 300 denarii – the equivalent to one year's wages at that time. Judas Iscariot complains that the woman's money should have been given to the poor instead, but Jesus disagrees, accepting it as an act of honour.

John is not trying to describe accurately an incident that occurred in Jesus' life. He characteristically exaggerates details to warn the reader not to take the story at its literal level. No one, however generous, would pour a litre of perfume over someone's feet or spend a year's wages on a gift. The point of the story is (at least in part) that anointing signifies Jesus' messiahship ('Messiah' means 'anointed'), and that the story anticipates Jesus' death and resurrection – the perfume anticipates the even more lavish quantity that Joseph of Arimathea provides for Jesus' tomb (John 19.39), and the presence of Lazarus, whom Jesus had raised from the dead (John 11.1–44), anticipates Christ's resurrection. It is important not to read John – or indeed any of the gospel writers – as simply a set of short stories.

Christians have sometimes been criticised for their expensive buildings, and the money that is spent on altar pieces, stained glass, icons, fine organs, and elaborate robes worn by the clergy. Perhaps we could convert our English cathedrals into blocks of flats for the homeless, and have our clergy dress in potato sacks instead of expensive chasubles, copes and mitres, as a way of expressing our Christian humility and generosity.

There are some denominations who keep costs down, having simple, unadorned meeting places, and who do not robe up to conduct Sunday worship. Perhaps they have a point but, if we decided to abandon our high art and architecture, we would put many skilled craftspeople out of work, or else only enjoy secular forms of art. (And we could equally well argue that the money we spend on going to the opera or theatre could be spent instead to help the poor.) If we value our culture, why should we not use it in the service of our faith, rather than for some other purpose, or not at all? Paul said, 'whatever you do, do it all for the glory of God' (1 Corinthians 10.31).

The saying that 'money is the root of all evil' is a misquotation of the Bible, which says, 'the love of money is a root of all kinds of evil' (1 Timothy 6.10). Christians may legitimately be wealthy, if they are fortunate enough and have acquired their wealth honestly, but our money should be used wisely, and for good purposes. Jesus said, 'No one can serve two masters... You cannot serve both God and Money' (Matthew 6.24). This does not mean that we should give away all our possessions to serve God, but rather that God, not money, should be the object of our devotion.

Chapter 16

MEN AND WOMEN

The Ashkenazi morning prayer includes thanking God for not having been made 'a gentile, a slave or a woman'. The woman thanks God 'for having made me according to his will'. Does this indicate that Jews devalue women? Does the Christian faith do any better? Timothy, one of the early Church leaders, is instructed not to allow women to preach or to assume positions of authority (1 Timothy 2.12). The Qur'an significantly refrains from considering Eve as having been created from Adam's rib, and regards Eve and Adam as sharing an equal responsibility for eating from the forbidden fruit. Yet it also states that men are superior to their wives, permits polygamy under certain conditions, and only allows women half the share of inheritance with men. Do we all need to improve the relationship between the sexes?

DAN

In modern times women have gained an increasingly important role in Jewish life. In biblical times, however, very few women were mentioned in Scripture, suggesting that they played a relatively insignificant part in the Jewish community. There are nonetheless several notable exceptions including the matriarchs, Sarah, Rebecca and Rachel; Miriam the prophetess; Deborah the judge; Huldah the prophetess; Bathsheba, who married King David; and Esther. The Bible records that at Mount Sinai women were present, yet the covenant was formulated in such a way that it bound men to fulfil the requirements of the law and to ensure that members of their household including wives met these requirements as well. In this way, the covenant included women indirectly.

In biblical times marriage and family law favoured men over women. For example, a husband could divorce a wife, but a wife could not divorce her husband without his consent. The practice of levirate marriage applied to widows of childless deceased husbands but not to widowers of childless deceased wives (Deuteronomy 25.5–6). In general women were subordinate to men in biblical society. Nonetheless men had specific obligations they were required to perform for wives including providing clothing, food and fulfilling sexual relations.

In talmudic and midrashic sources very few women are explicitly mentioned, and none are known to have written a rabbinic text. Those who are referred to are portrayed as having a strong influence on their husbands. Occasionally they had a public presence. During the Middle Ages Jews were viewed as second-class citizens in the Christian and Muslim worlds. Conditions made it even more difficult for women to establish their own status. Yet during this period prohibitions against teaching women the Torah were relaxed, and there was an emergence of women's prayer groups. In synagogues women were confined to their own section, frequently in the balcony. As a consequence, the role of women in the synagogue was severely limited.

With the Enlightenment and emancipation, the role of women dramatically changed. As Jewish men extended their influence, many Jewish women took advantage of similar opportunities. As Jewish women gained more rights, they sought to improve society. In the twentieth century the role of women underwent major change. Regina Jonas was privately ordained a Reform rabbi in Berlin in the 1930s. In 1972 Sally Priesand was ordained a Reform rabbi by the Hebrew Union College. The following year the Conservative movement ruled that women were to be counted toward making up a quorum for prayer (*minyan*). In 1985 Amy Eilberg became the first woman Conservative rabbi, ordained by the Jewish Theological Seminary. Reconstructionist and Humanist Judaism similarly advocated equal rights for women and ordained female rabbis.

Orthodox Judaism, however, proved the least responsive to women's demands. Compelled to pray behind curtains or in balconies outside the sight of men, Jewish women were unable to take an active role in Jewish worship. As a consequence, some women left Orthodoxy; others established women's prayer groups. Orthodox Jewish women perceive religious study as a key to greater participation in Jewish life.

In recent times there has been a growth of women's yeshivot and study groups. Yet despite these advances, there is a growing awareness within the Orthodox community that a number of *halakhic* (legal) practices are degrading to women.

USAMA

The role of women in Muslim life mirrors much of the Jewish experience, as explained by Dan.

Islam emerged in the tribal Arabian society of the seventh century CE, where public and powerful roles were dominated by men, whilst women concentrated on home-making, bringing up children and some manual labour in the scattered oases. Family wealth and tribal power were concentrated amongst the menfolk, with only sons inheriting – daughters were generally excluded from inheritance. There were occasional exceptions that proved these rules. Women had a complementary role to men in society: the respective gender roles could be summarised as being private and public, respectively.

Qur'anic references to women reflect the above realities. Maryam (Mary), mother of Jesus, is the only woman mentioned by name in the entire Qur'an, and there is even a *sura* named after her. She is referred to as Maryam bint Imran (bint denoting 'daughter of'), or simply Maryam. Her mother is never named, but referred to as 'the wife of Imran'. Other notable women in the Qur'an are similarly given titles relating them to their menfolk: the wives of Noah, Abraham, Lot, Moses and Pharaoh. There are also the mother and sister of Moses. Many such women are named in Islamic tradition, often borrowing from 'Israelite sources', but not in the Qur'an. Thus, Abraham's wives are Sara and Hajar or Hajira (Hagar). Moses' wife is Safura. The 'wife of the minister' in the story of Joseph is Zulaykha. The Queen of the tribe of Saba (Sheba) is Bilqis. All of these are common Muslim female names.

Even the Prophet's wives, and there were 12–15 of them (the exact number is uncertain), are not named in the Qur'an, but referred to as his wives or women. They played a leading role in Mecca and Medina. Khadija was a successful businesswoman who employed and then married Muhammad. Aisha is one of the great scholars of Sunni Islam: she and Umm Salama transmitted thousands of hadiths or traditions about the teachings and practice of the Prophet. Aisha became a political leader in Sunni Islam too: mounted on a camel, she led an army against Caliph Ali for the 'Battle of the Camel' during the civil war that ensued from the murder of the third caliph, Uthman.

The Qur'an treats women equally to men in a spiritual sense, since our essential humanity and spirituality transcends gender. Some Sufis teach that the Most Beautiful Names of God in the Qur'an are reflected differently by the genders: men reflect the names of Majesty, Power and Outwardness whilst women reflect the names of Beauty, Mercy and Inwardness. However, in financial matters, women are not treated the same as men: their share of inheritance is generally half that of men, and their testimony is worth half that of men.

Gender roles are one of the hotly contested topics in contemporary Islam. Burning questions are:

- Are traditional, complementary gender roles mandated by Islamic theology and scripture, or does the egalitarian spirit of Islam apply here also?

- Is the Qur'anic treatment of women in inheritance and testimony related to essential inequality, or is it the beginning of a move towards gender equality in the context of male-dominated seventh-century Arabia?

GEORGE

Like the Jewish and Islamic faiths, Christians have traditionally assigned women a subordinate role to men. Some conservative Christians appeal to the Old Testament, where Eve is portrayed as Adam's helper and the temptress who is the first to sin. Those who are opposed to the ordination of women have pointed out that all Jesus' disciples were male, and that Paul said that women should not teach, but should cover their heads during worship, and ask their husbands if there was anything they did not understand (Genesis 2.18–23; 1 Timothy 2.14; 1 Corinthians 14.33–35). ('Mansplaining' goes back to ancient times and, contrary to Dan Brown, it is unlikely that Mary Magdalene was the one portrayed as sitting next to Jesus at the Last Supper!)

However, if one looks at other parts of the Bible, women are accorded a much higher status. Paul writes, 'There is neither Jew nor

Gentile, neither slave nor free, nor is there male and female, for you are all one in Christ Jesus' (Galatians 3.28). Jesus spoke to women: his discussion with the Samaritan woman at the well (John 4.1–30) was a breach of social etiquette at the time. He allows himself to be touched by a woman who 'had been subject to bleeding for twelve years' (Luke 8.43) – one presumes the condition was vaginal bleeding, which would have made Jesus ceremonially unclean (Leviticus 15.19–27).

Jesus had at least one female disciple, and maybe more. Luke recounts that Mary of Bethany sat at his feet, listening to his teachings. When her sister Martha complains that she should be helping with the household chores instead, Jesus disagrees (Luke 10.38–42). Numerous other women, including Mary Magdalene, are named as following Jesus with his 12 disciples, indicating that they were his students, rather than providers of hospitality when Jesus happened to be in their area (Luke 8.1–3). Matthew relates that three women called Mary (including Jesus' mother and Mary Magdalene) remained at the foot of the cross when most of the male disciples had fled (Matthew 27.55–61).

Perhaps most surprising is the Gospels' portrayal of women as the first witnesses to Jesus' resurrection. Traditionally, women's testimony tended to be disparaged – Luke says 'their words seemed…like nonsense' (Luke 24.11) – thus it is remarkable that women are assigned the role of the first witnesses to Christianity's central event.

Some Christians view the Virgin Mary as an important demonstration of God's use of women to fulfil his purpose, and in the Roman Catholic and Orthodox traditions she provides a female focus of devotion, as a counter-balance to God the Father and Jesus Christ the Son, both of whom are portrayed as male. Protestants are uncomfortable with Marian veneration, however, and not all feminist scholars agree that Mary does women a service. Some have seen her as being passively obedient rather than 'highly favoured', when the angel Gabriel informs her that she will bear a son, having been impregnated by the Holy Spirit. Gabriel does not ask Mary whether she is happy with the idea – Mary's expression of joy only occurs afterwards (Luke 1.26–55).

Christians, then, have different views about the role of women. Conservative Christians draw on biblical passages that suggest a subservient role to women, contending that the Church should not follow secular trends such as feminism. Other more liberal Christians welcome what they see as a recovery of a lost tradition, which highlights the role that women have played in the biblical narrative.

DAN

We have been discussing the role of men and women – I want to focus here on leadership in the Jewish community. In Scripture, kings, prophets and priests played a major role in Jewish life. But there is no mention of rabbis. It was only during the Hellenistic period that the institution of the rabbinate emerged. Rabbis (which means teachers) were Pharisaic scholars. With the destruction of the Temple in 70 CE by the Romans, the Pharisees became the dominant group in the Jewish world. For thousands of years Pharisaic rabbis served as the leaders of the community.

Traditionally only men could serve as rabbis. However, in the 1880s Reform Jewish leaders proposed the idea that women could become rabbis, but it was not until 1922 that the concept of women in the rabbinate was discussed by the Central Conference of Reform Rabbis. The discussion focused on two issues: (1) the position of women rabbis within traditional Judaism, and (2) the question of whether the Reform movement should follow tradition. Reform leaders considered ordaining women as violating *halakhah* (Jewish law) and were concerned that ordaining women would give the Orthodox grounds for delegitimising Reform Judaism. In addition the Reform rabbinate believed that ordaining women would be detrimental to family life.

In the twentieth century the role of women underwent major change. Orthodox Judaism, however, wrestled with the issue of women's ordination. In 1973 the Conservative Jewish Theological Seminary (JTS) halakhic-decision-making body passed a law allowing women to count in *minyanim* (the quorum for prayer). But a year later the committee voted against ordaining women as rabbis and cantors. Eventually the Conservative Rabbinical Assembly and the JTS joint committee agreed that there is no direct halakhic objection to training and ordaining of women rabbis. In 1983 the JTS faculty voted to admit women to the rabbinical school. Adopting a similar policy, the Reconstructionist movement has ordained women from 1974.

Despite the opposition of Orthodox traditionalists, a few women have broken through the barriers to become rabbis. At least two women have openly declared that they have received Orthodox *semicha* (rabbinic ordination) and several others are studying in Israel in pursuit of this aim. Writing in *Moment* magazine, the Orthodox Jewish writer Blu Greenberg wrote that Orthodox women 'should be ordained because it would constitute a recognition of their intellectual accomplishments and spiritual attainments; because it would encourage great Torah study; because it offers wider female models of religious life; because women's input into *p'sak* (interpretation of Jewish text), absent for 2,000 years, is sorely needed; because it will speed the process of re-evaluating traditional definitions that support hierarchy; because some Jews might find it easier to bring halakhic questions concerning family and sexuality to a woman rabbi. And because of the justice of it all.'[40]

In opposition to such innovations, Orthodox critics argue that the ordination of women rabbis is against the tradition. Zevulun Charlop, dean of the Rabbi Isaac Elchanan Theological Seminary of Yeshiva University, for example, argues that women cannot receive *semicha* because it originated with Moses and was passed down only to men. There is thus a seemingly unbridgeable gap between the role of women in Orthodox Judaism and the non-Orthodox movements.

USAMA

I will say something about the veiling of women, a practice that is now particularly associated with Islam.

Surah al-Nur (Chapter: *Light,* no. 24) begins with a passage about a scandal that rocked the Prophet's own household: his favourite wife Aisha got left behind in the desert en route back from a military expedition; she was rescued and brought home by a virgin young man, Safwan. Tongues began wagging, accusing Aisha of adultery with Safwan. This passage prescribed harsh punishment for fornication, adultery or accusing a woman of unchaste behaviour without having four eyewitnesses to support the accusation. It also exonerated Aisha of any wrongdoing.

The *surah* continues with rules relating to gender interaction, with the aim of preventing such scandals in the future. These rules include the command, to both male and female believers, in that order, to 'lower their gazes and guard their private parts (chastity)'. It also orders women 'not to display their charms, except for what ordinarily appears'. The idea is that women, who are called the 'fair sex' in English, are a reflection or manifestation of God's Divine Name of Beauty, and that some of this beauty must be kept hidden through veiling, except to close male relatives who are listed in the verse.

The classical commentators differed as to whether 'apparent' beauty or charms, which women were allowed to display, referred to outer garments or parts of the body such as the face and arms that would normally be visible in public. This dispute leads to the variety of Muslim women's dress styles: all agree on modesty in public, based on the story of Moses and some young women, one of whom was to become his wife. However, the style of this modest dress is disputed: some authorities refer it to local tradition and custom; others insist on the covering of the head or even the face.

The term *hijab*, meaning veiling, is wrongly used nowadays to refer to a headscarf, for which the Qur'anic word is *khimar*. Veiling of women in the Qur'an refers to a curtain that veiled the Prophet's wives from male believers, except for close relatives, to avoid temptation. However, even the only verse mentioning a headscarf or headcover is ambiguous: 'Let them (the female believers) draw their headscarves over their bosoms.' Is this a command to cover the chest only, or does it include the head? Different understandings of the verse result in different contemporary practice. Note that *hijab* in the Qur'an ultimately refers to the mystical idea that we are all veiled from God by creation: when this veil is lifted in the afterlife, one has a vision of God.

The only other verse referring to women's clothing is a command to female believers to wear a *jilbab*, which may be an outer covering such as a shawl or a cloak, in public. This was in response to sexual harassment by sick-minded men: 'That makes it more likely that they will be recognised (as noble women), and not harassed.'

The question is: how can we stop sexual harassment, and if women cover up in public, are they more or less likely to be harassed? Is the essential objective of the verse to prescribe covering up, or to warn against sexual harassment?

GEORGE

I recently had a conversation with a young woman who belonged to the Christian Union (a student organisation for predominantly conservative Christians). She told me that she found the final chapter of Proverbs particularly 'empowering' for women. I was somewhat surprised. This chapter contains a description of the ideal wife, who gets up early in the morning to prepare food for the household, spins wool and flax, makes clothes for her family, shows hospitality to the needy, and earns her husband's approval for all her hard work. Meanwhile, her husband is a respected elder in the community, who appears to be exempt from these menial tasks (Proverbs 31.10–31).

In fairness, this ideal wife is also portrayed as being commercially astute: she buys a field in which she plants a vineyard, engages in trade, and is a wise teacher. It should be remembered, however, that this passage is an acrostic poem, and that the editor of Proverbs personifies Wisdom in female form (e.g. Proverbs 8.1). So perhaps the passage is not a statement about the role of women, but about the ideals to which any wise person – male or female – should be metaphorically wedded. As Usama suggests, femininity can refer to the manifestation of God, and Christians have also used the metaphor of male–female relationships, specifically marriage, to symbolise the mystical union between Christ and the Church (meaning the entire body of Christians) (Revelation 21.2, 9).

Like the Qur'an, the Bible suggests that women should dress modestly. Paul (or someone writing in his name) says, 'I also want the women to dress modestly, with decency and propriety, adorning themselves, not with elaborate hairstyles or gold or pearls or expensive clothes...' (1 Timothy 2.9). However, it is only nuns who cover almost their entire bodies, and Paul's advice is as much about refraining from flaunting one's wealth as it is about personal modesty.

The passage then goes on to forbid women to hold positions of authority. Yet there are several places in the New Testament where we read of women leaders: Tabitha (also known as Dorcas) (Acts 9.36), Phoebe, Priscilla, Junia (Romans 16.1, 3, 7), Eudonia and Syntyche (Philippians 4.2). Dan has discussed the issue of women rabbis, and these references are frequently cited in favour of women's ordination. Christians who adopt a more conservative stance will point out that

Jesus' 12 disciples were all men, and argue that the 2000-year-long tradition of all-male clergy should be maintained. In 1988 the papal encyclical *Mulieris Dignitatem* ('On the Dignity and Vocation of Women') contended that feminism is a modern secular movement, and that the Church should not bend its ideas to secular ideologies: John Paul II declared that women should reclaim true forms of femininity, rather than assume traditionally masculine roles.

Some conservative Protestants have adopted a similar stance. Promise Keepers is a Christian men's organisation that began in the US, and is committed to traditional family life, as they believe is portrayed in the Bible, with the husband the head of the household, to whom his wife is subordinate. This is in accordance with Paul's statement, 'For the husband is the head of the wife as Christ is the head of the church, his body, of which he is the Saviour' (Ephesians 5.23). By contrast, one (non-mainstream) denomination, the Unitarian Universalists, have set up a men's group – UU Men – to support women against gender injustice. While women's initiatives have been important in improving their status, it is equally important that men are persuaded to accept a more equitable role for women.

Chapter 17

WAR AND PEACE

Both Judaism and Christianity uphold peace as an ideal. The word 'Islam' derives from the same root as the Arabic word for peace, 'Salam'. Yet all three religions have been substantially involved in wars. The God of the Hebrew Bible is portrayed as belligerent and bloodthirsty, and Hebrew Scriptures have numerous accounts of Israel's expansionist policies, which sometimes involved the complete elimination of other nations. The God of the New Testament is said to be a God of love, although Christians cannot claim a good track record of peacekeeping. 'Jihad', which literally means 'an effort', is often differentiated into the 'small Jihad' (war for the cause of God) and the 'big Jihad' (a spiritual personal path to God, which involves overcoming internal obstacles). How is it that the 'small Jihad' seems to be better known?

GEORGE

I suppose I have been fortunate, living at a time when my country did not have conscription or military service. I was born just at the end of World War II, and National Service was abolished in 1960, when I was still at school. My mother was an uncompromising pacifist, and would not allow my brother and me to join the school corps, which was an expectation. I was quite relieved, but other pupils asked me awkward questions like whether I would have allowed Hitler to invade Britain unopposed.

I did not have good answers, and I am not sure that I do now. The commandment 'Thou shalt not kill' (Exodus 20.3, King James Version) seemed at odds with all the wars – sometimes genocides – in which the ancient Israelites engaged, apparently with God's approval. I soon discovered, of course, that the verse really meant 'You shall not murder', not that one should not engage in military combat. On the other hand, the Bible talks about peace as an ideal. Isaiah's vision of God's ideal world is one where swords will be beaten into ploughshares, and spears to pruning knives, and he speaks of a child being born who will be called the Prince of Peace, and whom Christians identify with Jesus Christ (Isaiah 2.4; 9.6).

The New Testament does not teach unqualified pacifism. Jesus certainly says, 'Blessed are the peacemakers, for they will be called children of God' (Matthew 5.9), and he seems to suggest that his disciples should not physically resist his arrest when he says, 'My kingdom is not of this world. If it were, my servants would fight to prevent my arrest by the Jewish leaders' (John 18.36). At the Last Supper, Jesus explicitly encourages his disciples to procure swords, and when the disciples produce two, Jesus replies, 'That's enough' (Luke 22.38). Was he suggesting that a limited amount of self-defence was permissible? Yet, when one of his disciples uses a sword and cuts off the high priest's servant's ear, Jesus says, 'No more of this!' and miraculously restores the amputated organ (Luke 22.49–51).

In places Jesus appears to make remarks that oppose peace, for example, 'I did not come to bring peace, but a sword' (Matthew 10.34). This should be understood figuratively, though: Jesus meant that his message was challenging and likely to be divisive.

Because of the Bible's ambiguity about war, it is not surprising that Christians should take different stances. A few Christians are out-and-out pacifists, while most would probably agree that there are circumstances in which war can be justified. The doctrine of the Just War, defined by the Roman Catholic Church, entails that a war should only be fought when the following conditions are satisfied: the aggressor is likely to inflict damage that is 'lasting, grave and certain'; all other ways of ending the conflict have failed; there must be a reasonable chance of success; and the evil produced by war must not be greater than the evil to be eliminated.[41]

This is certainly an advance from the ancient biblical wars in which the desire to acquire land was sufficient justification for using force. However, particularly with the proliferation of nuclear weapons, we must consider whether any large-scale war could satisfy the above conditions. Also, although one's cause may be just, wars do not necessarily bring about justice, but merely establish which party is the stronger.

DAN

During my second year at rabbinical seminary, all students in my class were required to register with the military chaplaincy. This was in preparation for graduation, when those of us who had not married would be required to enter one of the branches of the armed services. I was summoned to the Dean's office for an interview. 'I am against war,' I declared. 'Peace is all important. This is what the biblical prophets taught. The Bible prophesies peace for all nations… The lion will lie down with the lamb.'

For the next half hour my teachers pointed out that Judaism is not a pacifist religion. Indeed, the Hebrew Bible prescribes that war should take place against Israel's enemies. Wars of extermination, for example, are referred to in several of Judaism's biblical commandments:

- Do not leave alive any individual of the seven Canaanite nations. (Deuteronomy 20.16)

- Exterminate the seven Canaanite nations from the land of Israel. (Deuteronomy 20.17)

- Always remember what Amalek did. (Deuteronomy 25.17)

- The evil done to us by Amalek shall not be forgotten. (Deuteronomy 25.17)

- Blot out the name (or memory) of Amalek. (Deuteronomy 25.19)

The extent of such extermination is described in Deuteronomy 20.16–18, which orders the Israelites not to leave alive anything that breathes.

In the history of ancient Israel, wars other than those of extermination often took place with Israel's enemies. Such conflicts were condoned on the grounds of self-defence. Nonetheless there are strict rules about such warfare. Jewish law prohibits the use of outright vandalism. The twelfth-century rabbinic scholar Moses

Maimonides wrote: 'On besieging a city in order to seize it, it must not be surrounded on all four sides but only on three sides, thus leaving a path of escape for whomever wishes to flee to save his life.' The Jewish philosopher Nachmanides, writing a century later, strengthened the rule and added a reason: 'We are to learn to deal kindly with our enemy.'

This is the biblical and rabbinic background to modern warfare between Israel and its surrounding neighbours. In 1992 the Israel Defence Forces (IDF) drafted a Code of Conduct that combines Israeli law, the Jewish heritage and IDF's own traditional ethical code. Outside of Israel there has also been concern about the rules for war in contemporary circumstances. In 2006 during the Lebanon War, for example, leaders of the Rabbinical Council of America issued a statement suggesting that the Israeli military should review its policy of trying to spare the lives of innocent civilians, because Hezbollah puts Israeli men and women at risk by using their own civilians, hospitals, ambulances and mosques as human shields, cannon fodder and weapons of asymmetric warfare. Such discussion and debate is predicated on the assumption that armed struggle is justified when the lives of Jews are at stake.

What we can see, therefore, is that Jewish attitudes to war are grounded in the biblical narrative and expanded in rabbinic sources. In biblical times warfare was a constant feature of Jewish life. However, with the destruction of the Temple in 70 CE and the dispersion of the Jewish people among the nations, this preoccupation ceased. However, with the creation of a Jewish state in modern times, Jews have again been obliged to search their ancient sources for instruction on how warfare is to be waged against their enemies.

USAMA

In 1990, when I was a 19-year-old university student, I travelled to Afghanistan with the leaders of my radical British Muslim group. We spent a week at a spiritual, physical and weapons training camp for Arab *mujahideen* (jihad fighters). We travelled to the front line and briefly fought Afghan communist forces, exchanging artillery fire.

Our British group sent dozens of fighters to Afghanistan and hundreds to the Bosnian civil war, 1992–1995. We wished to defend

Muslims and 'Muslim lands' – thousands of Muslims had been massacred in both wars. Some fighters went to other conflict zones: Burma, Chechnya and Kashmir. A couple of my friends were killed in action.

I returned to Afghanistan in 2010 as a delegate of the British government, and with far more pacifist views. We met ex-Taliban leaders, who were now trying to mediate between the Taliban and the Afghan government. A young British soldier was killed in action and we attended a memorial service for him in the NATO/ISAF military base, Helmand. It was the afternoon, and the British chaplain's Bible readings were accompanied by the Muslim call to prayer from several mosques outside the compound. The medley of sounds went something like:

> God is Greater, God is Greatest... The Lord is my shepherd, I shall not want... I bear witness that there is no god but God (Allah)... He makes me to lie down in green pastures... I bear witness that Muhammad is the Messenger of God (Allah)... Yea, though I walk through the valley of the shadow of death, I will fear no evil.

This situation was very poignant, and I wondered for how long Abrahamic believers would continue to kill each other whilst reciting similar texts.

The essential Qur'anic teaching about jihad is that it is a non-violent struggle for goodness of all kinds, and against evil of all types. 'Struggle in God, as the struggle (jihad) deserves...' (*Pilgrimage*, 22:78).

During his 13 years in Mecca, the Prophet and his followers were subjected to persecution, but were ordered to remain non-violent: 'Withhold your hands (from violence in self-defence): establish prayer and give in charity' (*Women*, 4:77).

During the Prophet's ten years in Medina, military jihad in self-defence was eventually permitted:

- 'Permission has been given to those who were fought (to fight back), because they have been oppressed...' (*Pilgrimage*, 22:39)

- 'Fight, in the way of God, those who fight you, and transgress not...' (*The Heifer*, 2:190)

Even the most apparently belligerent verses about jihad are in self-defence: the command to 'Prepare against them your strength to the utmost' is followed by the exhortation to accept overtures of peace from the enemy: 'If they incline towards peace, then also incline towards it' (*Spoils of War*, 8:60–61).

The command to 'Fight them: God will punish them at your hands' was preceded by the cause: 'They violated their oaths and…attacked you first' (*Repentance*, 9:12–15).

Military jihad was always conditioned by strong ethical restrictions. Numerous hadiths speak of the obligation of avoiding the killing of women, children, old people, peasants, monks and others in war – in the seventh century CE, these were advanced, civilised teachings. Further hadiths forbid the chopping down of trees, burning of orchards, poisoning wells or other water supplies as war tactics.

The twelfth–thirteenth century CE Andalusian philosopher and jurist, Ibn Rushd (Averroes), in his short *Book of Jihad*, discusses ten issues related to the philosophy and ethics of war. Thus, Islam has a long tradition of warfare ethics, and leading Muslim authorities endorse the Geneva Conventions.

GEORGE

I remember our English teacher at school setting us an essay on the quotation: 'Peace hath her victories no less renowned than war.' The quote comes from John Milton, in a letter to Oliver Cromwell, and it is a salutary reminder that we should not define our history in terms of military conquest. When I reflect on my school history classes, many of them seemed to be about knights in armour, war casualties and the conquest of land. It was much more interesting when we got on to the Renaissance, when the focus was more on Europe's intellectual and cultural achievements, such as art, architecture, music, literature and human invention. I cannot help thinking that, if only humankind could channel its efforts away from manufacturing weaponry and destroying property, we could see much greater advance in eliminating diseases, making land more productive, and advancing our technology even further for human benefit.

Dan and Usama both draw attention to the role of violence in the histories of their religions, and sadly Christians have done no better.

In 312 CE the Roman Emperor Constantine purportedly had a vision of a cross in the sky, and was commanded – presumably by God – 'In this sign conquer.' And of course, the Crusades are invariably cited as one of the black spots in Christian history.

Dan rightly draws attention to the parts of Hebrew scripture where God not only condones but explicitly instigates genocides. When Joshua invades Jericho, he is instructed to spare only Rahab the prostitute and her household, since she had helped the Israelite spies (Joshua 6.17). God rejects King Saul precisely because he fails to carry out his instructions to exterminate every man, woman, child and animal (1 Samuel 15.3). Saul's mistake, evidently, is to spare King Agag and to appropriate some of the Amalakites' best cattle. It is left to his successor King David to finish off the task.

Stories like these make the Bible a source of embarrassment. Scholars have sometimes described the biblical narrative as 'salvation history' – the story of how God has brought salvation to the people – but it is also a history of sin, and it is sometimes encouraging to learn that the heroes of the Bible could commit gross misdeeds. Maybe I am not so bad after all! When I learnt such stories in Sunday School as a child, Joshua and David were presented as great heroes. Joshua won the Promised Land, and King David represented the golden age of God's approval for his people. I think we need to reappraise the idea that everything that is condoned in Scripture is morally acceptable. Such perceptions of Jewish history continue to fuel the conflict in the Middle East, as well as the support for the Jews that comes from Christian Zionists.

Perhaps too we need to reappraise our perception of Islam, which is often portrayed as a violent religion that teaches the duty of 'holy war', which is often how the notion of jihad is portrayed. It is appropriate that Usama reminds us that Muhammad taught that violence was for self-defence rather than aggression, and that his response in Mecca to persecution was non-violent.

Changing our perceptions is perhaps the most difficult task, particularly when there are extremists within all three religions, and it is the actions of the terrorist that receive media attention and thus tend to shape public attitudes. Much rethinking is needed if humanity is to live in the peaceful paradise to which prophets like Isaiah have looked forward.

DAN

Although, as I noted previously, Judaism provides criteria for waging war, the ideal is peace. The Torah as well as the rest of Scripture contain extensive discussions of the concept – these are a few examples in the Bible where it is extolled:

- The Priestly Blessing in Numbers 6.24–26 ends with: 'May God lift up his face upon you and grant you peace.'

- 'And I shall place peace upon the land.' (Leviticus 26.6)

- 'Behold I give him my covenant of peace.' (Numbers 25.12)

- 'Peace, peace to the distant and the close.' (Isaiah 57.19)

- 'Seek peace and pursue it.' (Psalm 34.14)

- 'Grant peace to those who love your Torah.' (Psalm 119.165)

- 'Peace upon Israel.' (Psalm 125.5; Psalm 128.6)

According to the Jewish tradition, the messianic age will be one of global peace and harmony, an era free of strife and hardship, conducive to the furtherance of the knowledge of the Creator. The theme of the Messiah ushering in an era of global harmony is encapsulated in two of the most famous scriptural passages from the Book of Isaiah:

> They will beat their swords into ploughshares
> and their spears into pruning hooks.
> Nation will not take up sword against nation,
> nor will they train for war any more. (Isaiah 2.4)

> The wolf will live with the lamb,
> the leopard will lie down with the goat,
> the calf and the lion and the yearling together;
> and a little child will lead them.
> The cow will feed with the bear,
> their young will lie down together,
> and the lion will eat straw like the ox.
> The infant will play near the cobra's den,
> and the young child will put its hand into the viper's nest.
> They will neither harm nor destroy

on all my holy mountain,
for the earth will be filled with the knowledge of the Lord
as the waters cover the sea. (Isaiah 11.6–9)

Despite the endorsement of warfare, Jewish religious texts overwhelmingly stress the importance of compassion and peace. Even though the tradition permits waging war and killing in certain circumstances, the requirement is that one always seeks a just peace first. As the 1947 Columbus Platform of the Reform movement explains: 'Judaism, from the days of the prophets, has proclaimed to humankind the ideal of universal peace, striving for spiritual and physical disarmament of all nations. Judaism rejects violence and relies upon moral education, love and sympathy.'[42]

As I noted previously, when the time for war has arrived, Jewish soldiers are expected to abide by specific laws and values when fighting. Jewish war ethics seek to balance the value of maintaining human life with the necessity of fighting a war, demanding adherence to Jewish values even while fighting. The Torah provides the following rules for engaging in battle:

1. Pursue peace before waging war.

2. Preserve the ecological needs of the environment.

3. Maintain sensitivity to human life.

4. The goal is peace.

Shalom, then, is a key principle. Proverbs 3.17 declares: 'Her ways are pleasant ways and all her paths are *shalom*.' The Talmud explains: The entire Torah is for the sake of the ways of *shalom*. The twelfth-century philosopher Maimonides comments in the Mishneh Torah: 'Great is peace, as the whole Torah was given in order to promote peace in the world, as it is stated: "Her ways are pleasant ways and all her paths are peace."' In modern times, Rabbi Moshe Avigdor Amiel, the former Chief Rabbi of Tel Aviv, wrote that military restraint is an absolute demand of Torah law. In his view, the commandment not to murder applies irrespective of whether the victim is Arab or Jew, and is the basis of Jewish ethics.

USAMA

It is worth noting Qur'anic angles on some of the biblical stories cited by George and Dan. Genocide is condemned, for people must always behave justly, even with enemies: 'Let not the hatred of a people make you transgress...and swerve you from doing justice: Be just, for that is closest to piety.' However, Moses promises the Israelites that 'Your Lord may destroy your enemy and make you successors in the land, to see how you act.' The classical commentator Tabari says that 'your enemy' here refers to Pharaoh and his people, that is, the Egyptians, at the time.

The Prophet-King David (Dawud), does not commit genocide, but takes part in justified warfare. David appears alongside King Saul (Talut), whose army faces its enemy. 'They routed them, by the permission of God. David killed Goliath [Jalut], and God granted him kingdom and wisdom, and taught him of whatever He willed. Were God not to check some people by others, the earth would become corrupt...'

Prophet-King Solomon (Sulayman) threatens overwhelming force against the polytheistic Queen of Sheba: she later submits to God alongside Solomon.

The phrase from the David–Goliath verse above, 'were God not to check some people by others,' was repeated when the persecuted Muslims were finally given permission to fight back:

> Permission has been given to those who were fought (to fight back), because they have been oppressed... And were God not to check some people by others, then monasteries, churches, synagogues and mosques, where God's name is mentioned often, would surely be demolished.

Thus, military jihad was legislated to protect the religious freedom of Muslims, Jews and Christians, according to the explicit text of the Qur'an. Muhammad bin Qasim, the eighth-century CE Muslim commander who first brought Islam to India, extended this religious protection to Zoroastrian and Hindu temples.

Several Qur'anic verses that speak of war and peace are addressed in the singular to the Prophet, for example, *Women*, 4:84 and *Spoils of War*, 8:61. This is because only he, as the legitimate ruler of the city-state of Medina, had the authority to declare a state of war or peace.

Islamic jurists have always agreed that only a legitimate authority can declare a state of war. In modern times, this means that only legitimate states have such authority: non-state actors have no Islamic authority whatsoever to issue a call to arms in the name of jihad. As Dan notes, non-state actors, such as Hezbollah and Hamas, are notorious for violating warfare ethics, although state actors are also guilty of this sometimes.

Inner jihad or *jihad al-nafs* (struggle against the self's base desires) has always been understood as a prerequisite for taking part in the outer jihad, or struggle for goodness and truth in the world. The Qur'an promises heaven to whoever fears standing before God and 'forbids their self from base desires'. A hadith states, 'The true *mujahid* (holy warrior) is the one who struggles against their own self for the sake of God.'

Ibrahim bin Abi Ablah, an early ascetic, remarked after a military expedition, 'We have returned from the lesser jihad to the greater jihad', that is, from the lesser, military jihad to the greater jihad of lifelong struggle against evil. This teaching was widely favoured by Sufi mystics, keen to preserve spiritual dimensions of Islam during the early centuries of astonishing military conquests and worldly success.

Chapter 18

OTHER FAITHS

Jesus said, 'No one comes to the Father except through me' (John 14.6). Many Christians have claimed that it is only through Christianity that one can gain salvation. According to Muslim belief, on the Day of Judgement, all will be annihilated save those who accept Islam. Judaism, by contrast, has claimed that salvation is offered to all nations (Genesis 22.18), without their having to convert to the Jewish faith. Is Christian and Islamic exclusivism unduly narrow, and can Christians and Muslims really believe in a God who would consign everyone to eternal punishment for failing to find or follow the one 'true' religion?

USAMA

Traditional Islamic theology takes an exclusivist view of salvation: only true Muslim believers go to the Garden (heaven), whilst everyone else goes to the Fire (hell). This belief is based on an exclusivist view of verses that also have inclusivist interpretations favoured by many mystics and rationalists, such as the following from the third *surah*, in which submission (*islam*) is a major theme, just as faith (*iman*) is paramount in the second *surah*:

1. Truly, religion with God is submission (*islam*).

2. So then, do they seek other than the religion of God, when to Him have submitted everyone in the heavens and the earth, willingly or unwillingly, and to Him they will be returned? … Whoever seeks other than submission (*islam*) as a religion, it will never be accepted of him: in the hereafter, he will be amongst the losers.

But what exactly are these verses saying? Are they saying that Islam is a separate, tribal religion, and the only way to salvation? Or are they saying that the true path(s) to God is rooted in submission to all that is divine? The Arabic text plausibly carries both meanings, and I try to translate it accordingly.

To me, it is very clear that the latter is the case: the second pair of verses (2 above) are separated by the following verse that repeats the Qur'anic notion that all the biblical prophets and their followers were true submitters to God (*muslim*):

3. Say: We have put our faith in God, and in what has been revealed upon us; and in what has been revealed upon Abraham, Ishmael, Isaac, Jacob and the [Twelve] Tribes; and in what was given to Moses, Jesus and the [other] prophets from their Lord. We do not differentiate amongst any of them, and we, to Him, are submitters (*muslim*).

The context of *surahs* 2 and 3, that address these issues whilst together making up almost a seventh of the Qur'an in length, is a critique saying that the previous inheritors of this message, Jews and Christians, have become largely tribal and sectarian, as opposed to the universal nature of God's message. The following verses illustrate this:

4. They said: No one will enter the Garden, except a Jew or Christian. Those are their fancies! Say: bring your proof, if you are truthful. Nay, whoever submits his face to God and is excellent in nature: he will have his reward with his Lord; no fear shall be upon them, nor will they grieve. The Jews said that the Christians have no basis, and the Christians said that the Jews have no basis, whilst they recite the same scripture!

5. They said: Become Jews or Christians, and you will find guidance. Say: Nay, [follow] the way of Abraham in monotheism, for he was not of the polytheists.

This verse is immediately followed by 2:136, which is almost identical to 3 above.

The following important verse, repeated elsewhere in the Qur'an almost verbatim, has both exclusivist and inclusivist interpretations.

I understand it as transcending religious tribalism and emphasising the essential path to God:

> Truly, those who believed, and those who followed Judaism, Christians and Sabians: whoever believed in God and the Last Day and worked righteous deeds, they shall have their reward with their Lord – upon them shall be no fear, nor shall they grieve.

GEORGE

On the issue of other faiths, Christians have tended to fall into two different camps: exclusivists and inclusivists. The exclusivist view is, bluntly, that the Christian faith has the sole truth and that other faiths are in error. Supporters of this position will frequently cite Jesus' words, 'I am the way and the truth and the life. No one comes to the Father except through me' (John 14.6), or Peter's defence to the Jewish authorities, 'Salvation is found in no one else, for there is no other name under heaven given to mankind by which we must be saved' (Acts 4.12). The missionaries of the nineteenth and early twentieth centuries preached the Gospel precisely because they were exclusivists, and often portrayed those of other faiths as heathens living in darkness. As Paul wrote, 'The god of this age has blinded the minds of unbelievers, so that they cannot see the light of the gospel that displays the glory of Christ, who is the image of God' (2 Corinthians 4.4). The missionaries' aim was therefore 'that at the name of Jesus every knee should bow, in heaven and on earth and under the earth' (Philippians 2.10).

On the other hand, the inclusivists can point out that Jesus says, 'My Father's house has many rooms' (John 14.2), which some see as a hint that God's final kingdom will contain Hindus, Buddhists, Jews and Muslims as well as Christians. Inclusivists can argue that the Bible describes God as just and loving, and these characteristics would be incompatible with a God who decided to condemn all non-Christians – the vast majority of the world's population – to the fires of hell, or (less painful) annihilation. Such a God would be a far worse tyrant than Vlad the Impaler, Adolf Hitler, Pol Pot, Idi Amin, and all the other genocidal political leaders combined.

Some forms of inclusivism have gone so far as to claim that 'all paths lead to God', or even that all religions ultimately teach the same thing – a sentiment that one often finds in interfaith circles. The famous Indian teacher Ramakrishna (1836–1886) is well known for his statement:

> God can be realized through all paths. All religions are true. The important thing is to reach the roof. You can reach it by stone stairs or by wooden stairs or by bamboo steps or by a rope. You can also climb up by a bamboo pole.

While it can be good to find points in common, and to realise that different religions may not be as different as one previously imagined, I think such sentiments are misguided attempts at tolerance, and must be subjected to critical scrutiny. Do all paths really lead to God? God does not feature prominently among Buddhists and Jains, and can God really be reached through Satanism, or the Ku Klux Klan?

Religions do not teach the same tenets. Hindus typically believe in reincarnation, while Christians do not; Christians hold that Jesus is the Messiah, while Jews do not. They cannot all be right. Those who want to bring religions too close together conceptually have a somewhat mistaken view of tolerance. Tolerance is not about claiming that we all believe the same; on the contrary, we are only truly tolerant when we recognise differences but agree to live together and co-operate with each other, despite different beliefs and practices.

DAN

In the Hebrew Bible God is depicted as making a covenant with the Jewish nation. As his chosen people they are forbidden to worship other gods. Non-Jews on the other hand are free to engage in idolatrous practices. Thus, although Israel's covenant with God is considered superior to the religious beliefs and observances of foreign peoples, such superiority did not impel the Jewish nation to condemn those who engage in idolatry.

However, in the rabbinic period, such leniency underwent a major transformation. According to the rabbis, all Jews are obliged to observe the whole Torah, while every non-Jew is a 'son of the covenant of Noah'. In theory the Noachide laws which all human beings are obliged to follow are based on the commandments given to Adam and Noah. As progenitors of all human beings, the obligations placed on them are universal in scope. Traditionally these laws are: the prohibition of idolatry, blasphemy, bloodshed, sexual sins, theft, eating from a living animal, and the injunction to establish a legal system.

On this view, non-Jews are perceived as culpable if they engage in idolatrous practices, since the prohibition against idolatry is understood as prior to God's special covenant with his own people. However, a fundamental distinction is drawn between conventional idolatry as opposed to the symbolic worship of idols. The differences between Israel and the gentiles is not that Israel worships the one God whereas gentiles worship other gods. Rather Israel worships God directly whereas the nations of the world approach him through visible intermediaries, which function symbolically. In this view pagans should be understood as polytheists in practice but monotheists in theory if they worship the one God through religious objects of their own religious system.

Given such an understanding of polytheism, gentiles are guilty of violating the Noachide ban against idolatry only if they believe in the divine nature of the objects they worship. However, if these idols are conceived as signs or symbols of the one supreme God, such behaviour is acceptable. In short, gentiles are permitted to engage in polytheistic activity as long as they perceive that God is the ultimate object of their concern – in such cases they are not literally idolaters.

The notion that gentile idolatry is not necessarily polytheistic in principle became a dominant motif of rabbinic Judaism. How is this distinction between the notion of pure idolatry and symbolic idolatry to be understood? Pure idolatry consists in the elevation of what is finite to the level of the divine. The finite in such a case is perceived as the object of worship – it is in no way symbolic. Rather the idol is a representation of a divine being's power and wisdom: it itself is the object of devotion and veneration. Symbolic idolatry, on the other hand, is legitimate in pagan religions when the objects of devotion are not elevated in this way. Monotheism demands that God alone is the ultimate object of worship.

Here then in rabbinic Judaism we can see the emergence of an inclusivist understanding of other religions. In the Bible the gods of other nations are ridiculed, and the Israelites are warned not to turn away from the true worship of the God of Israel. Yet such Jewish exclusivity does not entail the need to persuade foreign peoples of their misguided ways. Instead the Jewish nation is simply to remain loyal to the covenant. Gentile idolatry was tolerated in the expectation that in the end of days all peoples would acknowledge the God of Israel as the Lord of history. In time such an exclusivist stance was superseded by a Jewish form of inclusivism, which accepted pagan observance as legitimate as long as non-Jewish worshippers acknowledge its symbolic function.

USAMA

Many people ask why the Qur'an only offers salvation to Abrahamic faiths. This is not the case: it opens the door to others also. Qur'an 2:62 and 5:69 promise salvation to anyone that believes in the One God and in the Last Day, and, crucially, does good works.

The Magians (Zoroastrians) get a mention in the Qur'an, in neutral terms alongside the Abrahamic faiths, the Sabians and the polytheists: God will judge between them all on the Day of Resurrection.

There is a good reason why polytheists, Jews and Christians dominate references to non-Muslims in the Qur'an: they were the main faith communities that the early Muslims encountered in Arabia, the Levant and Abyssinia.

When the Muslims later encountered Magians in Eastern Arabia and Persia, they were generally regarded as 'semi-People of the Book': only some of the concessions that Jews and Christians received were given to them. For example, the Magians were entitled to state protection in return for a protection-tax (*jizya, cf.* Qur'an 9:29), but intermarriage with them was forbidden and their slaughtered meat was prohibited to eat. However, I agree with those authorities who regarded them as fully People of the Book, and gave them full concessions, because they had a divinely revealed scripture (Book) and divinely inspired prophet (Zoroaster). It is striking that the Qur'an refers to the Jews (*yahud* or *alladhina hadu*, 'those who turned to God through Judaism') and Christians (*nasara* or 'Nazarenes') in their own right, but also speaks of the 'People of the Book' (*ahl al-kitab*). The general nature of the latter term indicates, to me, that this covers every major world religion, since these all have scriptures, presumably inspired by God.

I therefore agree with those Muslim authorities, and there were and are many in India who took this view, that Hindus and Buddhists are also 'People of the Book'. A young Hindu priest once told me that he respects Christianity and Islam because Jesus and Muhammad are prophesied in the Hindu scriptures. This confirms for me that the Hindu scriptures have a divine origin.

George further asks whether the Ku Klux Klan or Satanism can really be paths to God. A famous Sufi teaching holds that, 'There are as many paths to God as the number of human souls.' However, this must be restricted by some conditions, otherwise Satanism would indeed be a path to God. The mediaeval theologian Ibn Taymiyyah explained the teaching to refer to paths within Islam. I think a Qur'anic restriction would be an acceptance of monotheism in some form, that even some Hindus, Magians and Sabians believe in, and, importantly, good or righteous works. This is because goodness is not just in belief, but manifested through actions, or our dealings and mutual interactions with other beings around us.

The Qur'an does teach a supersessionist view: Islam, as brought by the Prophet Muhammad, peace be upon him, supersedes and replaces the paths of the previous biblical prophets, that were also known as Islam, and their followers as *muslim*. In history, large numbers of polytheists, Christians, Magians, Hindus, Buddhists and Confucians converted to Islam, as did a number of Jews. However, many others did not. I agree with those authorities, such as the mystic Ibn Arabi and the syncretist Mughal Emperor Akbar, who took a pragmatic approach to this theological dilemma: although Islam in theory has superseded other religions, in practice, the partial corruption of Islam from within and the continuing presence of goodness in other religions means that Muslims must not insist on exclusivity, and must indeed accept an inclusivist view of divine salvation.

GEORGE

Dan discusses the notion of covenant, and Usama mentions supersessionism. The two ideas are linked, since supersessionists hold that God's covenant was transferred from the Jews to the Christians. Supersessionism is also associated with the idea that religions progress and evolve, with newer ones surpassing the older. The theory can be discerned in some parts of the Christian Bible, and it has a history in religious scholarship and in Christian mission.

Influenced by Charles Darwin's *Origins of Species (1861)*,[43] scholars such as E.B. Tylor (1832–1917), J.G. Fraser (1854–1941), R.R. Marett (1866–1943), and others believed that religions progressed from the 'primitive' to the more advanced, Christianity being the culmination point. J.N. Farquhar (1861–1921), a missionary to Calcutta, wrote a book entitled *The Crown of Hinduism* (1913), contending that the Hindu faiths looked forward to fulfilment in the Christian gospel.[44]

If it were true that religions progress on an evolutionary path, then Usama would be right to place Islam above the Jewish and Christian faiths, since Islam comes historically later, and arguably presents a more thoroughgoing monotheism than Christians, who espouse the doctrine of the Trinity. Of course, one could take this argument further and place the Baha'i at the pinnacle, since it is even more recent, and claims to complete the traditions of all three faiths, with their prophet Bahá'u'lláh progressing beyond Moses, Jesus and Muhammad, as God's messenger for the present age.

When we turn to Christian scriptures, we seem to find conflicting messages about the respective positions of Christians and Jews. The Bible is certainly clear that God entered into a covenant relationship with the Jewish people – first with Noah, then Abraham, Isaac and Jacob, and most importantly Moses (Genesis 9.11; Exodus 31.18; Leviticus 26.42) – and of course the Jews are described as God's chosen people (e.g. Deuteronomy 7.6–8). However, the New Testament goes on to describe the emergent Christian communities as God's new chosen people (Colossians 3.12; 1 Peter 2.9), which some Christians regard as a transfer of God's favour from the Jews to the Christians, sometimes using terms like 'new Israel' or 'second Israel' to describe their status.

Such terms are not biblical, however. The Bible speaks about a new covenant, not a new Israel. The 'new covenant' prophecy is found in Jeremiah (Jeremiah 31.31–33), and it is later cited in the New Testament in the Letter to the Hebrews (Hebrews 8.7–12). The latter passage adds: 'By calling this covenant "new", he has made the first one obsolete; and what is obsolete and ageing will soon disappear' (Hebrews 8.13). Thus, Christians have therefore frequently interpreted Jeremiah's prophecy as supersessionist. However, this would be a misreading of Jeremiah, who spoke of a new relationship between the Jewish people and God, who would 'write [the Law] on their hearts' (Jeremiah 31.33). As Paul points out, God does not renege on his promises: 'I ask then: Did God reject his people? By no means!' (Romans 11.1), although he expresses the desire for God's people to be saved through Christ (Romans 10.1–4).

Christianity's attitude to Jews has therefore been somewhat ambiguous. On many occasions throughout its history, the Church has shown extreme hostility to Jews – and also to Muslims. Attitudes have changed, however, and to give one important example, Pope Paul VI's Declaration *Nostra aetate* ('In Our Time'), which was overwhelmingly approved by the Second Vatican Council in 1965, decisively condemned all forms of antisemitism, and affirmed the esteem in which God holds the Jews as well as the Christians.[45]

DAN

We have been discussing various notions of exclusivism and inclusivism. But I want to go further, and suggest an alternative approach to the world's religions, which is generally referred to as 'pluralism'. According to the Christian theologian John Hick, what is now required is a Copernican revolution in theology.[46] It demands, Hick wrote, a paradigm shift from a Christianity-centred or Jesus-centred to a God-centred model of the universe of faiths. In this light the great world religions should be understood as different human responses to the one divine reality, embodying different perceptions that have been formed in different historical and cultural circumstances.

Turning to Judaism, it is possible to pose a Jewish pluralist model similar to what has been espoused by Hick and others. In such a view, it should be recognised that in each and every generation and to all peoples of the world, the Divine is considered in distinctly different ways. Thus neither Judaism nor any other religion contains an absolute and universally valid conception of the Divine. Rather, in each case the view of ultimate reality is conditioned by such factors as history, climate, language and culture. For these reasons the doctrine of divine reality is characteristically different in each case.

Such a conception of the ultimate serves as the basis for a pluralistic model in which the Divine, rather than the Jewish tradition, is at the centre. Judaism, like other religious faiths, encircles the Divine, intersecting only at those points at which the nature of divine reality is truly reflected. The advantage of this vision of Judaism in the context of the world's faith is that it is arguably theologically more coherent with the Jewish understanding of God as the Lord of creation, and it also paves the way for interfaith encounter on the deepest levels.

There are thus three models for understanding the relationship between Judaism and the world's religions. According to the first model – Jewish exclusivism – Judaism is at the centre of the universe of faiths. Such a view can be presented diagrammatically:

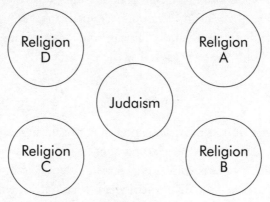

Figure 18.1: Jewish exclusivism

Jewish inclusivism, however, assumes that God revealed himself not only to the Jews but to others as well; this model can be represented in this way:

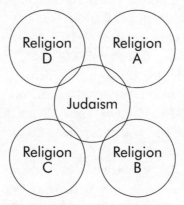

Figure 18.2: Jewish inclusivism

The third model – pluralism – places the Divine at the centre of the world's faiths. All religions are viewed as lenses through which divine reality is conceptualised:

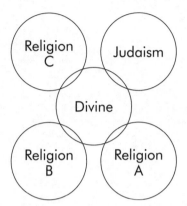

Figure 18.3: Jewish pluralism

Already Jews work together with members of other faiths on common projects of fellowship and charity. Yet this pluralist model emphasises that Jews need to free themselves from an absolutist Judeo-centric position. On this basis the way is open for interfaith encounter of the most profound kind. With the Divine at the centre of the universe of faith, Jewish dialogue with other religious traditions can assume an altogether different character.

Chapter 19

PERSECUTION

The Christian and Muslim characterisation of Jews has tended to be uncomplimentary. They have been portrayed as spiritually blind, as a stubborn people who would not listen to God's message, and as 'Christ-killers'. By contrast, Christians have often portrayed the Church as the New Israel or the Second Israel; and Muslims regard Islam as conveying the true message of God, falsified by the Jews and misinterpreted by Christians. How have our interpretations of scriptures prejudiced our different faiths against each other, leading to persecution, physical violence and even genocide? What hope is there of reconciliation and repairing the damage that erroneous scriptural exegesis has caused?

DAN

Looking back over two thousand years, it is possible to isolate a number of causes of antisemitism. Jews have been detested because they were different, despised on account of their financial success, and feared for their connections with Jewry in other lands. In addition to the various social, economic and psychological explanations for humanity's longest hatred, the Christian roots of Jewish antipathy run very deep.

In the Greco-Roman world, the early Church utilised a number of Hellenistic ideas that had penetrated the Jewish religion to denigrate Judaism itself: the allegorical interpretation of Scripture was transformed into a justification for separating religious meaning from ritual practice; revival movements served as a basis for the belief that the Christian faith was the fulfilment of biblical teaching; the quest to harmonise Hellenistic thought with the Jewish tradition led to the denigration of the God of the Hebrew Bible; and the universalisation of Judaism intensified the Christian conviction that the gospel should be spread to all people.

With the emergence of Christianity, the followers of Jesus believed themselves to be the true heirs of the covenant. For these Christians Jesus' messiahship was understood as bringing about a new age in which the true Israel would become a light to the nations. Given this eschatological vision, the Jewish people were regarded with animosity. Later, the Fathers of the Church developed an *Adversos Judaeos* tradition, which vilified the Jews. According to the Fathers, Jews were guilty in the past of indecent actions, and they have continued to be a contemptible people.

The tradition of Christian antisemitism as created by the Church Fathers continued through the centuries. Later, during the time of the Crusades, Jewish communities were decimated throughout Western Europe. Through the Middle Ages the Jew was represented as a dark, demonic figure. Repeatedly Jews were accused of possessing the attributes of the Devil. As the personification of evil, they were regarded as sub-human.

In later centuries, such hatred of Jewry continued to foster antisemitic outbreaks. In the early modern period, centuries-old Christian prejudice combined with commercial interests provoked widespread antipathy. Despite the influence of the Enlightenment, Jews continued to suffer in lands where they had settled. In Germany, for example, the Jewish community suffered outbreaks of hostility during the second half of the nineteenth century. Various racist publications attacked Jews, and the researches of Christian biblical scholars undermined the traditional belief that the Torah was given by God to Moses on Mount Sinai. Eventually such hatred crystallised in Adolf Hitler's view of the Jewish people as an evil nation that sought world domination.

In Arab lands, the Jewish community was never subjected to the same hostility as in Christian countries. Nonetheless, the ongoing struggle between Israel and the Palestinians has intensified Arab antisemitism in modern times, and has led to the destruction of Jewish communities in Arab lands. Throughout the Arab world, Jews are continually vilified – as a consequence, the Zionist aspiration to solve the problem of antisemitism by creating a Jewish state in the Middle East has proved an illusion. Today the Arab community has become the greatest proponent of anti-Jewish attitudes, and has transformed the demonic image of the Jew to suit its own purposes.

GEORGE

It is perhaps inevitable that the topic of persecution homes in on the Holocaust. Hitler, of course, was no Bible scholar, although it is arguable that post-Enlightenment trends in biblical scholarship – much of which was German – provided a *zeitgeist* in which anti-Jewish prejudice could be unleashed. The German scholar Julius Wellhausen (1875–1965) pioneered source criticism by postulating a theory of multiple sources of the first books of Hebrew scripture, which a later editor collated. This hypothesis called into question the traditional Jewish view that the Torah was given on Mount Sinai. In his *The Quest of the Historical Jesus* (1910), Albert Schweitzer portrayed Jesus as a failed end-time prophet – a theory that gave impetus to more sceptical scholarship, much of which was German, and which implied that little hard historical fact emerged from Scripture.[47]

Dan mentions the influence of Christian scholarship on Nazi ideology, but curiously he also seems sympathetic to the approach of scholars like Wellhausen. As he has said earlier with regard to Jewish Scripture, 'Most is myth; some may be true.'

Hitler's incursions into biblical interpretation were much less sophisticated. In *Mein Kampf* he alighted on the story of Jesus cleansing the temple, in which he cast out the money changers with a whip (John 2.12–25). Hitler believed that the story demonstrated the Jews' mercenary character: they used their religion for profiteering, and Jesus was crucified in retaliation for demonstrating his disapproval of such practices.

However, in common with much popular belief, too much of a contrast is drawn between first-century Jews and Christians. To what religion did Hitler think Jesus belonged? If Jesus and the early apostles had been around during the Third Reich, they would undoubtedly have been sent to death camps. When the first Christian martyr, Stephen, was stoned to death by some synagogue worshippers (Acts 6.8–8:1) it should be remembered that Stephen was also a Jew, preaching about the Messiah – a Jewish expectation.

Dan mentions early Christian interpretations of Jewish scriptures. Certainly much of their exegesis would be firmly rejected by most Jewish and Christian scholars today. For example, when Paul refers to Moses striking the rock at Rephidim, he declares, 'and that rock was Christ' (1 Corinthians 10.4), as if the incident was a cryptic portent of what was to happen 1500 years later. However, Paul too was a Jew, having studied under the renowned Jewish teacher Gamaliel (Acts 22.3), and his way of interpreting Hebrew scripture must have had some credence in its day.

It is true that some Christian biblical exegesis has given rise to antisemitism, and fuelled persecution of Jews. However, it is important to recognise that all three Abrahamic faiths have done their share of persecuting those of other persuasions. While Hebrew scripture portrays the Jews as slaves of the Egyptians and captives of the Assyrians and Babylonians, it also mentions their own genocidal tendencies. As I have previously highlighted, Joshua and – later – King Saul are instructed to kill every Canaanite and Amalekite respectively. In another incident, King Jehu and his foreign supporter Jehonadab conspire against the Baal worshippers by proclaiming an assembly in Baal's honour and, after murdering all the participants on their exit, convert the Baal temple into a latrine (2 Kings 10:27). So much for inter-religious relations!

All three faiths have persecuted and been persecuted. The Bible portrays Christians as the victims of persecution, but sadly, once Christianity became the dominant religion of the Roman Empire, Christians took advantage of their new-found power and transformed themselves from victims of violence to perpetrators.

USAMA

I agree with George that the three Abrahamic religions have all been persecuted and persecutors throughout their chequered histories. They all agree that persecution and oppression is very wrong. As I explained in Chapter 17, military jihad was allowed partly to defend synagogues, churches and mosques (cf. Pilgrimage, 22:39–41).

Another reason given was that 'Persecution is more severe and serious than killing [an oppressor in war]' (*The Cow*, 2:191, 2:217).

I agree with Dan that Arab and Muslim antisemitism has increased over the past century and a half, and particularly after the dawn of the Zionist movement and the establishment of the State of Israel with the help of colonial, Western and European powers. Sadly, Qur'anic passages such as the following are sometimes misused nowadays to incite Muslims against Jews:

> You were the best of nations brought forth for people: you enjoin goodness, you forbid evil and you have faith in God. Were the People of Scripture [primarily Jews and Christians] to have faith, it would be better for them. Amongst them are believers, but most of them are wicked... Humiliation has been stamped upon them wherever they are found, unless they have a rope [protection] from God and a rope [covenant] from people. They have deserved anger from God, and poverty has been stamped upon them. This is because they used to reject the signs of God and kill the prophets unjustly; this is because they disobeyed and transgressed. (*The Family of Imran*, 3:110–112; *cf.* also *The Cow*, 2:61)

This is reminiscent of Jeremiah and Jesus' excoriations of the Israelites. The early commentator of the first Islamic century, Hasan of Basra, illustrated this passage with reference to the domination of Byzantine Christians and Persian Jews by Persian Magians (Zoroastrians): for Abrahamic monotheists to be subjugated by neo-polytheistic, dualist Zoroastrians was utter humiliation.[48]

But those who misuse this passage ignore its ending, which reiterates that some Jews and Christians are godly people, as good as the best Muslims:

> They are not all the same: amongst the People of Scripture are a steadfast people who recite the verses (signs) of God by night whilst in prostration. They believe in God and the Last Day, they enjoin goodness, they forbid evil and they compete in good works: they are amongst the righteous. (*The Family of Imran*, 3:113–114)

However, I think that Dan should acknowledge the parallel increase in Jewish Islamophobia over the past century. Extremist rabbis and parts of the Israeli public regularly invoke the Torah's justification of genocide against the enemies of the Israelites, and extreme anti-Gentile teachings in the Talmud, to call for a genocide of Gazans and other Palestinians. A number of Hollywood films, since the late twentieth century, with substantial Jewish influence, such as *True Lies* starring Arnold Schwarzenegger and Jamie Lee Curtis, have stereotyped Arabs and Muslims as terrorists, and there have even been racist anti-Arab lines in some of these films. I studied at some of London's top, private secondary schools by the grace of God, and about a third of the pupils were Jewish. I experienced much anti-Arab racism and anti-Muslim bigotry from them. Israeli Arabs, both Muslim and Christian, who comprise about 20 per cent of the Israeli population, complain that they are treated as fifth- or sixth-class citizens, after the higher classes such as Western Ashkenazi, Russian, Sephardic and Falasha Jews. The Palestinians in the West Bank and Gaza are arguably subject to apartheid policies. If our Jewish friends wish to complain about persecution, they should first take a long, hard look in the mirror.

DAN

It is unquestionable that Christianity has been the primary source of anti-Jewish attitudes for nearly 20 centuries. This is so despite the fact (as George points out) that Jesus himself was Jewish, as was Paul, the disciples and a number of early Christians. This is a terrible blight on the Christian tradition, and a cause for shame. Fortunately the Church in recent times has acknowledged guilt for the crimes it has committed against Jewry, and has sought reconciliation in numerous ways. Today as never before there is genuine sympathy and understanding between Jews and Christians.

As far as Muslim-Jewish relations are concerned, it is a tragedy that today there is deep hostility on both sides. Usama is right that we Jews need to look at our own recent dealings with the Palestinians. Israel is not guiltless in causing great suffering in the Occupied Territories and Gaza. Amongst Jews in the Jewish state and the diaspora there is considerable animus directed against Muslims and Islam. We are not guiltless. Yet, we should remind ourselves that the Arab world has been largely sympathetic to the plight of Jews through the centuries. However, in the early decades of the twentieth century, the indigenous Arab population in Palestine was fiercely antagonistic to Jewish settlers. These Jews were regarded as usurpers who had stolen the land from Arabs. As early as 1920 during the annual Palestinian festival of al-Nabi Musa, civil unrest erupted into demonstrations against Jewish immigration.

From that time to the present, the Arab world has refused to accept the existence of a Jewish state in the Holy Land, and has attempted to drive Jews into the sea. In the Arab world Jewry is portrayed in the most offensive fashion. During the last 50 years a vast quantity of antisemitic literature has been published in Muslim countries utilising religious as well as racial motifs. Some of this literature, such as Hitler's *Mein Kampf,* Henry Ford's *The International Jew* and *The Protocols of the Learned Elders of Zion,* has been translated into Arabic and is widely available.[49] Other writings have exploited stereotypical images of the Jew inherited from the past. In all cases, these native depictions of Jewry have been reinterpreted to express Arab antipathy towards Jews.

Repeatedly the Jew is portrayed as an evil force determined to corrupt and exploit the society in which he lives. In addition, Jews are presented as forming a global conspiracy intent on dominating world affairs. Such denunciations of Jewry parallel medieval polemics. As a result of such perceptions, many fundamentalist Muslims are intent on carrying out a jihad against the Jewish community.

As humanity's most persistent hatred, antisemitism thus continues to flourish in the modern world. Nearly 4000 years of antipathy towards Jews has not diminished despite the determination of the Jewish people to free itself from the scourge of prejudice and misunderstanding. Even though the Jewish people are now empowered in their own country, Jewish security is as imperilled as it was in previous centuries. In a world now faced with the very real threat of mass destruction, the flames of such hostility continue to burn bright, with the threat of Jewish extermination as great as ever.

GEORGE

Much Christian antisemitism stems from the incident when Jesus appears before Pontius Pilate, who is reluctant to sentence him to death.

The crowd cry, 'His blood is on us and on our children' (Matthew 27.25). In the past many Christians interpreted this to mean that subsequent generations of Jews were collectively responsible for Christ's death. The notion of collective and intergenerational rather than individual guilt was already inherent in Jewish thought: the second of the Ten Commandments describes God as 'punishing the children for the sin of the parents to the third and fourth generation' (Exodus 20.4).

If Christian history has been wrong in interpreting the Bible in this way, we must equally avoid the same error if we try to make Christians collectively and intergenerationally responsible for the persecution of Jews in past ages. Yes, I thoroughly deplore the statements of figures like Martin Luther, who recommended that Jews' houses be burnt, synagogues destroyed, and that the Jewish community should be denied safe passage. But twenty-first-century Christians collectively cannot be held responsible for the remarks of Luther and other otherwise well-respected figures in Christian history. Indeed, most present-day Christians thoroughly reject such ideas, and I am certainly not proud of our past. However, I cannot share collective guilt unless I condone it, but can only be held responsible for my own words and deeds.

There are at least two main causes of persecution. One occurs when perpetrators feel threatened by the other's lifestyle or ideals. By their very nature all our religions challenge the status quo by pointing out the wrongs and injustices that we find within the world. Inevitably we can make ourselves unpopular. This is no doubt why Jesus said, 'Blessed are those who are persecuted because of righteousness, for theirs is the kingdom of heaven' (Matthew 5.10). If persecution results from our convictions, perhaps that suggests that we are practising our religion effectively.

The other principal cause of persecution is simply xenophobia. Human beings typically find it difficult to accommodate the 'other' – people who are inherently different from themselves, because of their appearance (maybe the colour of their skin), their lifestyle, and their values. Jesus was no xenophobe, however. We can find accounts of his welcoming Samaritans, Romans, Greeks, and on one occasion a Syro-Phoenician woman, as well as the marginalised members of society, such as tax collectors and prostitutes.

It is understandable that Dan should mention the Holocaust as the most horrendous example of persecution. Yet, without wishing in any way to minimise the way in which the Jews were treated by the Third Reich, I think one must beware of exaggerating the threats that they are now under in a post-Holocaust era. One recent report from the International Society for Human Rights in fact suggested that 80 per cent of acts of discrimination and persecution are directed, not against Jews or Muslims, but against Christians.[50]

Usama mentions Zionism, and I believe that the supporters of the Zionist cause pose a much more serious threat to political stability and world peace than the antisemites, influencing US foreign policy as they do, and abetting the sale of arms to Israel. As far as the Christian Zionists are concerned, of course, they are not aiming for a State of Israel in which the Jews retain their own religious identity, but rather hoping for their conversion to the Christian faith in preparation for the world's end.

Dan is encouraging when he says that mutual understanding between Jews and Christians has never been better. If only we could experience more of it.

USAMA

I think we are now in danger of competing as to which of our faiths is facing the most persecution. This is not appropriate or dignified for monotheist believers, especially since we are all aware of how God has always tested humanity, a basic theme of the Qur'an.

According to one hadith, God tests people according to how much He loves them: this is why the prophets and messengers of God, the greatest men and women in history, were often persecuted the most: their stories are recounted repeatedly in the Qur'an. In one passage, the response of the disciples of Israelite prophets to persecution is summarised thus:

> they did not falter because of what befell them in the path of God, neither did they weaken or give up; God loves those who patiently persevere. Their only word was that they said, 'Our Lord, forgive us our sins and our excesses in our matter; consolidate our feet; help us against disbelieving people.' So God granted them immediate (worldly) rewards, and the goodness of the rewards of the hereafter, for God loves those who act with excellence.
> (*The Family of Imran*, 3:146–148)

This prayer begins with introspection and a humble confession of one's own mistakes and weaknesses.

This is not to justify discrimination or oppression. Legally and morally, all our faiths support societies that promote truth, justice and equality. But spiritually speaking, God promised to help us grow through tests and calamities.

Tests come through comfort also: 'We test you with evil and good, as a means of purification' (*The Prophets*, 21:35). This is why early Muslim authorities declared that true faith comprised equal measures of patience and gratitude: patience when tested by evil, and gratitude when tested by goodness. It is also why the Qur'an repeatedly praises those who are 'very patient and very grateful' (*cf. Abraham*, 14:5; *Sheba*, 34:19; *Consultation*, 42:33).[51]

Also, calamities and tribulations are sometimes signs of God's love, but at other times, they are manifestations of divine displeasure: 'Calamities that befall you: they are from what your own hands have earned, although God overlooks many (transgressions)' (*Consultation*, 42:30).

As for current Arab/Muslim-Jewish relations, I think we need to recognise that both groups have a claim to the holy land of Israel/Palestine, and to build friendship and affection between the two communities, so that a political solution is easier to find.

I urge Dan to think about the Arab/Muslim narrative: for centuries, Jews escaping Christian persecution in Europe found refuge with Muslim rulers in North Africa, the Ottoman Empire and Asia. Maimonides and other great Jewish figures flourished under Islamic rule, and often wrote in Arabic. Islamic rule over Jerusalem and its surrounding areas was the longest in history, exceeding that of any other people.[52] The State of Israel was approved by the United Nations, an undemocratic body dominated by former Western, Christian, European powers who had colonised most of the Islamic world. It is no wonder then, that the Zionist expansion in Palestine was seen as usurpation, and the establishment of Israel as Arabs, mainly Muslim but also Christian, paying a partial price to help Christian Europe assuage its guilt over the Holocaust.

Let's be friends, understand each other's viewpoints, and work together to find a religio-political solution.

PART 5

HOPE

Chapter 20

SUFFERING

The Bible promises prosperity to God's chosen people as a reward for obedience. Yet the Jews have suffered throughout the ages, culminating in the horrific experience of the Holocaust. Where was God when such things happened? What might Christian interpretation of Scripture contribute to the understanding of Jewish suffering? Jewish suffering has been due in a substantial degree to Christian prejudice and hostility: what might we do to rectify the past? Although the Holocaust does not challenge Islam in this way, it raises serious questions about the problem of evil. How do we explain evil and suffering, and reconcile them with a benevolent God?

GEORGE

Suffering has been with us since the world began, and is probably the greatest intellectual barrier to belief in an all-powerful and loving God. The story of Creation suggests that God made a perfect paradise for Adam and Eve, but when they fall into sin, God tells Eve that the consequences will be pain in childbirth, and that Adam must engage in 'painful toil' in cultivating the land (Genesis 3.16–17).

The Christian faith teaches that we have all inherited Adam's sin but, as I suggested in my previous exchange, the notion of collective and intergenerational guilt and punishment seems unjust. At times, Hebrew Scriptures present the view that good fortune is the result of righteous living: 'Blessed is the one who does not walk in step with the wicked…whatever they do prospers' (Psalm 1.1, 3). And the books recounting Jewish history seem to suggest that the 'good kings' are rewarded with prosperity, while the 'bad kings' experience national disaster. One of the Psalmists notes the lack of correlation between good living and prosperity, when he urges God to fulfil his role as avenger: 'Rise up, Judge of the earth; pay back to the proud what they deserve…how long will the wicked be jubilant?' (Psalm 94.2–3).

The Book of Job is the most sustained scriptural attempt to resolve the problem of suffering. Job is faultless, and God appears to have rewarded him with large flocks, a large happy family, and many servants. One day, however, enemies attack his herds, lightning destroys his sheep and servants, raiders make off with his camels, and his eldest son's house collapses, killing his seven sons and three daughters (Job 1.1–19). Three friends visit Job and discuss the possible reason for his misfortune, which they attribute to sin, and which Job denies. In the end God intervenes and tells Job that it is impossible to understand his ways, causing Job to confess: 'I am unworthy – how can I reply to you? I have no answer… I will say no more' (Job 40.4–5). (The story has a happy ending: Job ends up with twice as much by way of material assets, and a new set of sons and daughters – a slightly strange scenario, which contradicts the book's initial statement of the problem of suffering. Incidentally, the ending of the story makes an important point about women's rights: the three new daughters are granted equal rights of inheritance along with their brothers; Job 42.15.)

When we turn to the New Testament, we find a somewhat enigmatic passage in Paul's Letter to the Romans, when he writes: 'We know that the whole creation has been groaning as in the pains of childbirth right up to the present time' (Romans 8.22). The reference to childbirth alludes to the punishment given to Eve, but Paul also expresses a hope for the radical transformation of the world, which he relates to the death and resurrection of Jesus Christ: 'Now if we are children, then we are heirs – heirs of God and co-heirs with Christ, if indeed we share in his sufferings in order that we may also share in his glory' (Romans 8.17).

These are difficult ideas, which are not easily unpacked within a short exchange like this. One of the key concepts here is the notion of vicarious suffering – the idea that one person or group can suffer on behalf of another. The idea was not invented by Christians, but can be found in several places in Jewish Scripture also.

DAN

For Jews the problem of human suffering has always been of critical importance. If God is all powerful, then surely he would be capable of curtailing human misery. If he is all good, then he would wish to eradicate it altogether. But human suffering exists. Hence the puzzle. The ancient Israelites were acutely aware of this dilemma, and the Book of Job seeks to provide an answer (as George has indicated).

According to tradition, Job was a wealthy man who lived in the land of Uz. The purpose of the book is to explain the suffering of the righteous. Job is initially portrayed as a person of integrity and faith. The scene then shifts to a discussion between God and Satan. Convinced that Job's piety is due to his prosperity, Satan wishes to test him, and God agrees. His children, wealth and health are then taken from him. Later his friends confront him and seek to persuade Job that his misfortunes are his own fault.

Throughout the book, Job complains of his fate. Eventually God speaks to Job out of a whirlwind, challenging his presumption. 'Brace yourself like a man,' he is told. 'Would you discredit my justice? Would you condemn me to justify yourself?' (Job 40.7–8).

Recognising his inability to understand God's ways, Job declares:

I know that you can do all things;
no purpose of yours can be thwarted.
You asked, 'Who is this that obscures my plans without knowledge?'
Surely I spoke of things I did not understand,
things too wonderful for me to know. (Job 42.1–3)

Notice that here there is no appeal to reward and punishment in the Hereafter as a solution to the problem of suffering. Yet, this dilemma continued to haunt Jewish scholars in the post-biblical period. Why, they asked, is it often the case that the virtuous suffer and the wicked prosper? Eventually rabbinic sages argued that the righteous will be rewarded in the World to Come. God's justice, they believed, could only be served if there is another life in which the balance is redressed. It is only fair, they maintained, that the good should receive their just reward and that the wicked should have cause to regret their misdeeds. Since this does not happen in this life, then clearly it must be a feature of the World to Come. As the rabbis of the Talmud put it: 'This world is a place where the commandments are obeyed: the World-to-Come is the place of reward for keeping them.'

According to these Jewish theologians, when the Messiah arrives, there will be a general resurrection of the dead; this will be followed by a final judgement. Then the righteous will enter into Gan Eden (Heaven), and the wicked will be subjected to eternal torture. This doctrine of reward and punishment in the afterlife sustained Jews through the centuries. Yet, in the modern period, the Jewish community has largely abandoned such belief. It is striking that when faced with the enormity of the Holocaust, in general Jewish scholars have not turned to these traditional doctrines to find some sort of explanation for God's silence.

USAMA

The best answer I know to the problem of evil is by Frithjof Schuon, the twentieth-century metaphysicist: 'There is evil in the world, because the world is not God.' In other words, God is all good and although creation (the world) manifests this goodness, it is not perfect, unlike God: its imperfection includes evil and suffering.

Schuon's aphorism is based on the Qur'an: 'Say, "I seek refuge with the Lord of Daybreak, from the evil of what He has created"' (*Daybreak*, 113.1–2). These verses are known to almost every Muslim child, being part of daily prayers.

A mystical approach such as Schuon's can be paradoxical: the existence of evil is admitted, but the mystic is taught to see goodness everywhere.

A more practical Muslim approach to the problem of suffering is based on the idea of the world as a testing-place: the Hereafter is the commensurate place of reward and punishment. I outlined the Qur'anic doctrine of divine testing through good and evil in Chapter 19, with better people being tested more.

Although the Prophet Job (Ayyub) is praised repeatedly in the Qur'an, his story is recounted very briefly, in only a handful of verses. The traditional commentators draw on 'Israelite traditions', that is, biblical sources, to expand upon the story. The prophets in general are seen as paragons of patience in adversity, including the Prophet Muhammad himself, peace be upon him, as he and his followers faced persecution. They were comforted by stories of Israelites, including

Christians such as those who were tortured in fiery trenches by the polytheistic 'Companions of the Ditch' (*Zodiacal Signs*, 85:4–10).

I hold, on the basis of the universal Qur'anic teachings about suffering, that victims of genocides and holocausts are martyrs.

The Holocaust destroyed a very large proportion of the modern Jewish people. In terms of numbers, millions of Muslims also died during the first half of the twentieth century, particularly during the two world wars, anti-colonial independence struggles and associated population movements. Hundreds of thousands of Muslims have also died since the late twentieth century in the wars in Afghanistan, Iran, Iraq and Syria, as well as numerous natural disasters such as major earthquakes and tsunamis affecting Iran, Pakistan, Turkey and Indonesia, the world's most populous Muslim country. Throughout, Muslims have drawn on their profound scriptural teachings about suffering, regarding victims as saints and martyrs being tested by God, and their monotheistic faith has generally remained unshakeable.

Friends and I took part in disaster relief efforts after the 2004 Indian Ocean earthquake and tsunami that killed a quarter of a million people, and the 2005 Pakistan earthquake that killed 150,000. We were utterly heartbroken upon seeing the devastation and suffering, but never doubted God. I'm saddened that the 1755 Portugal earthquake and tsunami (that also devastated Morocco and Algeria) caused such a crisis of faith in Western Europe, even for the Pope. After the 2004 tsunami, the Archbishop of Canterbury admitted that those events had also shaken his faith. Belief can be very bizarre!

GEORGE

I said in my previous exchange that suffering was the greatest intellectual barrier to faith. Dan and Usama mention possible solutions: the view that injustices and sufferings will be redressed in an afterlife, and the idea that suffering is ennobling and character-building. We shall discuss the afterlife in a later chapter, so let me focus first on the argument that suffering fosters the development of virtues.

If suffering is a test, some people appear to pass with distinction, while others fail miserably. I know of people who have abandoned their faith merely because one of their parents died. Losing a parent is sad, but what do such people expect? If they had any faith at all, they would be familiar with the obvious truth that 'people are destined to die' (Hebrews 9.27). On the other hand, there are some who positively welcome very serious sufferings and disabilities. I once knew a Church of Scotland minister who had been involved in a motorcycle accident, causing him to lose a foot. His comment was, 'I wouldn't have missed it for anything.' I must admit that I don't understand that reaction either; I am sure I would be devastated if that happened to me. The problem about regarding suffering as testing is that we do not all receive the same test. If we were to set different students different examinations of different levels of difficulty, we would justly be accused of gross unfairness. God is said to be a just judge, so why do we not all receive the same testing?

We cannot realistically offer a solution to the problem of suffering in these short exchanges, so let me return to the theme of positively welcoming suffering. Paul writes, 'we also glory in our sufferings' (Romans 5.3–4). We do not know the full extent of Paul's suffering: he was certainly persecuted and imprisoned, and he had a mysterious 'thorn in the flesh' (2 Corinthians 12.7), which may have been some persistent physical ailment, although we cannot be certain.

In the letter to the Romans, which I quoted above, Paul continues by relating suffering to hope, which he argues is made possible through Christ's suffering. I mentioned vicarious suffering in Chapter 20, and, for the Christian, suffering on someone else's behalf is a key concept: Christ's crucifixion was an ignominious experience and, as Paul argues, ought logically to have been a cause of great shame for himself and his followers. Yet Christians proudly proclaim that this event takes away the sins of the entire world. This opens up all sort of questions about the meaning of the Atonement, but it is sufficient to say that the Church (that is, the entirety of Christians) is the body of Christ (1 Corinthians 12.27), and there is therefore a mystical sense in which our sufferings are Christ's sufferings. As Paul says, we are 'crucified with Christ' (Galatians 2.20). The writer to the Hebrews, speaking of Christ's atoning sacrifice, urges the faithful to persevere and to endure hardship, just as Christ sacrificed himself. If this involves suffering on behalf of others, then we have a supreme precedent in Jesus Christ.

Usama aptly says that faith can be bizarre, and I don't know how much sense all this makes to someone outside the Christian faith.

Paul said Christ's crucifixion was 'a stumbling block to Jews and foolishness to Gentiles' (1 Corinthians 1.23). Is it mumbo-jumbo or saving truth?

DAN

In my last exchange I mentioned that the Holocaust poses a major challenge to the Jewish faith. Not surprisingly there have been a wide variety of theological responses to the horrific events of the Nazi era. A number of Jewish thinkers appeal to the notion of redemptive suffering, paralleling Christian thought. Kalonymus Kalman Shapira, for example, was the rebbe of the Warsaw ghetto. In *The Holy Fire*, he rejects the explanation that the Holocaust was due to Israel's sins. Instead, he argues that God suffers on behalf of his chosen people:

> the Talmud states, 'When a person suffers, what does the Shekinah (God's presence) say? "My head is too heavy for me, my arm is too heavy for me."' Our sacred literature tells us that when a Jew is afflicted, God, blessed be He, suffers, as it were much more than the person does. It may be that since He, blessed be He, is not subject to any limitation – for which reason no conception of Him is possible in the world – therefore His suffering from Israel's troubles is also boundless.[53]

Arguing along similar lines, the contemporary British Reform rabbi Colin Elmer argues in 'Suffering – A Point of Meeting' that although he is unable to accept the doctrine of the Incarnation, he believes that the Jewish tradition speaks of a God who suffers with his chosen people:

> Is there a sense, then, in which a Jew can talk of the power of suffering love? If we speak of a God who cares, who loves his people, of God as a loving parent, then we have also to speak of God who suffers. In the same breath that the biblical prophets establish a connection between abandonment of the covenant and consequent suffering, they also speak of God's continuing love. The Shekhinah (God's presence), the divine presence, has gone into exile with the people. God will be with them, and will not abandon them and will ultimately return them to their land and former glory. To match the tears we weep by the waters of Babylon, God also weeps.[54]

For the Jewish theologian Hans Jonas in 'The Concept of God After Auschwitz', the idea of divine impassability must be set aside in a post-Holocaust age:

> If anything in what I have said makes sense, then the sense is that the relation of God to the world from the moment of creation, and certainly from the creation of man on, involves suffering on the part of God... Bound up with the concepts of a suffering... God is that of a caring God – a God not remote and detached and self-contained but involved with what He cares for.[55]

These writers in various ways draw on the tradition of divine suffering in seeking to provide a religious response to the horrors of the death camps. With different emphases, they appeal to the idea of God sharing this terrible tragedy with his chosen people.

USAMA

I love George's anecdote about the minister who lost his foot in an accident but did not regret it: he sounds like a saint, utterly content with God's will, no matter how painful, for that is the mark of a true lover of God.

Both George and Dan mention that God suffers along with His people sometimes. This idea seems to have been articulated and explored much further in Judaism and Christianity than in Islam. However, the concept is not absent from Islam, and needs to be highlighted nowadays, since many Muslims are losing their faith over doubts around evil and suffering.

As ever in Islam, it is mystical teaching that helps with this problem. Ibn Arabi, the thirteenth-century Andalusian mystic, points out that God may be hurt: 'Truly, those who hurt God and His Messenger...' (*The Confederates*, 33:57). In a previous chapter, I mentioned the hadith where God says to people, 'I was ill, but you did not visit Me. I was hungry, but you did not feed Me. I was thirsty, but you did not quench My thirst. I was naked, but you did not clothe Me.'

As the translator of Ibn Arabi's short discussion of Job puts it in his introductory note:

The chapter opens with an explanation of the all-embracing nature of the Reality. It is pointed out that God is to be found not only in what is 'high,' 'above,' and 'lofty,' but also in what is traditionally thought of as profane, 'low,' 'below,' and 'beneath,' so that wherever you turn, there is the face of God [Qur'an 2:115] ... In discussing Job's plight, our author suggests that true patience is not simply the stubborn refusal to voice a complaint, but rather that it is the intelligent refusal to be tempted by the illusion that any other but God is able to bring relief of suffering. Indeed, supplication to God is, for him, not a sign of impatience, but rather an indication of the essential reciprocity between himself and God, God in him and he in God.[56]

Such a reciprocal relationship between humanity and God directly implies that when a person suffers, God suffers in some sense, which is why the above discussion is in the context of Job.

Theoretically and experientially, there is thus a multi-level Muslim reaction to suffering, with a rich interaction of the different levels of response. Also, people's faith and belief are at different levels, so each person will respond uniquely. Firstly, suffering is partly a result of sin. Therefore, one accepts it with humility. But the suffering itself is an opportunity to be purified of any such sin, as atonement or expiation. Therefore, one accepts this with gratitude for the forgiveness of sins. But if one is trying to lead a good life, one hopes that most of the calamities and suffering befallen in life are God's way of testing us and improving us. As Muslim sages often remind us, metal ore is purified through fire. Scientists know all about the stress and high temperatures and pressures needed to remove impurities from iron and gold. Similarly, God purifies the believers' hearts by putting them through immense but not unbearable stress, for *God does not burden a soul beyond what it can bear*, a repeated Qur'anic principle (e.g. *The Cow*, 2:286). This stress is made all the more bearable by the comforting thought that we are not alone: by the reciprocity principle, God Almighty is very near to us, with all the concomitant love and mercy, when we suffer.

Chapter 21

PROPHECY

In biblical times the prophets were charismatic figures who communicated messages revealed to them by God. Frequently prophets prefaced their utterances with the expression, 'Thus says the Lord.' The New Testament accepts Hebrew prophecy, but perceives it as culminating in Jesus Christ, and his proclamation of the kingdom of God. Islam extends the prophetic tradition beyond Jesus, regarding Muhammad as the final prophet. The Islamic concept of prophethood appears broader than the biblical one, and suggests a difference between a prophet and a messenger. So how do we understand prophecy, and in what ways has it relevance in the twenty-first century?

USAMA

'About what do they ask each other? About the magnificent news (of the future), wherein they are in disagreement. Nay! They will soon know! Again, nay! They will soon know!' (*The News*, 78:1–5)

This dramatic *surah* opening refers to the cataclysmic events of the end of the world and the establishment of Judgement Day. The *surah name al-Naba'* (*The News*) is the source of the Qur'anic term for a prophet (*nabi*): a prophet is given visions of the unseen world, directly or via an angel, usually Gabriel. Thus, the prophet is able to tell his people about God's work in the past, present and future. A related term is *rasul*, meaning a messenger or literally, 'one who is sent with a message'.

The prophets, most of whom are also described as messengers of God, are the great heroes of the Qur'an, featuring in almost every major story, replete with moral teachings about good and evil, courage, determination and perseverance in the face of persecution. One *surah* (*Joseph*, no. 12) is entirely devoted to that prophet's dramatic life, and described as the 'best of stories' (*Joseph*, 12:3) Another *surah*, simply entitled *The Story*, mostly recounts the tale of Moses and the Pharaoh (*The Story*, 28).

Most of the prophets named in the Qur'an are also biblical, with the important addition of two Arabian prophets, Hud and Salih, associated with the Nabatean Arabs who populated northern Arabia and built Petra. The Midianite prophet Shu'ayb, possibly the same as Jethro, is also Arab. The following is a generally accepted list of prophets mentioned in the Qur'an: Adam, Idris (Enoch?), Nuh (Noah), Hud, Salih, Ibrahim (Abraham), Isma'il (Ishmael), Ishaq (Isaac), Ya'qub (Jacob), Yusuf (Joseph), Shu'ayb (Jethro), Lut (Lot), Yunus (Jonah), Ayyub (Job), Musa (Moses), Dawud (David), Sulayman (Solomon), Ilyas (Elias), al-Yasa' (Elijah?), Yahya (John the Baptist), 'Isa (Jesus) and Muhammad.

In addition, there is a prophet called Dhul-Kifl (meaning, 'having a portion' – of what?), who may be Ezekiel. There are also figures who may or may not be prophets, such as Luqman the Wise, Dhul-Qarnayn ('the two-horned one', possibly Cyrus or Alexander the Great) and Moses' spiritual teacher, named in the hadith as *Khidr* ('the Green').

The great Qur'anic dramas involving prophets include: Adam and Satan, Nuh and the Flood, Ibrahim and the Fire, Joseph and his brothers, Moses with the Pharaoh and Israelites, and Jesus' miracles.

The Prophet Muhammad's, peace be upon him, own account of his first vision of Gabriel includes that the latter squeezed him until he could hardly breathe, whilst commanding him to repeat the verses of the first Qur'anic revelation. Ibn Khaldun, in his *Introduction to History*,[57] explains that the squeezing refers to the Prophet being transformed from his human nature to an angelic nature, in order to be able to receive the message from an angel.

There is almost no criticism of any prophet in the Qur'an. Later Islamic theology developed the doctrine of the 'infallibility of the prophets', and Muslims tend to reject biblical stories about the supposed drunkenness, incest and adultery of Noah, Lut and David.

Muhammad is the 'Seal of the Prophets' (*The Confederates*, 33:40), generally understood to mean that there is no prophet after him.

The Ahmadiyya Muslim sect is persecuted because they are accused of believing that their founder is a prophet after Muhammad.

A handful of authoritative theologians argued that there were female prophets also, notably the mother of Moses (Safura), the wife of the Pharaoh (Asiya) and Mary, mother of Jesus.

DAN

In biblical times prophets were charismatic figures who were able to receive and communicate messages revealed to them by God. A number of prophets were reluctant to take on this role (such as Moses, Jeremiah and Jonah), yet the prophet was obligated to serve as God's spokesman. Frequently prophets prefaced their utterances with the expression, 'Thus says the Lord.' The second section of the Hebrew Bible is called Neviim (Prophets). The first part of this is referred to as 'Former Prophets' consisting of the Books of Joshua, Judges, Samuel and Kings. These historical works contain accounts of the pre-classical prophets including Nathan, Elijah and Elisha. The second part – the Latter Prophets – consists of the books of the three Major Prophets (Isaiah, Jeremiah and Ezekiel), and the 12 Minor Prophets (Hosea, Joel, Amos, Obadiah, Jonah, Micah, Nahum, Habakkuk, Zephaniah, Haggai, Zechariah and Malachi).

The early prophets were sometimes referred to as 'seers'. During the period up to the eighth century BCE, there were schools of prophets who gathered together to engage in prophetic experience. Thus 1 Samuel records: 'When they came to Gibeah, behold, a band of prophets met him, and the spirit of God came mightily upon him [Saul], and he prophesied among them' (1 Samuel 10.10). Some of the pre-classical prophets chastised the rulers for their iniquity. For example, Nathan rebuked David for his wrongdoing in the matter of Bathsheba (2 Samuel 12), and Elijah condemned Ahab for the murder of Naboth and the confiscation of his vineyard (1 Kings 21).

The period of classical prophecy extended from Amos to Malachi (mid-ninth to mid-fifth century BCE). Coming from all sectors of society, these prophets reproved the leaders of the nation, and as a result were sometimes persecuted and subjected to hardship. Often they employed symbolic acts to illustrate their message. Although the prophets accepted the Temple cult, their criticisms were directed against those who were meticulous in performing ritual but failed to live up to the moral law. According to tradition, prophecy ceased after the time of Haggai, Zechariah and Malachi.

In the Middle Ages, Jewish philosophers gave two different explanations to the phenomenon of prophecy. Rationalistic thinkers (such as Abraham ibn Daud (twelfth century), Maimonides (twelfth century) and Gersonides (thirteenth to fourteenth century) argued that a prophet was endowed with perfection of reason, imagination and moral character. Inspired by the Active Intellect, the faculties of reason and imagination were activated, culminating in prophetic experience. Other writers such as Judah Ha-Levi (eleventh–twelfth century) and Hasdai Crescas (fourteenth–fifteenth century) maintained that prophecy is a divine supernatural gift. The intellectual qualifications of a prophet are thus irrelevant.

Turning from Jewish prophecy to other faiths, how are prophets in other religions to be viewed? According to some Jewish thinkers, prophecy was not restricted to Israel. Nathanael al-Fayyumi (twelfth century), for example, argued that God established an eternal covenant with Moses and the children of Israel, but also established a covenant with Muhammad and the Muslim community. According to al-Fayyumi, Muhammad was given prophecies meant for non-Jews. The revelation for the Jewish people, however, is binding. If a prophet comes to change the laws of the Torah, he should not be viewed as a prophet for the Jewish people.

GEORGE

I would agree largely with Usama and Dan about the characteristics of a prophet. However, to Christians it seems somewhat strange to identify Adam and Noah, Abraham, Isaac and Jacob, and Joseph as prophets. For someone to be a messenger of God, he or she (Miriam is a prophetess, see Exodus 15.20) must have a message. Noah and Ishmael have non-speaking parts in the Genesis story, and there were few people around to whom Adam could deliver any divine message. We would prefer to describe Abraham, Isaac and Jacob as patriarchs: they are part of a historical narrative, rather than preachers. Jacob and his son Joseph have dreams (Genesis 28.10–17; 37.5–11), but the prophet Jeremiah makes it clear that recounting one's dreams is not prophecy (Jeremiah 23.25–32). As for David and Solomon, they were kings of Israel, and the psalms and wisdom literature which are traditionally attributed to them respectively, are different literary genres from prophecy.

A biblical prophet was not just anyone who could find a soap box, or whatever the ancient equivalent was, and rant against the status quo. Typically, a prophet's career began with an inaugural vision from God. Samuel, whom Dan mentions, received an auditory commissioning rather than a vision in the Tabernacle at Shiloh (1 Samuel 3). Although Samuel is not afraid to chastise King Saul, he appears to be part of the establishment, since he officially anoints both Saul and David as kings of Israel (1 Samuel 13.13–14; 10.1; 16.13). We do not know enough about ancient Jewish society to know exactly how prophets fitted in. Some appear to have been ecstatics: this may have been what happened to Saul when he joined the procession of prophets (1 Samuel 10.10). Others seem simply to have preached, typically prefacing their message by affirming that it was 'the word of the Lord'. In some cases the role of prophet may have been an official position: Elijah appoints Elisha as his successor by anointing him, just as he appoints King Jehu (1 Kings 19.16).

At a popular level, Christians tend to associate prophecy with prediction, but most biblical scholars regard this as a misunderstanding. Isaiah did not set up a tent in the marketplace and read people's fortunes! The prophet's role was more typically that of a political commentator and, when he made predictions, he was speaking of imminent rather than distant happenings. The idea that the prophets predicted the coming messiah is problematic. Many Christians would be surprised to learn that the word 'messiah' occurs nowhere in Hebrew scripture. The only possible allusion is Daniel's enigmatic statement that 'the Anointed One will be put to death' (Daniel 9.26). Someone once said that prophecy is best interpreted with hindsight, and Christians perceive that the Hebrew prophets were pointing towards some significant future state, which was not clearly defined. When the two disciples at Emmaus dined, unbeknown to themselves, with the risen Christ, they only recognised with hindsight the meaning of their scriptures' prophecies (Luke 24.25–27).

Finally, Dan asks whether there can be prophets outside one's tradition. For the Christian, Christ is the fulfilment of prophecy, and there is nothing further outside Scripture that is needed for salvation. Christians have tended to react negatively to subsequent extra-biblical prophets, whether it is Muhammad, Joseph Smith, or Sun Myung Moon. Certainly, there can be teachers and writers with messages that are worth heeding, but they cannot be accorded an equal, let alone superior, status to Jesus Christ.

USAMA

It is good to learn from Dan that Nathaniel al-Fayyumi, whose name implies an Egyptian connection, accepted the prophethood of Muhammad, albeit only for non-Israelites.

George correctly implies that the Islamic doctrine of prophethood is unique. However, as I indicated in my section earlier in this chapter, there are people whose prophethood is disputed. Adam's main role in the Qur'an is as the father of humanity and as the object of God's honour and Satan's envy. In one hadith, one of the Prophet's Companions asks him, 'Was Adam a prophet?' showing that this was not clear to him. In Islamic tradition, Adam and Eve (Hawwa') have many offspring, and Adam's prophetic role is also a fatherly one, reminding his children of their duty to God. But Noah is the first of the great messengers and major prophets: 'Truly, We inspired to you as We inspired to Noah and the prophets after him' (*Women*, 4:163).

I agree with the contemporary Professor Seyyed Hossein Nasr, that history proves that the Prophet Muhammad, peace be upon him, is the last divinely inspired messenger: there is literally no one comparable to him since. The Prophet was 'founder of twenty terrestrial empires and one spiritual empire' in the words attributed to Thomas Carlyle. George's mention of two relatively unknown people in the same breath as the Prophet is rather ridiculous. And of course, according to Trinitarian Christians, no one can be of a status equal to Jesus, since they believe that he is uniquely the only human who is also God. We have discussed Muslim responses to that claim elsewhere.

I would like to turn to the issue of how prophethood affects us now. For Muslims, an important aspect is the personal example of the Prophet Muhammad, peace be upon him, the *Sunnah*, that is an inspiration as to how to practically live a life dedicated to God. This goes into great detail of ritual worship, dress, food and drink and economic activity. But the most important aspect of the *Sunnah* is the internal states of the person and one's character, especially the importance of cultivating the qualities of patience, forbearance, kindness, generosity, altruism, forgiveness and love.

An intriguing hadith states that having 'true dreams', in the sense of seeing true realities or events before they actually occur, is one of the 46 parts of prophethood (*Sahih Muslim*, hadith nos. 2263–2264). A strange number, one might think. But it may be a spiritual genetics: we all have 46 chromosomes (23 pairs), so the prophetic qualities are a 'spiritual DNA'.

The literal, defining feature of a prophet is prophecy. There are many hundreds, if not thousands, attributed to the Prophet himself. Many of them are intriguing because they were written down by the ninth century CE and appear to have come true later. These include the prediction of a major fire in the Hejaz that would be visible in Syria, that literally happened in the year 654/1256,[58] after a major earthquake and volcanic eruption near Medina.[59] Another is the conquest of Constantinople by Muslims, predicted in the hadiths and occurring in 1453 CE.

There are many other Islamic prophecies found in dubious, less authentic hadiths: these include the 'descent' of Jesus Christ to fight and defeat the anti-Christ, alongside a Muslim messianic figure known as the Mahdi. Contemporary Muslim militant and terrorist groups use these hadiths to recruit fighters to the Middle East, since the above events are supposed to occur there. My view is that these prophecies are Judaeo-Christian in origin, fabrications wrongly put into the mouth of the Prophet Muhammad, peace be upon him.

DAN

Since biblical times Jews have been prepared to challenge injustice, immorality and iniquity. As I noted, the prophets were the first who took on this role, speaking in the name of God. In ancient times this included the foretelling of future events. In time, however, Jewish social critics abandoned the quest to predict the future. Instead, they drew on the Jewish ethical tradition to protest against oppression and corruption.

In modern times, such individuals frequently cited the biblical prophets as exemplars of the highest moral values of the faith. This has certainly been so within the religious community. Rabbis and others drew on spiritual values in proclaiming their message. But, it should be noted that the prophetic spirit extends beyond religious boundaries. Karl Marx, for example, was descended from a long line of talmudic scholars. At an early age he was baptised, yet arguably his views were to some degree shaped by his Jewish inheritance.

Several scholars have suggested that Marx used the fury of the prophets to convey his message about social injustice and conflict. In their view, it was his role as a prophet that stirred the imagination of millions of workers throughout the world. Although Marx's views have been vilified, there is no doubt he fulfilled the prophetic tradition by condemning the social injustice he saw as inherent to capitalism. So, even a Jew who has rejected the faith of his ancestors, can retain the truthful aspect of the Hebrew prophets and uphold the tradition, which is central to the identity of the Jewish nation.

More recently several events have caused a resurgence of the prophetic spirit. The first is the Holocaust. Reflecting on the significance of the Shoah, the novelist Elie Wiesel warned of the sin of complacency and the dangers of apathy in the face of evil. Those in power, he stated, are responsible for defending those who cannot defend themselves. In making this claim, he cited the legacy of Amos and Hosea by stressing the need for the empowered to come to the rescue of the powerless.

The second event was the founding of Israel. Abba Hillel Silver, president of the Zionist Organisation of America from 1945 to 1947 called for Jews around the world to support the creation of a Jewish state in their ancient homeland. Speaking at the United Nations General Assembly, he reminded those in power of the sufferings of the Jewish people and asserted that this new nation will be their salvation. In making this claim, he called for the ultimate triumph of great moral principles. These, he said, were the values that the biblical prophets tried to instil in the people in ancient times.

The third event was the emergence of the Civil Rights movement, which stimulated many American Jews to remonstrate against the plight of African Americans. The Jewish theologian Abraham Joshua Herschel protested against segregation, claiming that it was easier for the children of Israel to cross the Red Sea than for a black person to cross certain university campuses. In making such a statement he saw himself as following in the footsteps of the prophets of the biblical period.

The legacy of the ancient prophets thus continues to animate the lives of many contemporary Jews. Their message is an inspiration for those who are deeply troubled by the injustices of the modern age. Like the prophets of old, they passionately care for those at the margins of society and seek justice for those who suffer.

GEORGE

The juxtaposition of Muhammad's name to these twentieth-century figures – to which Usama seems to react badly – was not to suggest that they are in any way of equal importance or influence. My point was – and I think Usama agrees – that it is important to define a cut-off point at which prophecy ends. Unless we do this, we risk suggesting that our faith is incomplete, or that we should give equal credence to some later teacher whose message might turn out to be suspect or ephemeral. This has certainly happened in the case of Sun Myung Moon, many of whose followers have become disillusioned with new disclosures about his past life.

Paul wrote, 'where there are prophecies, they will cease' (1 Corinthians 13.8), and the writer to the Hebrews suggests finality regarding prophecy when he writes: 'In the past God spoke to our ancestors through the prophets at many times and in various ways, but in these last days he has spoken to us by his Son' (Hebrews 1.1–2). This does not mean that we cannot learn from other teachers or from each other's traditions, but it does mean that Christ's life, death and resurrection are all that is needed for salvation, and that the teachings of the Bible, which points to Jesus Christ, are sufficient to deliver the world from sin. Christians believe that Jesus Christ was the greatest human who ever lived, and is unsurpassable by any other teacher or prophet.

Usama seems impressed by the predictive powers of prophets. While there are many Christians who believe that prophets could see into the distant future, I think such belief conflates prophecy with clairvoyance, as I mentioned in Chapter 21. There are Christians who have claimed to find cryptic references in Scripture to Napoleon, Hitler, an Anglo-American alliance – and even Muhammad. Tellingly, such allusions only appear to be recognised in hindsight. What is the point of making a prediction if it cannot be understood in advance? Those who have made clear predictions about the world's end, like Mother Shipton, William Miller, Joseph Franklin Rutherford and – more recently – Harold Camping, have been thoroughly discredited.

Usama, interestingly, mentions the anti-Christ (antichrist) at the end of his exchange. I do not know whether the dubious Islamic properties to which he refers draw on the Christian tradition. However, it is important to correct some popular misunderstandings of the word. The term occurs four times in John's letters in the singular (1 John 2.18, 22; 4.3; 2 John 1.7) and once in the plural (1 John 2.18). Contrary to popular supposition, the word never appears in the Book of Revelation. The word does not necessarily refer to an evil person who will appear in the end times, an unwarranted supposition made in the popular end-time *Left Behind* novels by Tim LaHaye and Jerry B. Jenkins.[60] John himself explains what the word means: 'deceivers, who do not acknowledge Jesus Christ as coming in the flesh' (2 John 1.7), of whom there can be many. John clearly believed they were around in his time, and was not writing prophetically about the twenty-first century. We must be very wary of trying to interpret the Bible and its prophecies as an almanac of events in world history.

Chapter 22

LAND

In Genesis, God promises Abraham that he would inherit the land of Canaan (Genesis 12.7), and under Joshua's leadership the Jewish people wrested the 'Promised Land' from the Canaanites, regarding the land of Israel as an inalienable gift for God's chosen people. Christians differ in their understanding of the Promised Land, some favouring the Zionist stance, while others see God's covenant as having been transferred to themselves. Islam, having emerged in Arabia, acknowledges Mecca as the origin of the Prophet Muhammad, peace be upon him, whose night journey took him to Jerusalem, which Muslims also regard as sacred. In this chapter we explore the issue of the Promised Land and the acrimonious disputes and conflicts that have centred on it.

DAN

Throughout history, the Jewish people have longed for a land of their own. In Genesis, God called Abraham to travel to Canaan where he promised to make him a great nation: 'Go from your country, your people and your father's household to the land I will show you. I will make you into a great nation' (Genesis 12.1–2). This same declaration was repeated to his grandson Jacob who, after wrestling with God's messenger, was renamed Israel (meaning 'he who struggles with God').

After Jacob's son Joseph became a vizier in Egypt, the Israelite clan settled in Egypt for several hundred years. Eventually Moses led them out of Egyptian bondage, and the people settled in the Promised Land. There they established a monarchy, but due to the corruption of the nation, God punished his chosen people through the instrument of foreign powers who devastated the northern kingdom in the eighth century BCE and the southern kingdom two centuries later.

Though the Temple lay in ruins and Jerusalem was destroyed, Jews were sustained by their belief that God would deliver them from exile. In the sixth century BCE a number of Jews sought permission to return to their former home. In 538 King Cyrus of Persia allowed them to leave. Under the leadership of Joshua and Zerubbabel, restoration of the Temple began. After the destruction of the First Temple the nation had strayed from the religious faith of their ancestors. To combat such laxity, the prophet Nehemiah asserted that the community must purify itself. In this effort he was joined by the priest Ezra. Although religious reforms were carried out, the people continued to abandon the Torah, and the Temple was destroyed a second time in the first century CE by the Romans.

After Jerusalem and the Second Temple were devastated, the Jews were bereft of a homeland. The glories of ancient Israel had come to an end, and the Jews were destined to live among the nations. In their despair the nation longed for a messianic figure of the House of David who would bring them back to Zion. Basing their beliefs on prophecies in Scripture, they foresaw a period of redemption in which earthly life would be transformed and all nations would bow down to the one true God. Such a vision animated rabbinic reflection about God's providential plan for his chosen people.

According to rabbinic speculation this process would involve the coming of a messianic figure, Messiah ben Joseph, who will serve as the forerunner of the second Messiah. The second Messiah will bring back all the exiles to Zion and complete earthly existence. Eventually at the end of the messianic era, all human beings will be judged; the righteous will enter into heaven whereas the wicked will be condemned to eternal punishment. This eschatological vision served as a means of overcoming the nation's trauma at suffering the loss of its sacred home and institutions.

In modern times, this eschatological vision has generally lost its hold on Jewish consciousness. Yet, the longing for a Jewish home did not diminish. Increasingly Jewry came to believe that this eternal quest could only be realised through the labours of the Zionists. The early Zionist pioneers were infused with hope and enthusiasm. Their task was to create a Jewish society that would be a light to the nations.

Yet, such a scheme was vehemently opposed by Arabs living in Palestine, and for over a century the country has been soaked in blood.

USAMA

As is often the case, the Qur'an affirms in general outline the biblical narrative that is summarised by Dan.

Moses asks his people, the Israelites, to 'enter the land made holy, that God has written for you'. When they refuse, out of cowardice and fear of its inhabitants at the time, Moses prays to God to save him and Aaron from 'wicked people', and God makes the Holy Land prohibited for the Israelites for 40 years, during which time they will wander in the desert (*The Last Supper*, 5:20–26).

In another *surah*, of which one name is *The Children of Israel*, the story is summarised of the two-time destruction of the Israelite temple, referred to as a mosque (Arabic: *masjid*, meaning simply a place of prostration or worship) (*The Night Journey* or *The Children of Israel*, 17:4–8). In this *surah*, the story of Moses and Pharaoh is also summarised, and it is stated that afterwards, God 'said to the Children of Israel to live in the land' (*The Night Journey* or *The Children of Israel*, 17:101–104).

However, as the divine 40-year ban illustrates, a right to land is conditional upon righteous conduct: 'We had surely written in the Psalms, after the Reminder, that the earth will be inherited by My righteous servants' (*The Prophets*, 21:105). The Reminder (*Dhikr*) here refers to the Torah, and this verse alludes to the teaching of the Torah and Psalms that 'the righteous shall inherit the earth'.

The Qur'an repeatedly warns the followers of the Prophet, peace be upon him, that if they turn away from godliness, they will be replaced by other people (cf. *The Last Supper*, 5:54; *Muhammad*, 47:38; *Victory*, 48:16–17). Later theologians argued that this had indeed happened throughout Islamic history: the Arabs, Persians, Africans, Central Asians, Indians and Turks have all taken turns at being the torch-bearers of Islam. In terms of the bigger picture, the mantle of being God's chosen people had passed from the followers of Moses to those who followed both Moses and Jesus, and then to those who followed Moses, Jesus and Muhammad.

And this is why the Zionist narrative, whilst being partly true, is also deeply flawed. Zionism insists on a controversial, divine right to the Holy Land of Israel–Palestine that belongs to modern Jews only, who constitute only two of the original 12 Israelite tribes. It ignores the other ten Israelite tribes, many of whom converted to Christianity and later Islam, and helped populate the entire Middle East, as we know it today. Every so often, we hear about Israelite roots of people as diverse as Gypsies, some Indians and Afghan Pathans, which illustrates this point.

Zionism also ignores the principle, 'the righteous shall inherit the earth', in favour of a racial principle. Dan's language is not helpful: his account is Judeo-centric, as though other peoples have had no connection to the land of Israel–Palestine over the past few millennia. He speaks of Zionists being opposed by 'Arabs living in Palestine' as though the latter were incidental observers, although the Muslims, led originally by the Arabs and later by Persians, Kurds and Turks, ruled Jerusalem and the surrounding holy land for longer than anyone in history. When I was last there, my Palestinian driver told me that his ancestors were Kurds who had come there with their leader Saladin (Salah al-Din al-Ayyubi) in the twelfth century CE. He regarded Ashkenazi Zionists, who dominate power in Israel, as recent arrivals. There are deep roots, and blood-soaked culpability, on both sides of the conflict there.

GEORGE

The account of Jewish history and the quest for the Promised Land, which Dan presents, is of course familiar to Christians. As Sunday School children we enjoyed the stories of the patriarchs' and Moses' journeyings, Joshua's capture of Jericho and David's establishment of his kingdom in Jerusalem. Many years on, I have deep concerns about these narratives. Joshua kills every man, woman, child and animal in the city – a plain act of genocide (Joshua 6.21). As far as we know, the Canaanites were doing the Israelites no harm, and when David captures Jerusalem, he has no obvious claim over the Jebusites, who already occupied the city (2 Samuel 5.6–7).

Dan himself earlier expresses reservations about the historicity of the Torah (2.5), and I wonder if he might agree that such parts of the Bible narrative are myth rather than history. When God is said to make a covenant with Abraham, promising him the entire land of

Canaan (Genesis 17.8), this cannot be regarded as history, since good historiography does not make claims about actions of supernatural beings, but sticks to the empirical and the verifiable. If they are myths rather than historical happenings, then can the Jewish people legitimately lay claim to a Promised Land? Such myths, I believe, are dangerous ones: as Usama points out, they perpetuate the idea that the Jews have a right to the land of Israel, describing them as 'exiles', even though the vast majority have never inhabited the country.

If the Jewish claim to Israel is based on divine covenant, it should be remembered that divine covenants were conditional on each side fulfilling their obligations, and that God reserved the right to disperse the Jewish people from the land if they disobeyed him (Deuteronomy 29:28). As Dan acknowledges, the Bible portrays God's people as guilty of corruption, with dispossession as a consequence.

I would largely agree with Usama's comments on Zionism. While there are Christians who support the Jews' return to Israel as divinely approved, and a prelude to Christ's return, there are no passages in Scripture that state this. Those who make such claims cite biblical prophecies – such as Ezekiel 37.21 – which refer to the regathering of the Jews from the Babylonian exile that began in the late seventh century BCE, and which are misapplied to the present day. Other Christians, particularly in the Adventist tradition, have applied spurious numerological calculations to biblical dates, and consequently concluded that events such as the 1917 Balfour Declaration must be significant.

Christians make no claim for their own physical territory. The eleventh chapter of Hebrews recounts the story of the faithful Israelites of old, stating that Abraham 'was looking forward to the city with foundations, whose architect and builder is God' (Hebrews 11.10). The writer asserts, 'yet none of them received what had been promised, since God had planned something better for us so that only together with us would they be made perfect' (Hebrews 11.39–40). The Bible concludes with John's vision of a new heaven and earth, in which a new holy city, the 'new Jerusalem' comes down from heaven, inaugurating a new kingdom, which the faithful will inherit (Revelation 21.1–2, 7). The wanderings of the ancient Hebrew patriarchs and the Israelites who were led by Moses through the desert in a quest for a country of their own metaphorically symbolises the

Christian's position as merely passing through the present world, in the hope of a transformation into a perfected state in a world to come. As Paul writes, 'our citizenship is in heaven' (Philippians 3.20), where territorial disputes will end.

DAN

Is George right? Are the stories in the Bible about the conquest of Canaan historically true? Or are they myths? How are we to understand the Bible? Traditionally Jews believed that the Hebrew Bible is a completely reliable record of the Jewish past. This is so because of the doctrine of *Torah mi Sinai* (the belief that God revealed the Torah (Five Books of Moses) to Moses on Mount Sinai). Throughout our trialogue, I have emphasised the centrality of this doctrine for the Jewish people. It provides a framework for understanding our ancestral past, God's dealing with the Jewish nation, and how to live in accordance with God's will.

Rabbinic sages later commented on the Hebrew Bible in volumes of midrashic sources. Their speculations form the basis for the development of Jewish theology. Alongside this scholarly outpouring, rabbinic scholars debated the meaning of the commandments and applied them to daily life. From generation to generation their debates were passed on through an oral tradition and later collected together in both the Palestinian and Babylonian Talmuds. Subsequently the *Shulhan Arukh* (Code of Jewish Law) was produced to guide Jews in their daily lives.

Traditionally, therefore, the stories in the Bible about creation, the Exodus, the revelation on Mount Sinai, and the conquest of Canaan are viewed as revealed by God himself. The suggestion that these narratives are myths is thus completely appalling. Today strictly Orthodox Jews adhere to this understanding of Scripture: as a result, there is no way for these Jews to accept George's interpretation of the Jewish past. When Scripture states that God chose the Jews as his special people and promised that they would inherit the land of Canaan, this is both a matter of history and faith. Not myth. And it is not surprising therefore that strictly Orthodox Jews view the conflict with the Palestinians in religious terms. The land belongs to the Jews by divine right.

Most non-Orthodox Jews, however, do not share such a conviction. Unlike the Orthodox, who view the Torah as divinely revealed, they regard the Torah (Genesis, Exodus, Leviticus, Numbers and Deuteronomy) as well as the other books of the Bible as an epic composed by ancient Israelites. Even those who regard the Bible as divinely inspired adhere to such a view. As a result it is not abhorrent to think that the Bible contains both myth and history. There is no question that some of the incidents depicted in the Bible took place. There are archaeological remains that demonstrate their historicity.

What then can be said about the claim that God gave his special people the land of Israel in perpetuity? Certainly some Jews – Orthodox as well as others – believe this to be the case. But most Jews do not adhere to this belief as the basis of their conviction that Israel must exist. Rather than appealing to theological belief, they are persuaded that Jewry must have a state of their own if they are to survive. Reform Judaism has reinterpreted the notion of the Promised Land. It is not God who chose the Jewish people. Instead, we are the choosing people. We have chosen to believe in the God of Israel. And we have chosen to create a Jewish state in our ancient homeland.

USAMA

It is striking that whereas Jerusalem occupies a central role in biblical geography, Mecca is analogous in the Qur'an: it is the venue of the first house of worship for humanity, and hence of the annual pilgrimage (*The Family of Imran*, 3:96–97). Some hadith traditions speak of Mecca as being the first part of the earth that was created, with the rest 'spread out from under it', identical to certain Judaeo-Christian traditions about Jerusalem.

Mecca was the first sanctuary of Islam; a large area around it is designated in the Qur'an as 'the Sacred Mosque'. Medina was later designated by the Prophet Muhammad, peace be upon him, as the second sanctuary of Islam; the third is Temple Mount in Jerusalem. In Jerusalem in 2015, I was present when a Sikh leader addressed an international conference. He referred to Israel as '*this* holy land', implying that there are others, such as India, the sacred homeland of his ancestors. This illustrates that the entire earth is sacred, but different religions and cultures are especially attached to various regions.

I agree with George that our ultimate citizenship is in heaven – whether the original Garden of Adam and Eve was heavenly or earthly, Satan instigated their expulsion from the metaphorical and spiritual state of grace. 'Children of Adam, let not Satan seduce you, as he expelled your parents from the Garden' (*The Heights*, 7:27). An influential Arab poet said:

> Let your heart go wherever you like with love,
> But love is ultimately, only for the First Love [i.e. God].
> How many a home on earth may a young man build,
> But his yearning will always be for the First Abode [i.e. Heaven].

However, in this life, we live on the earth and whilst we have a spiritual aspect to our lives, that other-worldly citizenship is primarily reserved for the Hereafter. Attachment to land is a natural emotion, as in the concept of 'Mother Earth' that is also found in Qur'anic commentary (especially under *Earthquake*, 99:4). A popular Islamic teaching, even attributed to the Prophet himself, says that, 'Love of one's homeland is part of faith.'

But excessive devotion to land can result in jingoistic nationalism. Did the Prophet Muhammad, peace be upon him, really order the expulsion of all Jews and Christians from the Arabian Peninsula (understood to refer to the Hejaz region of Mecca and Medina only), something that he never himself did, despite having the power to do so, or was this a political move by his successors, with fabricated words put in his mouth afterwards? The Hindutva movement in India over the past century and a half has sought to expel 'non-Indian' religions, such as Islam and Christianity, despite the fact that Hinduism itself was originally an imported religion. Today, we see ethnic cleansing in Burma blessed by some Buddhist monks. And there are some genocidal Jews and Arabs in the land of Israel–Palestine, who each wish to exterminate the other.

In between being tied to a particular land or being tied to no earthly land, is the idea of recreating perfection, or at least aspiring to it, wherever you are. This is implied by the *Book of Revelation*'s 'New Jerusalem'. Medina, the Prophet's city, rather than Mecca, the House of God, is the equivalent Islamic archetype of the 'City of God' or Al-Farabi's 'Virtuous City'. And let's not forget the powerful ending of William Blake's *Jerusalem*, a favourite song of English nationalists:

I will not cease from mental fight,
Nor shall my sword sleep in my hand:
Till we have built Jerusalem,
In England's green and pleasant land.[61]

GEORGE

Dan says that for the Orthodox Jew the belief that God chose the nation of Israel is both a matter of history and of faith. As I argued earlier, statements about the presumed actions of supernatural beings are not historical statements. We can corroborate statements about history by examining archaeological evidence, and other contemporary documents. Modern textual criticism suggests that the earliest sources of the Torah were compiled around the eighth century BCE – many centuries later than the events they purport to describe. This fact has obvious implications about their reliability as historical sources.

However, even more problematic for the historian are the supernatural claims that the authors make. Did God really appear before Abraham and speak to him, promising him a land, and were God and Abraham really able to have a conversation about the topic (Genesis 15.7–19)? Did an angel really appear to Abraham, Lot, Jacob, Samuel and other biblical characters? Even in my childhood I had problems with these ideas. I imagined God shouting down from heaven in a stentorian voice, and dazzling angels appearing in front of Moses, Balaam and others, who must have been extremely surprised. I also wondered why, if such accounts were true, God and his angels no longer appeared to speak to people I knew.

There are those who claim that signs and wonders were authentic phenomena that belonged to a previous biblical age but have since died out. However, even if this were the case, supernatural claims do not fall within the historian's remit: history is about empirical verifiable facts, and claims that God chose the Jews or that he promised Abraham a land are not historical claims, but can only at best be matters of faith, and which can be contested by those who do not share that faith.

Dan seeks to redefine the relationship between God and the Jews by claiming that the latter chose God. This seems fair enough, until he continues with the claim that Israel is their homeland. While the Jewish people have had a substantial history of inhabiting Israel, the land has come under the control of various forces in the course of its history: Canaanites and Jebusites, Jews, Assyrians, Babylonians, Persians, Greeks, Romans, the Islamic Empire, Crusaders and the British. To whom does the land rightly belong? Claims to historical rights to territory are at best problematic, and at worst dangerous.

I cannot pretend to have the solution to the present Palestinian-Israeli conflict. If we turn to the Bible, we find God's words, 'the land is mine' (Leviticus 25.23), indicating a territory that transcends national ownership. The idea of a New Jerusalem that transcends national boundaries and claims to territory is appealing, but of course it is difficult to see how such a concept can resolve earthly territorial disputes.

The Bible also teaches concern for the stranger, the poor, and the dispossessed – principles that are less abstract, and which can be more realistically implemented. Where settlers in Israel, and indeed any other country, have dispossessed those who have rightly owned territory, this can only be deplored. I have visited Israel on several occasions, and unfortunately have seen the evidence that this has happened.

Chapter 23

LIFE AFTER DEATH

Where does it all end? Is death the final event in our lives, or can we expect our existence to extend beyond the grave? This chapter explores what our various faiths have claimed about life after death. For some, death marks the end of the story, while most believers hold that life would be pointless unless there is something beyond. So might we expect a final judgement, with rewards and punishments in an afterlife? If so, have we any concept of what these might be like? How credible is the idea of eternal torment? The Bible depicts God as both just and merciful, but is God either if he condemns even the worst offender to everlasting torture? In what follows we explore the question of life after death.

GEORGE

Life after death poses many problems. What might we expect? Is it souls or bodies that survive? Is it a paradisiacal perfected earth, or some kind of ethereal angelic state? Will there be rewards for the righteous and punishments for the wicked? And has God predestined the fate of the faithful and the unfaithful?

The Hebrew Scriptures have little to say about a life after death, and offer little hope:

> For the living know that they will die,
> but the dead know nothing;
> they have no further reward,
> and even their name is forgotten. (Ecclesiastes 9.5)

By the time of Jesus, ideas have moved on. The Sadducees, who espoused traditional Hebrew ideas, posed a conundrum to Jesus about a woman who had successively married seven brothers. Whose wife would she be in the resurrection? Jesus accepts the idea of a resurrection but rejects the idea that there will be marriage partners: 'they will be like the angels in heaven,' he declares (Mark 12.18–27).

Jesus does not elaborate on what angels are like – whether they have ethereal or corporeal bodies, and Christians have been divided as to whether disembodied souls survive death, or whether – as the traditional creeds state – we believe in the resurrection of the body. Each view has its problems. How would we recognise disembodied beings in the afterlife, since recognition depends on bodily characteristics? If bodies are resurrected, in what form would they be brought back to life? Augustine of Hippo speculated that we would all be restored as we were or would have been at the age of 30, being the ideal age at which Jesus began his ministry on earth. If so, we would all be – or look – the same age as our parents, grandparents and children!

The Gospels stated that Jesus' body was no longer in the tomb when he rose from the dead, thus suggesting a bodily resurrection, and Paul compares Jesus' resurrection with the general resurrection, describing him as 'the firstfruits of those who have fallen asleep' (1 Corinthians 15.20). The nature of Jesus' resurrection body is not altogether clear. His followers do not always recognise him, and he seems to have been able to materialise and dematerialise, at times passing through locked doors. On the other hand, Jesus eats breakfast with his disciples at the Sea of Galilee, and invites Thomas to feel his wounds, thus suggesting a physical body (John 20.27; 21.12). Paul suggests that it is a 'spiritual body' that is raised from the dead (1 Corinthians 15.44), since 'flesh and blood cannot inherit the kingdom of God' (1 Corinthians 15.50), but our earthly bodies will be transformed into a new body, which Paul finds himself unable fully to describe.

This is what the righteous can expect, but what about the wicked? The New Testament uses some disturbing metaphors to describe their state: 'outer darkness', 'weeping and gnashing of teeth', being cast into a 'lake of fire' (Matthew 25.30; Revelation 21.18). In my youth, our fundamentalist minister acknowledged that these were probably metaphors, but indicated that 'something very terrible' lay in store for those who rejected Christ. It is important, however, to take a wider view of God's attributes than to rely on individual Bible verses. God is both just and benevolent, and the idea of eternal torment would seem quite incommensurate with even the worst of crimes. Perhaps the references to fire indicate purification rather than torment. As the philosopher John Hick argued, most of us are probably insufficiently pure to enter God's presence, and require some refining process, since it is the pure in heart who will see God (Matthew 5.8).

DAN

Though there is no explicit reference to the Hereafter in the Hebrew Bible, a number of expressions are used to refer to the realm of the dead. In Psalms 28.1 and 88.5, *bor* refers to a pit. In Psalm 6.6 as well as in Job 28.22 and 30.23, *mavet* is used in a similar sense. In Psalm 22.16 the expression *afar mavet* refers to the dust of death. In Jonah 2.7 the earth (*eretz*) is described as swallowing up the dead, and in Ezekiel 31.14 the expression *eretz tachtit* refers to the nether parts of the earth where the dead dwell. Finally the word *she'ol* is frequently used to refer to the dwelling of the dead in the nether world. In addition the words *ge ben hinnom*, *ge hinnom* and *ge* are used to refer to a cursed valley associated with fire and death where, according to Jeremiah, children were sacrificed as burnt offerings to Moloch and Baal. In later rabbinic literature the word ordinarily used for 'hell' (*Gehinnom*) is derived from these names.

Though these passages point to a biblical conception of an afterlife there is no indication of a clearly defined concept. It is only later in the Graeco-Roman world that such a notion began to take shape. The concept of a future world in which the righteous would be compensated for the ills they suffered in this life was prompted by a failure to justify the ways of God by any other means. According to biblical theodicy, human beings were promised rewards for obeying God's law, and punishments were threatened for disobedience. Rewards included healthy children, rainfall, a good harvest, peace and prosperity; punishments consisted of disease, war, pestilence, failure of crops, poverty and slavery. As time passed, however, it became clear that life does not operate in accordance with such a tidy scheme. In response to this dilemma the rabbis developed a doctrine of reward and punishment in the Hereafter. Such a belief helped Jews to cope with suffering in this life, and it also explained, if not the presence of evil in the world, then at least the worthwhileness of creation despite the world's ills.

In modern times, however, traditional rabbinic eschatology has lost its force for a large number of Jews. In consequence there has been a gradual this-worldly emphasis in Jewish thought. Significantly this has been accompanied by a powerful attachment to the State of Israel. For many Jews the founding of the Jewish State is the central focus of their religious and cultural identity. Jews throughout the world have deep admiration for the astonishing achievements of Israelis in reclaiming the desert and building a viable society. As a result, it is not uncommon for Jews to equate Jewishness with Zionism and to see Judaism as fundamentally nationalistic in character. This is a far cry from the rabbinic view of history that placed the doctrine of the Hereafter at the centre of Jewish life and thought.

USAMA

The Qur'an strikingly and vividly describes an eternal afterlife: approximately 15 of the 114 *surahs* are named after different aspects of the 'Last Day', that itself has many names, including Judgement, Resurrection, Reckoning, Inevitable, and Mutual Profit and Loss.

People who have faith in God and do good works go to Heaven: in the Qur'an, it is mainly known as *jannah* or *jannat* (Garden or Gardens), *jannat al-firdaws* (Gardens of Paradise) or *jannat 'adn* (Gardens of Eden or Eternity). These gardens have rivers of water, ever-fresh milk, delicious wine that does not induce headaches or hangovers and pure honey. Their inhabitants are resplendent in silk, gold, silver and pearls, reclining upon luxurious couches, eating from low-hanging fruit and waited upon by handsome youths. The men of Paradise are each married to many beautiful, wide-eyed wives known as *hoor*, as well as to their earthly wives. Families are reunited in the Garden, as long as they were all people of faith. The hadith literature expands on these Qur'anic descriptions in even more graphic detail, and adds the idea of ascending levels of Heaven, depending on how good a person was.

Hell, on the other hand, consists of descending levels of punishment, torture and humiliation for evil-doers and enemies of God. Hell is known as *nar* (Fire), *jahannam* (Arabised from the biblical *gehennom* or *gehenna*), *jahim* (a bottomless pit), and *hutama* (The Bonecrusher), amongst other graphic names.

Although many devout Muslims continue to believe these descriptions literally, many others have always understood them metaphorically and advocated a higher reason for living a godly life, rather than eternal bliss or damnation. The female mystic Rabia of Basra famously taught, 'Do not worship God for fear of the Fire or seeking the Garden, but worship the Divine for its own sake.' The later theologians Ghazzali and Nawawi distinguished between the 'worship of merchants' (seeking Paradise) and the 'worship of the elect' (seeking God).

The twentieth-century Spanish orientalist, Asín Palacios, wrote a book arguing that Dante's vivid descriptions of Heaven, Hell and Purgatory in his *Divine Comedy* were substantially influenced by Islamic texts that were known to Christendom via Latin translations. He pointed out something that is obvious from our discussion: the Islamic texts are far more graphic about these matters than Judeo-Christian ones. During an interfaith discussion on Scripture in London some years ago, a Christian theologian described the Qur'an's description of idolaters being punished by the fire of their own idols as these burnt in the Fire alongside them (*The Prophets*, 21:98) as 'Dante-esque'. I replied that he had inverted the situation: in fact, Dante was Qur'an-esque!

The eternal bliss of Paradise is, of course, heart-warming. But the eternal torture of the Fire is terrifying and troubled all the great Muslim theologians. Their solutions to this problem were creative and radical: all agreed that the Qur'anic principle expressed in the hadith, 'My Mercy dominates My Anger' meant that the Garden and Fire could not be symmetric in nature. Ghazzali, Ibn Taymiyyah and Ibn al-Qayyim argued that only the Garden was eternal; a closer reading of the Qur'an showed that the Fire would last 'except as God wills' (*Cattle*, 6:128; *Hud*, 11:107): Divine Mercy meant that God would not allow the Fire to continue forever. Ibn Arabi pointed out that the Qur'anic terms for punishment (*'adhab*) and sweetness (*'adhb*) have the same linguistic root. He said that, even if the Fire was eternal, its inhabitants would become acclimatised to it such that what initially felt like punishment would become sweet and rewarding!

GEORGE

We are all discussing a subject about which, to be honest, we know nothing – at least not directly. To the best of my knowledge, I have never been dead, and if I have existed in some previous life or pre-mortal state – neither of which ideas are part of Christian teaching – I certainly do not remember them. Christians view accounts of people returning from the dead with suspicion: the Bible forbids necromancy (Deuteronomy 18.9), and spiritualism is decidedly unpopular, to put it mildly. Samuel does not welcome Saul's use of a spirit medium to bring him back from the dead (1 Samuel 3.25). Accounts of near-death experiences (NDEs) are contentious, and there is no firm scientific evidence that people who are clinically dead have had visions of an afterlife.

If we turn to the Bible, I agree with Dan that there is little in Hebrew scripture that suggests any general resurrection or a final judgement that will divide humanity into the righteous and the unrighteous, who will experience heaven and hell respectively. There are two glimmers of hope: one verse in Isaiah states that 'your dead will live…the earth will give birth to her dead' (Isaiah 26.19), and Daniel 12.2 declares that 'Multitudes who sleep in the dust of the earth will awake: some to everlasting life, others to shame and everlasting contempt.' However, Isaiah 26:19 may be a later interpolation, and the Book of Daniel is probably the latest book of Hebrew scripture to be written, thus indicating that ideas of resurrection only began to flourish during the intertestamental period. It is perhaps not surprising, as Dan mentions, that many Jews perceive divine rewards as this-worldly rather than other-worldly.

When the New Testament attempts to describe life after death, much of its language is metaphorical, as Usama regards the Qur'an's descriptions of heaven and hell. The Bible's accounts are also confusing: it talks about heaven, eternal life, everlasting life and (very occasionally) paradise, and words for its counterpart are variously rendered as hell, Sheol, Hades, Gehenna, the Abyss, and unquenchable fire. Confusingly, the Book of Revelation tells us that death and Hades were thrown into the lake of fire, which is the 'second death' (Revelation 20.14). Some Christians have speculated that the author regards physical death as the first death, and the destruction of the wicked as the second. A number of fundamentalist Christians have tried to construct timetables of events leading from the present time to Christ's final rule. According to some, Christ will return to do battle with Satan – the Battle of Armageddon – after which Satan will be bound and thrown into the Abyss. This will be followed by Christ's 1000-year rule (the Millennium), after which Satan will be released and will attempt to regain power, but will be defeated by fire from heaven, after which he will be thrown into the lake of sulphur (Revelation 20.6–10). (This timetable has variations in Christian fundamentalist thinking.)

Such views incur a number of problems. These fundamentalists regard the Book of Revelation as predictive, while John is writing in the past tense, and makes no claim to clairvoyance. More likely, he is writing to early Christians who were undergoing persecution, offering them hope. It may be surprising to learn that Armageddon, which looms large in fundamentalist apocalyptic thinking, is only mentioned once in the entire Bible (Revelation 16.16).

It is irresponsible to inflate single verses in Scripture to such great importance. I can only agree with Usama that we must take a wider view, relying on God to reconcile his attributes of justice and mercy.

DAN

George and Usama have outlined the various beliefs in a Hereafter in Christianity and Islam. As I noted, there is no explicit belief in eternal salvation in the Bible; hence the rabbis of the post-biblical period were faced with the difficulty of proving that the doctrine of resurrection of the dead is contained in Scripture. To do this they employed methods of exegesis based on the assertion that every word in the Torah was transmitted by God to Moses. Thus, for example, Eleazar, the son of R. Jose (second century) claimed to have refuted the sectarians who maintained that resurrection is not a biblical doctrine:

> I said to them: 'You have falsified your Torah. For you maintain that resurrection is not a biblical doctrine, but it is written (in Numbers 15.31ff) 'Because he has despised the word of the Lord, and has broken his commandments, that person shall be utterly cut off; his iniquity shall be upon him.' Now seeing that he shall be utterly cut off in this world, when shall his iniquity be upon him? Surely in the next world.'

According to rabbinic Judaism, the World-to-Come is divided into several stages. First, there is the time of messianic redemption. According to the Talmud the Messianic Age is to take place on earth after a period of calamity, and will result in a complete fulfilment of every human wish. Peace will reign throughout nature; Jerusalem will be rebuilt; and at the close of this era, the dead will be resurrected and rejoined with their souls; and a final judgment will come upon all mankind. Those who are judged righteous will enter into heaven, which is portrayed in various ways in rabbinic literature. Conversely, those who are judged wicked are condemned to eternal punishment.

On the basis of this scheme of eternal salvation and damnation – which was at the heart of rabbinic theology through the centuries – it might be expected that modern Jewish theologians would attempt to explain contemporary Jewish history in the context of traditional theodicy. This, however, has not happened: instead, many Jewish writers have set aside doctrines concerning messianic redemption, resurrection, final judgement and reward for the righteous and punishment for the wicked. This shift in emphasis is in part due to the fact that the views expressed in the narrative sections of the midrashim and the Talmud are not binding. While all Jews are obliged to accept the divine origin of the Law, this is not so with regard to theological concepts and theories expounded by the rabbis. Thus, it is possible for a Jew to be religious and pious without accepting all the central beliefs of mainstream Judaism. Indeed, throughout Jewish history there has been widespread confusion as to what these beliefs are.

The doctrine of the resurrection of the dead has in modern times been largely replaced in both Orthodox and non-Orthodox Judaism by the belief in immortality of the soul. The original belief in resurrection was an eschatological hope bound up with the rebirth of the nation in the Days of the Messiah, but as this messianic concept faded into the background so also did this doctrine. For most Jews the physical resurrection is simply inconceivable in the light of a scientific understanding of the world.

USAMA

I agree with George that we know nothing directly about this subject of the afterlife. For Muslims, faith in the afterlife is based directly on the visions and revelations granted to the Prophet Muhammad, peace be upon him – we simply take his word upon these matters, and believe that his astonishing, graphic visions and revelations about the afterlife came from the Divine and not the devil. Furthermore, the afterlife satisfies a logical and moral gap, for without it, there appears to be no real justice for evil-doers and their victims, and no real reward for courageous good-doers, although there is a 'Muslim humanist' position that doing goodness is its own reward. 'Is the reward of excellence, anything but excellence?' asks the Qur'an, in the context of a famous passage about Paradise. Many Muslims believe that this reward is Paradise, whilst others understand the verse to mean, 'doing goodness is its own reward'.

The Prophet's visions about the afterlife mainly occurred during his night-journey and ascension to God during the early years of his mission in Mecca. Theologians are divided as to whether or not this journey was only spiritual, or also physical. The twentieth-century Spanish orientalist, Asín Palacios, who argued that Dante was influenced by Islamic texts, also said that Dante's journey, accompanied by the poet Homer, to the Inferno, Purgatory and Paradise was influenced by the story of the Prophet Muhammad's, peace be upon him, night-journey and ascension, accompanied by Angel Gabriel.

Dan and George speak about apocalyptic or end-of-world issues as being part of the afterlife and its study (eschatology). Islamic traditions about the end of the world, found mainly in the hadith literature, are in my view heavily influenced by Jewish and Christian sources: the appearance of a messianic figure (the Mahdi) around Syria or Jerusalem, the 'descent' or return of Jesus Christ in Damascus, the appearance of the anti-Christ or 'false Christ' (al-masih al-dajjal or simply, Dajjal), and a final battle where Christ kills the anti-Christ. None of these are mentioned in the Qur'an, although many theologians believe that there are a few, indirect references in the Qur'an to the 'Second Coming' of Christ. In addition, there is a Qur'anic description of a 'speaking, crawling creature (or walking beast)' that may be related to the Beast in the Book of Revelation.

Discussing apocalyptic eschatology can help understand and solve real geopolitical-religious conflicts. For example, terrorist groups such as Al-Qaeda and ISIS regularly invoke traditional Islamic eschatology to try to justify their actions and stated goals in Syria and Israel–Palestine. Furthermore, when I first visited Jerusalem, our Palestinian guide showed us one of the gates to the Temple Mount or 'Noble Sanctuary' (al-Haram al-Sharif) that is walled up. He told us that, according to Orthodox Judaism, only their Messiah is allowed to reopen that gate. Thus, as long as the Messiah has not appeared, we avoid another escalation of the Jewish-Muslim conflict over Jerusalem.

Dan understandably says that a physical resurrection is difficult to understand scientifically. As a trained scientist, I would argue that we can still analyse resurrection concepts scientifically. For example, we know that life on earth is based on a breath-taking digital system known as DNA. (Richard Dawkins' excellent, readable book, *River Out of Eden*,[62] explains this well: DNA is the digital river.) And I agree with my fellow physicist Roger Penrose that our souls may be regarded as very complex systems and patterns that process and shape information: we may thus understand resurrection as God 'remembering and reproducing', in some way, these information patterns. However, this sounds rather dull, and I prefer the traditional religious language of standing before God for the final judgement.

Chapter 24

CONCLUDING REFLECTIONS

We have covered quite a great deal of ground in this short volume – but where has it got us? What have we learnt from our exchanges? Has it brought our three faiths any closer together? How might we continue our discussion in the future and – importantly – how might our readers take this dialogue further? In this final chapter we make some concluding observations about our conversations.

USAMA

I have thoroughly enjoyed these discussions, mainly because I have learnt so much from Dan and George about Jewish and Christian perspectives on important scriptural, religious and theological issues. This has increased my knowledge and respect for our fellow Abrahamic traditions. Doing the research and reflection, sometimes accompanied by prayer, in order to contribute my own perspectives from an Islamic viewpoint, has been very rewarding for me personally.

Over the past four decades of Abrahamic, interfaith engagement since my childhood, I have often felt that Muslims have an advantage in such discussions, and that Jews and Christians generally have yet to come to terms with Islam. This is because the internal logic of Judaism and Christianity is often exclusivist, so there is no need felt to consider another religion, that also came later, seriously. But because these two religions share the Hebrew Bible, they have much common ground over which to have shared discussions. The extensive Qur'anic retellings of biblical stories and the requirement in Islam to believe in the divine revelations of the Torah, Psalms and Gospel, mean that Muslims have historically paid a lot of attention to biblical stories. Our Qur'an-commentaries and hadith traditions have many, many quotations from Jewish and Christian sources. Thus, Islamic scholars naturally have a decent knowledge of the Judaeo-Christian tradition, although not necessarily of the theological nuances.

I hope that readers will be inspired and enriched by our discussions. I also hope that these will spur them to come to terms better with the other Abrahamic traditions, if they belong to one of them. Jews and Christians need to come to terms with the fact that Muslims also believe in large parts of the Hebrew Bible and of the New Testament and will stake a claim to truth about the meanings contained in these scriptures. The Qur'an is not seen as a stand-alone scripture by Muslims, but as a continuation and culmination of the previous scriptures, so Muslims naturally regard such Abrahamic discussions as internal ones, regularly cross-referencing Qur'anic teachings with biblical ones.

Muslims also need to come to terms with the fact that Jews and Christians often have different stories and understandings of Muslims' beloved Qur'anic prophets, most of whom are originally biblical prophets. Furthermore, the biblical accounts have some claim to historicity. However, the Qur'anic accounts do not pretend to be historical in the sense of being contemporaneous with events: rather, they are generally abstracted and summarised versions of biblical stories, focusing more on moral lessons rather than historical detail.

Our discussions have also illustrated, I think, that the internal debates within each Abrahamic religion around theology, scripture, law, ethics and other important topics are often mirrored in the other Abrahamic traditions. This also helps in mutual understanding and even cross-fertilisation of thoughts, ideas and beliefs. I would argue that there has been three-way, mutual enrichment for centuries, with Judaism, Christianity and Islam all influencing and learning from each other. This needs to continue, and in fact this is happening globally, not just as an intellectual and academic exercise, but as a God-given and God-inspired resource to help reduce and even solve the many contemporary geopolitical conflicts that involve our three great religions. I hope that our book will be a small but important contribution to this endeavour.

GEORGE

We have had an interesting set of exchanges, spanning a wide range of topics. What have we achieved, I wonder? Yogi Bhajan, the founder of the Sikh-derived Healthy Happy Holy movement once said, 'If you want to learn something, read about it. If you want to understand something, write about it. If you want to master something, teach it.'

All three of us have taught students, although I'm not sure that we can claim mastery of all the topics we have included here. However, putting together a book like this has certainly increased our understanding, both of each other's faiths, and also of our own. Yogi Bhajan's maxim suggests that reading is the first step, preceding understanding and mastery. It is likely that most readers have gone beyond that first stage. In a multifaith, multicultural society like Britain it is inevitable that we come across Christians, Jews and Muslims, as well as members of other faiths, in our educational establishments and workplaces. So there is ample opportunity for readers to continue our dialogue for themselves.

Inevitably, our exchanges have left several omissions and loose ends. Reviewers are often only too eager to point out areas that books fail to cover, so it might be useful to be one step ahead of them. One topic we have not discussed, perhaps surprisingly, is predestination. It is frequently presented as a fundamental Islamic doctrine: since the Qur'an is believed to have eternally existed in heaven, yet refers to events in human history, such events must be foreordained. Some Christian scriptures seem to suggest predestination: Paul states that 'those God foreknew he also predestined to be conformed to the image of his Son' (Romans 8.29), and he also speaks of a potter who makes pots that are fit for purpose and others that are only fit for destruction (Romans 9.19–24). Calvinists interpret these passages in a predestinarian manner, while others have suggested that the first quotation may mean that God's purposes cannot be thwarted, and that the second may refer to the relative positions of Jews and Gentiles, rather than to individuals being assigned inescapable eternal destinies.

Another area to which we may not have done justice is alleged antisemitism in Christian scripture. We touched on the theme in Chapter 19, but it is also frequently brought up in connection with John's gospel, where the author appears to contrast 'the Jews' with Jesus and his followers. I would have liked to have commented on this: briefly, as I pointed out in that chapter, Jesus and his 12 followers were also Jews, as were most (although not all) of his supporters. John can hardly be making a spurious contrast; he also describes Jesus as 'the King of the Jews' – scarcely an antisemitic title. This controversy, of course, is between Jews and Christians, leaving Muslims somewhat out of the debate, which is no doubt why we have not pursued the topic.

If space had permitted, we could have continued our discussion about the Promised Land. While I agree with Dan that the notion of 'chosenness' is often wrongly construed as meaning that God picked a favourite nation, the idea that the Jews have chosen a God who gave them Israel as their homeland remains highly contentious, to put it mildly.

Of course, we cannot do full justice to, let alone reach agreement on, such issues in these short exchanges. Readers will no doubt continue to reflect on and discuss the arguments that the three of us have presented on these issues – in a friendly, yet frank, manner, as we have attempted.

DAN

When I was five I was an angel in a nativity play in primary school. My Jewish parents were remarkably progressive in allowing me to join in. I remember wearing wings, but I had no idea what it was all about. Only much later did I learn about Jesus. I discovered that he is supposed to be the long-awaited Messiah who has come to redeem humanity. We Jews are not supposed to believe this. The concept of the Trinity is for us Jews incomprehensible. The Incarnation is not a mystery – it is a mistake. For Jews Christianity is dangerous foreign territory. Rabbis tell us that we should not have Christmas trees. No Easter egg hunts for us. We are not to marry Christians. Instead we should remind ourselves that for nearly 20 centuries we have been victimised, at times murdered, by the Church.

Our book has been written to challenge such assumptions and prejudices. Throughout, George has sought to enlighten me and fellow Jewish readers about the fundamentals of the Christian faith. In dialogue, he has cast light on a wide variety of theological, ethical and social topics. This has been done largely through questions (and challenges) posed by both Usama and me. At the end of this exploration, there is no doubt that my understanding of Christianity has been enlarged, and I hope other Jews will feel the same. Today we live in a global society, and it is vital that the ghetto walls that once separated Jews from Christians are broken down for all time.

In past centuries Jews and Muslims regarded one another as fellow Semites. In the medieval period Jewish theologians, such as Moses Maimonides, were deeply influenced by Islamic thought. This was a golden age of Jewish-Muslim dialogue. In subsequent centuries Jews living in Muslim lands were regarded as People of the Book. However, with the creation of Israel in the twentieth century, all this changed. The early Zionists were viewed by the Muslim world as usurpers of Palestinian land, and for nearly a century Arab nations have sought to drive Israelis into the sea. Today our two communities are in constant conflict. Arab antisemitism has now become a regrettable feature of modern life. And from the Jewish side, there is deep-seated distrust and fear of Muslims.

A central aim of this volume is to overcome such animosity and misunderstanding. In dialogue Usama has illuminated numerous subjects and has helped me (and I hope fellow Jewish readers of this book) to gain insight into Islamic Scripture. Although we Jews believe in the same God as Muslims, we do not share the essential theological assumptions of the Islamic faith. Technically we (along with Christians) belong to the Abrahamic *ummah*, but there is much that we Jews need to learn from our sibling religion.

Our book is thus designed to dispel ignorance and prejudice. It is written for Jews, Christians and Muslims who seek to gain an understanding and appreciation of one another's religious heritage. And for readers who stand outside these three traditions, we hope our three-way conversation will help them to appreciate the scriptural riches of our three faiths. We have deliberately used the model of dialogue to present ideas because we believe that it is through such encounter and exploration that true understanding and sympathy can best be achieved.

Glossary

Aggadah Rabbinic Teaching which is an application of biblical narrative, history, ethics and prophecy.

Ahle-e-Hadith 'People of Hadith'; the main branch of the salafi movement in the Indian subcontinent.

Amoraim Title of scholars in Palestine and Babylonia from the third to the sixth century.

apocalypse Originally the term meant 'unveiling', but it has come to be associated with the world's end.

Apocrypha Books Excluded from Hebrew Scriptures, written around the second and third centuries BCE. Roman Catholics, but not Protestant and Eastern Orthodox Christians, accept these books as part of the canon.

ayah **(pl.** *ayat***)** A verse of the Qur'an. The word literally means 'sign'.

Baha'i A religion originating within Islam in the 1860s, which proclaims its founder Bahá'u'lláh (Mírzá Ḥusayn-`Alí Núrí), as the prophet for the present age, and the culmination of the expectations of all faiths.

Bar mitzvah Term applied to the attainment of legal and religious maturity. It also refers to the occasion on which this position is assumed.

Bat mitzvah Ceremony for girls which corresponds to the boy's *bar mitzvah*.

canon The body of scripture formally approved as authoritative by a religion – the *Tanakh* for Jews, and the Old and New Testaments for Christians. Additionally, Roman Catholics acknowledge the Apocrypha as part of their canon.

catechism A manual outlining a religion's basic beliefs and practices, often in question-and-answer format.

Charismatic Movement An exuberant movement originating in the US in the 1960s, emphasising the power of the Holy Spirit, manifested in speaking in tongues, healing and prophecy.

covenant A legally binding agreement between two parties, particularly between God and the people of Israel, and subsequently the Christians.

encyclical A letter sent by the Pope to the entire Church.

eschatology Doctrines relating to the end of time.

eucharist The Christian sacrament of Holy Communion, commemorating Jesus' last meal with his disciples. It is known as the Mass in the Roman Catholic tradition.

Fatiha 'The Opening', referring to the short, opening chapter of the Qur'an (*Surah al-Fatiha*) that comprises seven verses. The *Fatiha* is in the form of a prayer, and is recited frequently in daily Muslim life.

fundamentalism Although the term has come to denote extremism in several religions, it was originally a conservative Christian movement that arose in the early twentieth century, affirming biblical inerrancy, among other doctrines.

Gan Eden Heaven (Garden of Eden).

Gehinnom (Gehenna) Hell.

Gemara Commentary on the Mishnah.

Great Commission Jesus' instruction to his disciples to preach the gospel to all nations, and baptise them in the name of the Father, Son and Holy Spirit (Matthew 28:19–20).

hadith A traditional report about a teaching, saying or action of the Prophet Muhammad, peace be upon him, and of his Companions and their disciples.

hafiz One who has memorised the entire Qur'an.

Haftarah Second reading in the synagogue on Sabbaths and festivals.

Haggadah Prayer book for Passover.

Halakhah Jewish law.

Hasidim Members of a strictly Orthodox sect of Judaism, which was founded by the Baal Shem Tov in the eighteenth century.

Hijra Sacred emigration, especially the Prophet's emigration from Mecca to Medina in 622 CE.

Hijri calendar The Islamic lunar calendar, dated from the Prophet's *hijra*.

Injil Qur'anic Arabic term for the gospel inspired to Prophet 'Isa (Jesus) by God. It is an article of faith for Muslims to believe in the divinely revealed *Injil*.

intertestamental period The timespan between events recorded in Hebrew scripture and the inception of Christianity, from Malachi (the last book in the Hebrew Bible, probably written around 420 BCE), to John the Baptist (early first century CE).

Isra'iliyyat Israelite traditions, especially reports providing commentary on the Qur'an or explanation of biblical stories.

Kabbalah Jewish mysticism.

Ketubah Marriage contract.

Ketuvim Hagiographa consisting of the third section of the Hebrew Bible.

King James Version Also known as the Authorised Version, this translation of the Bible was authorised by King James I, and was widely used mainly in Protestant churches until the second half of the twentieth century.

Kosher Term that is applied to food which is permissible to eat according to Jewish law.

Maariv Evening service.

Mass The term favoured by Roman Catholics for the sacrament of the Eucharist, or Holy Communion.

Matzoh Unleavened bread.

midrash Rabbinic interpretation of Scripture.

Minhah Afternoon service.

Minyan Term applied to the group of ten male Jews who constitute the minimum number for communal worship.

Mishnah Early rabbinic legal code compiled by Judah ha-Nasi in the second century.

Mitzvah Commandment.

Neviim Prophetic books in the Hebrew Bible.

Noachide Laws According to the Talmud, seven laws were given to Noah, and are binding on Gentiles as well as Jews.

Orthodox (1) Major Jewish tradition, involving strict adherence to rabbinical interpretations of the Torah; (2) Major Christian tradition, separating from Roman Catholicism in 1045.

Parashah Term applied to the weekly portion of the Torah, which is read in the synagogue on the Sabbath.

Passover *(Pesach)* Pilgrim festival commemorating the exodus from Egypt.

Peshat Literal meaning of a text.

Pharisees First-century Jewish teachers, who codified the Jewish Law.

Ramadan The annual, Islamic lunar month of fasting, lasting 29–30 days. Ninth month of the *hijri* calendar.

Rebbe Hasidic spiritual leader.

Rosh Hashanah Jewish New Year.

Sadducees First-century conservative Jewish school of thought, focused on the Jerusalem Temple and its rites.

salafi, salafism This refers to a puritanical, traditionalist, socially conservative interpretation of Sunni Islam, which claims to be based on the original scriptures and spirit of Islam.

Sanhedrin Jewish Court in biblical times, established in every major city.

Second Vatican Council Also known as Vatican II, the Council was convened by Pope John XXIII in 1962, and concluded under Pope Paul VI in 1965, and introduced numerous reforms.

Seder Home ceremony that occurs on the first night of Passover.

Semicha Rabbinic ordination.

Septuagint Greek translation of Hebrew Scriptures, sometimes referred to as LXX. The translation was undertaken during the third and second centuries BCE.

Seventh-day Adventism A Christian Protestant movement originating in the US in the nineteenth century, which taught the imminent return of Jesus Christ.

Shaharit Morning service.

Sharia Islamic law, derived from the Qur'an and the *hadith*.

Shavuot Pilgrim festival commemorating the giving of the law on Mount Sinai.

Shehitah Ritual slaughter.

Shekinah Divine presence.

Shema Central prayer in the Jewish liturgy.

Shulhan Arukh Code of Jewish Law.

Sidra Torah portion that is read in the synagogue on the Sabbath.

Sod Esoteric allegorical method of scriptural exegesis.

Sukkot Pilgrim festival which marks the end of the agricultural year.

Sunna, Sunnah The Way of the Prophet. It is held to embody the teachings of the Qur'an, so the Qur'an is understood and applied in life with reference to the *Sunnah*.

sura, surah Chapter of the Qur'an. There are 114 chapters of varying lengths, ranging from three *ayat* to 286.

synoptic problem The area of New Testament scholarship that seeks to determine the literary dependence between Matthew, Mark and Luke's gospels.

Talmud Name of the two collections of records of the discussion of Jewish law by scholars in various academies from c.200 to c.500.

Tanakh Hebrew Bible.

Tannaim Sages of the first and second centuries CE.

Tawrat Qur'anic Arabic term for the Torah inspired to Prophet Musa (Moses) by God. It is an article of faith for Muslims to believe in the divinely revealed *Tawrat*.

Torah mi Sinai Revelation of the Pentateuch on Mount Sinai.

typology A method of interpreting Scripture which contends that certain people or events ('types') prefigured later happenings ('antitypes').

Yeshivot Rabbinical academies.

Yom Kippur Day of Atonement.

Zabur Qur'anic Arabic term for the Psalms inspired to the Prophet-King Dawud (David) by God. It is an article of faith for Muslims to believe in the divinely revealed *Zabur*.

Zionism Initiated by Theodor Herzl, Jewish Zionism advocated a return of the Jews to Palestine. Jewish Zionism is secular, in contrast with Christian Zionism, which views the return of the Jews as a fulfilment of biblical prophecy, as a prelude to Christ's return.

Recommended Further Reading

JUDAISM

Blech, Benjamin (2003) *The Complete Idiot's Guide to Judaism*. London: Alpha.

Cohn-Sherbok, Dan (2017) *Judaism: History, Belief and Practice*. London: Routledge.

Cohn-Sherbok, Dan (2010) *Judaism Today*. London: Continuum.

de Lange, Nicholas (2010) *An Introduction to Judaism*. Cambridge: Cambridge University Press.

Hoffman, C.M. (2008) *Judaism*. London: Teach Yourself.

Lehman, Oliver (2011) *Judaism: An Introduction*. London: I.B.Tauris.

Solomon, Norman (2000) *Judaism: A Very Short Introduction*. Oxford: Oxford University Press.

CHRISTIANITY

Barton, John (2010) *The Bible: The Basics*. London: Routledge.

Chryssides, George D. (2010) *Christianity Today*. London: Continuum.

Chryssides, George D. and Wilkins, Margaret Z. (2011) *Christians in the Twenty-first Century*. Sheffield: Equinox.

Daughrity, Dyron (2016) *Roots: Uncovering Why We Do What We Do in Church*. Abilene TX: Leafwood.

Gregg, Stephen E. and Chryssides, George D. (eds) (2019) *The Bloomsbury Companion to Studying Christians*. London: Bloomsbury.

Molloy, Michael (2017) *The Christian Experience*. London: Bloomsbury.

Moyise, Steve (1998) *Introduction to Biblical Studies*. London: Cassell.

ISLAM

Esposito, John and Mogahed, Dalia (2008) *Who Speaks for Islam? What a Billion Muslims Really Think*. New York: Gallup Press.

Esposito, John (2011) *What Everyone Needs to Know About Islam*. New York: Oxford University Press.

Geaves, Ron (2011) *Islam Today*. London: Continuum.

Gilliat-Ray, Sophie (2010) *Muslims in Britain*. Cambridge: Cambridge University Press.

Hourani, Albert (1991) *Islam in European Thought*. Cambridge: Cambridge University Press.

Lings, Martin (1983) *Muhammad, His Life Based on the Earliest Sources*. Cambridge: Islamic Texts Society.

Ruthven, Malise (2012) *Islam – A Very Short Introduction*. Oxford: Oxford University Press.

INTERFAITH DIALOGUE

Braybrooke, Marcus (1992) *Pilgrimage of Hope: One Hundred Years of Global Interfaith Dialogue*. London: SCM.

Braybrooke, Marcus (1996) *A Wider Vision: A History of the World Congress of Faiths 1936–1996*. Oxford: Oneworld.

British Council of Churches (1983) *Can We Pray Together? Guidelines on Worship in a Multi-Faith Society*. London: British Council of Churches.

Cohn-Sherbok, Dan, Chryssides, George D. and El-Alami, Dawoud Sudqi (2014) *Why Can't They Get Along?* Oxford: Lion Hudson.

Küng, Hans and Kuschel, Karl-Josef (eds) (1993) *A Global Ethic: The Declaration of the Parliament of the World's Religions*. London: SCM.

Smock, David (2002) *Interfaith Dialogue and Peacebuilding*. Washington DC: United States Institute of Peace Press.

Notes

1. Alice Parmelee (1951) *A Guidebook to the Bible*. London: English Universities Press.
2. John Barton and John Muddiman (2001) *The Oxford Bible Commentary*. Oxford: Oxford University Press.
3. Moses Maimonides (1987) 'The Thirteen Principles of the Jewish Faith.' In J.H. Hertz (ed.) *Authorised Daily Prayer Book*. London: Bloch Publishing Co.
4. Verse: *ayah* (pl. *ayat*) also means 'signs' – hence, the Qur'an is literally also a 'Book of Signs'. The 'Signs of God' are known as '*ayat Allah*'.
5. '24 Light' refers to the *surah* named 'Light', the twenty-fourth surah of the Qur'an, etc.
6. John Hick (1973) *The Philosophy of Religion* (Second Edition). Englewood Cliffs, NJ: Prentice-Hall, p.52.
7. J.G. Hamann (1759) *Cloverleaf of Hellenistic Letters*. In Kenneth Haynes (2007) *Hamann: Writings on Philosophy and Language*. Cambridge: Cambridge University Press, pp. 33–59. Cited online at http://godspeaksbadgrammar.blogspot.co.uk/2011/04/tuning-our-ears-to-grammar-of-god.html (accessed on 4/4/2018).
8. Lavinia and Dan Cohn-Sherbok (1997) *A Short Reader of Judaism*. Oxford: Oneworld, pp.135–136.
9. Vatican (1994) *Catechism of the Catholic Church*. London: Geoffrey Chapman, 1785–1786.
10. Michael Drosnin (1997) *The Bible Code*. London: Weidenfeld & Nicolson.
11. Michael Drosnin (1997) *The Bible Code*. London: Weidenfeld & Nicolson.
12. Vatican (1994) *Catechism of the Catholic Church*. London: Geoffrey Chapman, 234.
13. Louis Jacobs (1973) *A Jewish Theology*. Springfield, NJ: Behrman House, p.28.
14. Moses Maimonides (1881) *Guide for the Perplexed*. New York: Dutton.
15. Eckstein, Jerome (1965) 'The fall and rise of man.' *Journal for the Scientific Study of Religion 5*, 1, p.80.
16. Shaar Ha-Yihud Ve Ha-Emunah, The Tanya, Chapter 2, pp.153–154.
17. *Sahih Muslim*, hadith no. 2569.

18. See   www.amazon.com/God-Jar-GIAJ/dp/B01B5RGA9Q   (accessed   on 4/4/2018).

19. The Gideons International (2017) Available online at: www.gideons.org.uk (accessed on 4/4/2018).

20. Twenty-nine of the 114 chapters (*surahs*) of the Qur'an, including the two longest ones, begin with letter-sequences comprising one to five letters. In the Arabic, they are recited as stand-alone letters, e.g. '*Alif. Lam. Mim*'. I follow the translator of the Qur'an, Abdullah Yusuf Ali, in rendering these in English as 'A.L.M.' etc. The letter-sequences are regarded as cryptical and mystical, referring to higher mysteries, and are the subject of much commentary. Exactly half of the letters of the Arabic alphabet (14 out of 28) are represented in these letter-sequences that open various *surahs*.

21. This prayer is recorded in a hadith transmitted by Bukhari and Muslim, two of the major sources of hadith in Sunni Islam.

22. *Encyclopedia Judaica* (2017) 'Jewish Concepts: The Seven Noachide Laws.' Available online at www.jewishvirtuallibrary.org/the-seven-noachide-laws (accessed on 4/4/2018).

23. Bukhari is generally regarded as the foremost canonical collection of hadiths in Sunni Islam.

24. The name of this *surah* is the same as the one-letter sequence that begins it (see footnote 20 above). Therefore, in English, it is correct to render it as '*S*'.

25. Imam Nawawi, *Forty Hadith*, nos. 1, 32 and 33.

26. This refers to the eighth century of the Islamic calendar and the fourteenth century of the Common Era or Christian calendar. (The Islamic calendar begins with the *hijra*, the emigration of the Prophet Muhammad, peace be upon him, from Mecca to Medina in c. 622 CE. Hence, Islamic centuries are roughly six centuries behind Christian ones.)

27. John Calvin (1559/1962) *Institutes of the Christian Religion*. 2 vols. London: James Clarke.

28. Church of England. *Thirty-Nine Articles / Articles of Religion*; in *The Book of Common Prayer*. Available online at: http://www.anglicancommunion. org/media/109014/Thirty-Nine-Articles-of-Religion.pdf (accessed on 28/5/2018).

29. *Iesous, CHristos, THeou, Uios, Sōter* (Jesus, Christ, of God, Son, Saviour).

30. Jami al-Tirmidhi, Sunan, Book on Food. Available online at https://sunnah. com/tirmidhi/25 (accessed on 4/4/2018).

31. Richard H. Schwartz (1988) *Judaism and Vegetarianism. Marblehead, MA: Micah Publications.*

32. Stephanie Kirchgaessner (2016) 'Pope endorsement softens stance on divorced Catholics.' *The Guardian*, 13 September. Available online at www. theguardian.com/world/2016/sep/13/pope-endorsement-softens-stance-on-divorced-catholics (accessed on 4/4/2018).

33. Victor Appell (2018) 'What does Reform Judaism say about homosexuality?' Available online at http://reformjudaism.org/practice/ask-rabbi/what-does-reform-judaism-say-about-homosexuality (accessed on 4/4/2018).

34. Cf. William Clarence-Smith (2006) *Islam and the Abolition of Slavery*. London: Hurst.
35. Cf. Benedikt Koehler (2014) *Early Islam and the Birth of Capitalism*. Lanham, MD: Lexington.
36. See www.bartercard.com.
37. Benedikt Koehler (2014) *Early Islam and the Birth of Capitalism*. Lanham, MD: Lexington.
38. Kerry Sproston, Bob Erens and Jim Orford (2000) *Gambling Behaviour in Britain: Results from the British Gambling Prevalence Survey*. Available online at www.nationalcasinoforum.co.uk/wp-content/uploads/2013/11/British-Gambling-Prevalence-Survey-1999.pdf (accessed on 4/4/2018).
39. Sanhedrin 24b.
40. Avi Hein (2018) 'Women in Judaism: A History of Women's Ordination as Rabbis.' Available online at www.jewishvirtuallibrary.org/a-history-of-women-s-ordination-as-rabbis (accessed on 4/4/2018).
41. Vatican (1994) *Catechism of the Catholic Church*. London: Geoffrey Chapman, 2309.
42. Jewish Virtual Library (2018a) 'The Columbus Platform: The Guiding Principles of Reform Judaism, 1937.' Available online at http://www.jewishvirtuallibrary.org/the-columbus-platform-1937 (accessed on 4/4/2018).
43. Charles Darwin (1861) *On the Origins of Species by Means of Natural Selection*. New York: Appleton.
44. J.N. Farquhar (1913/1930) *The Crown of Hinduism*. Oxford: Oxford University Press.
45. Pope Paul VI (1965) *Nostra Aetate* ('In Our Time'). Declaration on the Relation of the Church to Non-Christian Religions. 28 October. Available online at www.vatican.va/archive/hist_councils/ii_vatican_council/documents/vat-ii_decl_19651028_nostra-aetate_en.html (accessed on 4/4/2018).
46. John Hick (1973) *The Philosophy of Religion* (Second Edition). Englewood Cliffs, NJ: Prentice-Hall.
47. Albert Schweitzer (1910/1963) *The Quest of the Historical Jesus*. London: Adam and Charles Black.
48. Ibn Kathir, *Tafsir*, 2:61.
49. Henry Ford (1920/1970) *The International Jew*. Marietta, GA: Thunderbolt Print Press. Anon (1903) *The Protocols of the Learned Elders of Zion*. Available online at http://xroads.virginia.edu/~ma01/Kidd/thesis/pdf/protocols.pdf (accessed 4/4/2018).
50. Paul Vallely (2014) 'Christians: the world's most persecuted people.' *The Independent*, 26 July. Available online at http://www.independent.co.uk/voices/comment/christians-the-worlds-most-persecuted-people-9630774.html (accessed on 4/4/2018).
51. *Cf.* Qur'an, *Abraham*, 14:5, *Sheba*, 34:19, *Consultation*, 42:33. The verse in each case ends, 'In this there are Signs for every extremely patient one, given

to much gratitude.' The Arabic terms are *sabbar shakur*, both intensive active participles derived from *sabr* (patience) and *shukr* (gratitude), respectively.

52. Jewish Virtual Library (2018b) 'History of Jerusalem: Timeline for the History of Jerusalem (4500 BCE – Present).' Available online at www.jewishvirtuallibrary.org/timeline-for-the-history-of-jerusalem-4500-bce-present (accessed on 4/4/2018).

53. Kalonymus Kalman Shapira (2002) 'The Holy Fire.' In Dan Cohn-Sherbok (ed.) *Holocaust Theology: A Reader*. Exeter: Exeter University Press, p.151.

54. Colin Elmer (2002) 'Suffering – A Point of Meeting.' In Dan Cohn-Sherbok (ed.) *Holocaust Theology: A Reader*. Exeter: Exeter University Press, p.135.

55. Hans Jonas (2002) 'The Concept of God After Auschwitz.' In Dan Cohn-Sherbok (ed.) *Holocaust Theology: A Reader*. Exeter: Exeter University Press, p.138–139.

56. Ibn Arabi (1988) *The Bezels of Wisdom* (trans. R.A. Austin). Lahore: Suhail Academy, pp.212–213.

57. Ibn Khaldun (2015) *The Muqaddimah: An Introduction to History* (trans. F. Rosenthal and N.J. Dawood). Princeton, NJ: Princeton Classics.

58. As explained in footnote 26, the Islamic calendar and the Common Era or Christian calendar differ.

59. Peter Harrigan (2006) 'Volcanic Arabia.' *Saudi Aramco World*. March/April, 2–13.

60. Tim LaHaye and Jerry B. Jenkins (1995) *Left Behind: A Novel of the Earth's Last Days*. Wheaton, IL: Tyndale House.

61. W.M. Rossetti (1914) *The Political Works of William Blake*. London: Bell, p.142.

62. Richard Dawkins (2015) *River Out Of Eden: A Darwinian View of Life*. London: Weidenfeld & Nicolson, Science Masters.

Index